AF479919

Praise for Climbing to 49

"Tanner Burns has proved, beyond the shadow of a doubt that aggressive turkey hunting tactics work. Read just about any chapter in this book and you'll agree. While Tanner's low-crawl, sneak-up-on-em approach to the hunt works for him, many of us older hunters have dialed it back a little as we've aged, and now usually hunt more conservatively. It's apples to apples though-it's turkey hunting either way, and either way it's exciting. If you can read this book and not say "Wow!" a dozen times, there's something wrong with you."

– Jim Spencer, author of numerous books including the *Bad Birds* series. He also has written over a thousand newspaper and magazine features about turkeys and turkey hunting.

"Skillfully fashioned!" If you care about turkey hunting adventures and the unique places you get to visit, you must read this book. This is a turkey hunting book for turkey hunters. The stories allow you to go to places you've never visited but always wanted to explore for turkeys. If you decide to take an outing to one of the states, Tanner Burns has laid a path for you to follow as he ventures forward on his U.S. Super Slam. The author has captured Tanner's anecdotal stories and innovative strategies in a way that is helpful to newcomers or veteran turkey hunters. Each chapter ends with a "Lessons Learned" comment that is insightful and valuable. This is a wonderful mix of a turkey hunting quest, a travel odyssey and the excitement, frustration, and humor that makes turkey hunting so special."

– Al Stewart, Director of the Nimrod Education Center, former Michigan DNR Upland Game Bird Specialist, recipient of numerous awards, some of which include the NWTF Wayne Bailey Lifetime Achievement and NWTF Henry S. Mosby Awards.

"In climbing to 49, the reader travels along with Tanner Burns as he pursues the U.S. Super Slam. We get the opportunity to tag along on a ride that took the utmost in motivation, diligence, and determination. In the end, not only do we get to accompany Tanner on his quest, but we also obtain bits of knowledge learned through his experiences and tribulations. All turkey hunters will see value in how Tanner has documented his quest to reach such a difficult task in the turkey hunting world."

– Michael J. Chamberlain, Ph.D. is the Terrell Distinguished Professor of Wildlife Ecology and Management in the Warnell School of Forestry and Natural Resources at the University of Georgia.

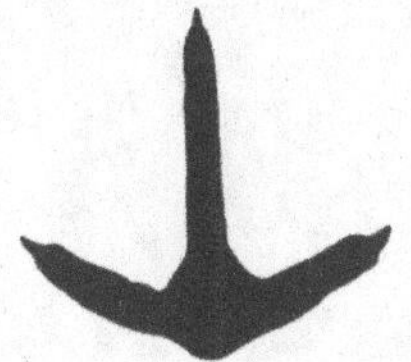

Climbing To 49

A Hunter's Completion of the U.S. Super Slam

TANNER BURNS
WITH DARIN POTTER

Copyright © 2024 by Darin Potter

Publisher: Outdoorwriter78@gmail.com

Cover photo by Dave Owens

ISBN 979-8-9882105-0-4

Printed in the USA

Contents

Prologue

The English dictionary defines "traveling" as "the action or activity of going from one place to another, typically over a distance of some length." What it fails to include are examples of travelers and hunters who have been etched into the fabric of this classification. Traveling is in a hunter's blood. Our ancestors who settled in America relied heavily on hunting in order to survive the harsh climate and the conditions they encountered while exploring new territories. Unforeseen challenges and danger were all part of exploring the rugged wilderness.

Sure, time has changed and technology has advanced hunting, but the urge and inner desire to travel and pursue game is still etched in the foundation of hunters. This desire is especially evident amongst turkey hunters as many travel out-of-state each spring extending their opportunities to pursue the wild turkey on unfamiliar soil. The appetite to travel and turkey hunt grows stronger with each passing year and when spring wanes and the season closes, plans are already in the works to venture into new places to go head to head with a gobbler or return to the familiar turkey woods we once hunted.

Some hunters take it one step further and set their sights on completing a Slam. There are six types of turkey hunting Slams according to the NWTF: Grand, Royal, World, Canadian, Mexican, and the U.S. Super Slam. Although the first five Slams mentioned require the hunter to harvest certain subspecies in a particular region or country the U.S. Super Slam is arguably the most intense and time consuming. In order to reach Super Slam status the hunter is required to shoot a gobbler in each of the 49 states except for Alaska, where conditions are too harsh for turkeys to exist.

On March 1, 2021 at just 30 years old, Tanner Burns from Buckhannon, West Virginia, shot an all white gobbler on a volcano in Hawaii, allowing him to complete the U.S. Turkey Super Slam. What makes this even more impressive is that he hunted all 49 states without going through any outfitters or hunting guides, with no decoys or blinds – all while working full-time as a teacher and running his business, "Full Draw Taxidermy," as a taxidermist. To top it off, the majority of these hunts took place on weekends and during spring break while teaching.

His pursuit of the wild turkey began early, when he was introduced to turkey hunting in the eastern panhandle of West Virginia. When Tanner was just nine years old, his next door neighbor and family friend Bob became his turkey hunting mentor. Bob was a farmer and also an avid turkey hunter who began hunting turkeys during a time when birds were scarce. He became an influential part of Tanner's passion for turkey hunting. Tanner would oftentimes hunt before getting on the school bus during the spring turkey season.

It wasn't until the spring of 2012 when Tanner decided to travel out-of-state to hunt wild turkeys and pursue his dream of accomplishing the Super Slam. This desire was fueled by two of his high school physical education instructors who also shared Tanner's passion for hunting turkeys. While a sophomore in college, Tanner finally had the opportunity to hunt with these two men during Alabama's spring turkey hunt in 2012. The stars had finally aligned and the stage was set for a journey which would soon take place. It was during this particular hunt he would meet another turkey hunting mentor and lifelong friend, Kenny Mount, aka, Chubbs. Kenny hunted turkeys in their purest form without the use of decoys or hunting blinds. Tanner would soon emulate this style throughout his journey on the Slam and credits Kenny with his success hunting turkeys.

In *Climbing to 49, A Hunter's Completion of the U.S. Super Slam*, Tanner Burns easily recounts each turkey hunt on new soil in such vivid detail that it comes to life on these pages like a roosted tom gobbling on a spring morning.

Throughout his journey Tanner takes you from the turkey woods of the West Virginia panhandle where he began hunting to an ancient volcano in Hawaii and all of the beautiful landscapes in between, oftentimes sharing his hunts with friends and detailing all of the kind people and characters he crossed paths with. You will feel as though you're right there beside him as he travels to each state, checking them off one at a time. His story is inspirational and will help you fill the void as you await the beginning of spring turkey season.

Despite many of the challenges, frustrations, and obstacles that come with the pursuit of turkeys, Tanner's humbleness, perseverance, and steadfast approach contains the right recipe for the dance of spring turkey hunting. Tanner's aggressive style and pure form of turkey hunting is evident throughout the pages of this book on his quest for harvesting a gobbler in each of the 49 states.

Each year prior to the season, Tanner meticulously devised a plan which would put him on track to finish the Super Slam in a record pace as he checked off numerous states each spring in the course of his nine-year quest. Each chapter concludes with some helpful tips in the "Lessons Learned" section, where he details some of the challenges he faced and provides helpful insight into some of the tactics which helped him close the deal on those elusive gobblers.

Where will you be traveling to hunt turkeys this spring? There are more choices than turkey calls in the aisles of a sporting goods store. Whether it's in your home state or thousands of miles away, it goes hand in hand with being in the subculture of turkey hunting and the desire to find new ground to hunt. For many of us, this yearning to travel all started the moment we entered a longbeard's turf and his gobble rattled us, shaking every twig and blade of grass through the entire spring turkey woods. For this young nine-year-old boy it meant swinging the barrel around a sapling as that gobbler closed the distance and stretched its neck out. The moment of truth was near, and *Climbing to 49* was on the horizon.

Chapter 1

West Virginia

A lthough my Dad wasn't a turkey hunting addict like me he would occasionally take a few turkeys in the fall, but never hunted them during the springtime. However, he did love to hunt his fair share of squirrels and deer in our home state of West Virginia. I would tag along with him every chance I could get at a very young age learning to hunt these animals. As a matter of fact, I cut my teeth on both types of hunting.

My first introduction to solo hunting came with a BB gun. This was my ticket to spending countless hours after school disappearing into the nearby woods and chasing mostly squirrels and rabbits. During these hunts I learned valuable skills that would soon carry over into the turkey woods. To this day, I still use these skills while hunting turkeys. Sneaking up on them to get into shooting range, patience, and persistence are a few traits that have stuck with me through the years as I continued to hunt other game in West Virginia.

1

When I was in first grade we moved from town out into the country. I spent a lot of time by myself hunting in these woods every chance I could. It wasn't long after moving when I was introduced to Bob Moran a farmer that lived down the road. He let my dad and me hunt on his property. In exchange, my dad did some chores for him like welding and whatever else Bob needed done on his farm. It just so happened that Bob was an avid turkey hunter who hunted in the surrounding area and grew up hunting them during a time when turkeys were pretty scarce. He quickly saw my passion for hunting and told me that he ought to take me turkey hunting during the spring time. I was not about to object to any type of hunting and my ears instantly perked up at the opportunity to try my hand at hunting an unfamiliar bird to me – the wild turkey. My dad said, "Well, I don't know anything about turkey hunting. Maybe you'll like it."

Who knew this would open the door to such an incredible passion and journey? During the weeks leading up to the spring turkey season when I was in the fourth grade and nine years old, Bob would take me up on a piece of property up in the mountains about 15 minutes from my house where we would listen for turkeys. It was during these outings where I heard my first turkey gobble.

Bob was in an accident when he was younger losing the use of one of his hands along with having some walking issues. He was already an older man at this time, so we did a lot of listening from the truck. Being new to the sport, I didn't know any better. I just thought this is how you went about preparing for turkey season. During this entire week I can remember Bob picking me up real early before school and driving up on the mountain to listen and try and find turkeys. Afterwards, we would come back and I would head on in to school. We had some great conversations in our travels up and down that mountain.

Opening day was approaching fast and my dad decided it was time for me to get ready for the season. The only shotgun my dad had was an old Remington 11-87 12 gauge, which he allowed me to use for the turkey hunt. Dad still has that gun in his possession today. Thinking back, that's a lot of gun for a nine year old kid. It was a real shoulder bruiser. We never patterned the shotgun, just abided by the "aim small miss small" mentality and prayed that I would hit my mark and kill my first wild turkey if given the opportunity.

Finally, opening day arrived. I was so excited the night before that I didn't sleep a wink. This lack of sleep was my introduction to the life of a turkey hunter. Because opening day in West Virginia always opens on a Monday, this meant that it would be on a school day. Fortunately, my dad told Bob if we find turkeys and time is running out, it was okay if I was late for school. With that said, we drove up the same familiar mountain that we had scouted prior to the season and started out the morning hearing turkeys on the roost right away. As we sat in Bob's truck we could hear a tom down below us gobbling pretty good. Bob thought that we should have a pretty good chance of killing this one so we went down the slope where we came upon a flat shelf and set up on this level piece of terrain. Bob began to do some calling and the tom began to answer.

This was my first turkey hunt so I didn't quite know what to expect. The bird flew from that adjoining ridge off the roost and landed on the same flat we were set up on, about 80 yards just out of sight. Bob whispered to me that the gobbler was probably going to come up this way once he did some calling. I remember laying eyes on the gobbler for the first time and it not being in range. Bob whispered, "Be real still!" Leading up to this he had already coached me on the steps I needed to take during a turkey hunt, however remaining motionless at this point was a top priority. Unfortunately, there was a branch to the right of my gun barrel and the turkey was starting to angle to the right so I was going to have to pull my gun barrel completely around this little sapling. Before making this move I waited until the turkey was completely hidden behind a tree. Bob had instructed me earlier that if you ever need to make a move you should wait until the turkey's head isn't visible. He also explained the importance of wearing a facemask, gloves, and the importance of being perfectly camouflaged. However, the one lesson from Bob that stood out the most was how even when you take all of these precautions there is the chance that a turkey can still see you.

Finally, the turkey came within shooting range and it was time to make my move. Bob quietly instructed me to swing my gun barrel around the sapling. Oftentimes a young kid wouldn't be able to get away with making a big move like that, especially around a sapling and at 30 yards. I guess I was a lucky nine year old. I finally got the gun swung around the sapling and Bob whispered, "He hasn't seen us!! Alright, as soon as he sticks his head up I want you to shoot him!" As the gobbler stretched his neck out, I placed the bead of my Dad's old 11-87 on his head and fired. The bird instantly hit the ground and began flopping around.

Now, one thing that I need to mention is up to that point Bob and I had never really discussed what to do after the shot. So, instantly after I took the shot Bob yells, "Go jump on him!" My initial reaction was, "What?!," but without hesitation I got up and ran out towards the turkey and got on top of the flopping bird. Eventually, Bob came over and we started high-fiving each other and celebrating my first turkey. I can remember thinking how cool it was that the turkey had gobbled, strutted into range, and put on a show for us, but most importantly it had been my first time turkey hunting. As Bob and I continued to stand there hovering over the gobbler I remember thinking, that was by far the greatest thing that has ever happened to me and the greatest thing I've ever seen.

Looking back now I think the stars aligned for me to become a turkey hunter and to experience that hunt. Killing a gobbler, let alone on my first hunt, was incredible. It lit the fire within me, which kept on growing each spring when turkey season arrived. It definitely set the stage for me to become a turkey hunter and instilled the passion for hunting them that I have to this day.

After the brief celebration Bob and I headed back down the mountain and went to my house to show my mom the turkey and get her to take a few pictures of Bob and me posed in the driveway with it. My dad was at work so we drove to his workplace with the turkey in my mom's car and I showed it to him. He was very proud of me. Normally, he isn't one to show much affection, but whenever I was hunting animals and successful he was a proud man. This isn't the reason I hunt anymore, but at the time it drove me to spend a lot of time hunting deer, turkeys, and other types of

The beginning of my passion for the wild turkey. March 24, 2001.

game. After showing my dad the turkey we left it at his work and he cleaned it for me while mom dropped me off to school on time. It's amazing all this happened and I still made it to school on time. Later on I can remember putting the turkey's beard and spurs in a zip lock bag and taking it to school the entire week and showing it off to all of my buddies and teachers.

After that spring turkey season it took me at least two or three more seasons to kill another turkey. However, it wasn't for a lack of trying. During this time Bob and I would continue our routine of hunting turkeys before school almost every single day of the season. ↓

LESSONS LEARNED

Never underestimate a first hunting experience. What happened on that hunt hooked me for life. If you get a chance to take someone hunting it doesn't have to end in a kill. Just make sure you engage them in a positive experience that makes them want to come back.

Chapter 2

Alabama

Throughout my youth and into my teenage years, my passion for hunting wild turkeys continued to grow. Each spring the woods of West Virginia called my name and oftentimes I would go afield with hopes of killing one before school. Up to this point I hadn't yet traveled out-of-state, but little did I know this would soon become a reality.

As my desire to hunt turkeys ramped up so did my interest in playing baseball. Unfortunately, baseball and turkey hunting don't mix. Although I was very involved in playing baseball I tried to not let that interfere with my time in the turkey woods. By the time high school rolled around I also began to play football. Coincidentally, my coach, Josh See., happened to be a big turkey hunter and was very passionate about it. Each spring he would travel down to Alabama to turkey hunt with the elementary gym teacher Roger Mongold and a retired high school gym teacher, Rick Perkins. They would also hunt with Greg Liller, who ran a local liquor store. (This was a good guy to have in turkey camp.) All four of these men were excellent turkey hunters. During their spring hunt they would also meet up with another fellow named Kenny Mount, who eventually became my turkey hunting mentor. Both Rick and Roger had met Kenny when he was young one spring while turkey hunting. They quickly befriended him and Kenny spent a great amount of time listening to them in camp and hunting with them every year on national forest lands. Kenny quickly recognized that Roger and Rick were turkey hunting in a way that intrigued him. No decoys, no blinds, woodsmanship, and getting in the right position was the essence of turkey hunting for them. Kenny quickly realized that if he wanted to be a better turkey hunter he needed to spend as much time as possible with these three guys.

Kenny lived next to where they camped and continued to absorb information like a sponge while roaming in the turkey woods and sitting around the campfire. Occasionally, Kenny had the opportunity to hunt with them, but mostly he would spend time listening to their stories and the tactics they would use while hunting gobblers in the national forest. Gradually, Kenny's collection of all of his mentor's information took his skills as a turkey hunter to great heights. I would put him up against anyone in the turkey woods.

Around the age of 16 I soon realized that my coach, Josh See., would head down to Alabama to hunt turkeys each spring. Josh knew of my love and passion for turkey hunting so after spring break when he had been turkey hunting he brought back a glass pot call and gave it to me. Kenny had heard about my interest in turkey hunting and had given the pot call to Josh to bring back home to me. Kenny had previously worked for a call company called Woodhaven.

Besides being my football coach, Josh also taught me in gym class. The rest of the school year, during class or whenever he had any down time, Josh would coach me on using this glass call. In time I started to become decent with it and finally began making turkeys gobble while using one, which I had never done before. Up to this point I had really struggled trying to get a tom to respond to any of my calling attempts. Josh would also accompany me on spring hunts in West Virginia, continuing to teach me turkey calling methods. Bob, who had called in my first turkey, was getting older and not able to hunt with me as often as he would like. During my middle school years I had killed turkeys, but was always hunting with someone. Eventually, when I was a junior in high school, I was finally able to call in and shoot my first turkey while hunting alone.

After graduating high school I was lucky enough to receive a scholarship to play baseball in college at West Virginia Wesleyan. Playing baseball at this level was definitely more demanding. As I said before, baseball and turkey hunting don't mix so my time in the turkey woods was extremely limited. However, during the spring time of my freshmen year I got permission to hunt on some private property and was able to hunt before classes and baseball practice. At this point I still didn't have a desire to travel and turkey hunt.

After baseball season and my classes had ended for the semester, there was still three weeks left in the West Virginia spring turkey season. This was the first time that I didn't have a time limit and other obligations so when I came home that spring I was able to hunt for two straight weeks. This extra time allowed me to fill both of my spring turkey tags.

During my sophomore year of college, I played baseball once again during the springtime. However, I had a falling out with my coach and at that point knew I wasn't going to play for him my junior year, but I still wanted to stay in college and finish my degree. In 2012 my junior year rolled around, and without baseball the door was wide open to be able to spend more time than ever in the turkey woods. Between classes and working a part-time job in town I was left with plenty of extra time I didn't have while playing baseball.

Throughout college I continued to stay in touch with my old high school football coach, Josh. One day I decided to give him a call and asked him what the chances were of me joining him in Alabama for a spring turkey hunt, basically inviting myself along on the hunt. Now this wasn't your basic turkey camp where you could just bring anyone you please. It was old school. His immediate reaction wasn't yes or no. He said he would talk with Rick and

Roger along with the other guys and see what they think. After a final discussion amongst all of them, Josh and the rest of the crew agreed to invite me down to their camp in Alabama. They gave me the dates that they would be heading down and we met up in Moorefield so we could ride to Alabama together. We were so excited to arrive at turkey camp we left early and drove ten hours straight through the night, arriving around 10 a.m. the following morning. As we rolled into camp everyone was already back and had finished hunting for the morning. To our surprise every single person in camp except Greg Liller had filled a tag that morning.

If you hunted during the spring of 2012 you probably remember that it was an exceptional year for hunting turkeys across the country due to early spring weather. The guys at camp said turkeys were gobbling everywhere. I met Kenny for the first time and it was good to see the others once again also. We exchanged high fives and celebrated the successful morning they had in the turkey woods. I instantly became a sponge like Kenny had been when he was a young turkey hunter, soaking up all the knowledge I could about turkey hunting. I made mental notes that to this day are still etched in my mind and are at my disposal for hunting turkeys.

The following morning Josh took me with him. We heard quite a few turkeys and even had a tom come within range, but I couldn't get a shot off. A couple days passed and we finally got on some turkeys, but still weren't killing any. On the third evening I decided to do some scouting on my own and had found an area with turkey tracks, droppings, and scratching. Afterwards, I came back to camp and told the guys. They suggested I hunt the area in the morning based on what they had seen while looking at a map and kindly pointed me in the right direction. This was before Google Maps was on phones, so the guys all had paper maps in camp to refer to. After some map game planning Rick told me he would go with me in the morning and hunt the area. At that time he had taken a few turkeys so he was willing to join me. The next morning rolled around and we arrived at this location. Rick did the calling and soon we heard some gobbles a couple ridges over. As we were just getting ready to top the second ridge I suggested to Rick that we should probably do some calling just in case the birds were closer to us than we thought. Rick agreed so we called to them and to our surprise they sounded as though they were almost within shotgun range. My guess is they were around 50 yards. After the gobbles sounded off we fell back to a lower elevation on the ridge and literally dove behind some trees for cover. Rick was a little bit forward of me and to the right, which wasn't ideal since I was the shooter, however he was still in a safe position. Once we set up, Rick let out another call and shortly afterwards two gobblers came up over the ridge and my first out-of-state turkey fell to the ground.

Kenny and I formed a lasting friendship in the turkey woods of Alabama. April 3, 2012.

Rick and I celebrated and I thanked him for taking me out that morning. I was super grateful for the opportunity to hunt with someone with so much knowledge. I must have thanked him a million times. Rick was just as excited for me as I was and it meant a lot to get to hunt with someone as accomplished as him.

The area that we hunted had several turkeys. Not only did we hear these two particular toms, but there was a chorus of gobblers throughout the surrounding area.

Back at camp that evening, everyone was talking turkey when they brought up Kenny. All of them mentioned that if given the opportunity to hunt with Kenny you'd better go. "School will be in session!" they said. I wasn't going to invite myself to hunt with him, but I thought if given the chance I would most certainly take it. That evening when it was almost dark Kenny asked me if I would like to hunt with him in the morning. I eagerly obliged. So the following morning we went back into that same area where Rick and I had hunted and right off the bat I noticed that Kenny was moving real fast. He was like lighting in the woods the way he moved and climbed hills and ridges. At this time Kenny was in his early thirties. I considered myself to be in pretty good shape, but at 20 years old I struggled to keep up with Kenny's pace in the turkey woods. Once we reached the familiar area we listened, but didn't hear anything close. Eventually, we heard one gobble on a distant knob.

We began walking straight for the turkey, closing the distance fast. 400, 300, 200, 100-up to this point we hadn't even called to this turkey. Meanwhile the tom was still up on the knob and we were still down below him. Finally, we reached 100 yards from the bird and I asked Kenny, "What are we doing?"

He responded, "If he's going to gobble like that, we're not even going to call to him. We're in a good position below him so we're just going to pop up over this ridge on the flat he's on and shoot him."

I was surprised that this was Kenny's strategy for killing a bird. However, I soon realized how effective this strategy is. To this day I use this tactic, especially on public land where you run the risk of a bird recognizing danger and ruining the hunt before you have a chance to kill him. Because this particular bird was so vocal, Kenny knew we would be able to crawl up there and shoot him without calling.

Just before we were about to break up over the ridge where the turkey was, a national forest vehicle drove by. It pushed the gobbler off the knob. We heard the crunch of the leaves as the turkey came closer, but we knew he was out of range so we dived down into some leaves, keeping our heads low as he walked by. Eventually the turkey walked further down into the valley. Kenny decided to give the bird some time, knowing that soon he would gobble again. Sure enough, it wasn't long before he gobbled off of a nearby ridge.

We decided to go after him again, sneaking to within 70 yards. Unfortunately, somewhere along the way he had picked up a hen, which made things even more challenging. The bird continued to gobble, so we decided to start calling to him. The hen began walking our way, which is usually a good thing. As it started to approach us, Kenny, who was hunkered down in a road bed behind me, whispered, "Get ready in case the gobbler is right behind her." Soon, she was right on top of us within shooting range. However, the gobbler was nowhere to be seen. With my shotgun at the ready I kept waiting for the gobbler to make an appearance. However, the gobbler continued to gobble from the same spot and refused to come to our setup. Then Kenny, knowing that the tom wasn't coming in and figuring the hen would probably go back to the gobbler, pulled a move that came from years of experience. Kenny purposely flushed the hen. Since then I've used this tactic when confronted with similar situations to rid the area of a hen. With the motion of Kenny's arms, the hen flew off in the opposite direction of the tom. Kenny called while the hen was flying in order to cover up the commotion, which caused the tom to let out a gobble. At that point it was one of the most bad ass moves I'd ever seen in the turkey woods. At the time I wasn't quite sure what had happened, because Kenny and I were far enough apart we couldn't communicate. After no progression from the gobbler we decided to go silent or go after the gobbler from a different angle. At this point he was around 50 or 60 yards out and holding.

I rolled on over to where Kenny was positioned, asking him what the plan was. Finally, I suggested crawling up to where the gobbler was and trying to take a shot at the turkey. Kenny looked at me and said, "Are you good at sneaking up on turkeys?"

Honestly, at the time I wasn't. I had snuck up on a couple of turkeys in the past, but wasn't the best at it. Little did I know that when I had slid to where Kenny was I had unintentionally made some scratching in the leaves. Up to this point we had ceased calling and suddenly heard some leaves crunching on the road bed where Kenny was. I looked up with my shotgun still on my knees and the tom came around the corner in full strut at 45 yards completely catching both of us off guard. Thankfully, I've always been good at making quick moves with a gun in high pressure situations. As the turkey approached closer and rounded the corner I was able to get the bead of my Mossberg 835 shotgun up on his head quickly. The gobbler noticed my movement, but by then it was too late.

During all of this commotion another turkey had begun gobbling across the valley several hundred yards away. I hadn't paid much attention to it, but Kenny had him on his mind while everything was playing out. Kenny didn't even miss a beat. As soon as I took the shot he said that he was up to bat on this gobbler. He knew this one was probably sneaking over to us while we were working the other bird. As the bird had flopped around on the ground Kenny called to cover up the noise. It was just a couple of minutes later when the gobbler came to within shotgun range, allowing Kenny to also fill his tag. After the shot we celebrated, sat with our turkeys, and began to talk. This became the first of many deep and meaningful conversations we would share in the woods.

It was at this point I watched Kenny engage in a ritual of sorts. After killing a gobbler he would set against a tree and smoke a cigar. A ritual I guess or maybe a way to pay respect to a truly magnificent creature. It was very intriguing to a young turkey hunter. He had an admiration for them like I had never seen. It became apparent this was a religion to him.

During my week long hunt in Alabama I ended up killing two turkeys. Before parting ways, Kenny and I exchanged contact information. I ended up heading back to West Virginia and also killed two birds in my home state a few weeks later. Kenny and I sent each other pictures of birds we had killed and shared our stories to each other throughout the various seasons.

The 2013 spring season rolled around and I returned to the same Alabama turkey camp for almost a week, killing a couple more turkeys with Kenny and learning more from him on our hunts together along with the other guys in camp. I also spent time hunting on my own trying to figure them out and continued to grow as a turkey hunter.

Toward the end of my 2013 trip to Alabama, Kenny asked me what I had going on the week of May 1. At this point I was still a senior in college. He wondered if I could skip a week of school to go hunt, which I figured I could. Kenny invited me to the Black Hills of South Dakota, an area where he hunted every spring. Up to that point I had never traveled out West in my entire life. I knew I had to figure out a way to make it work with my schedule. This experience was something that I didn't want to pass up.

On my way back from Alabama, I called my parent's excited about the news of this hunt with Kenny. I went to work, trying to figure out how to miss classes for a week and learn the ropes of flying to hunt. ↓

LESSONS LEARNED

When in doubt, call or blow a locator call before you break over a hill. You never know if a gobbler is on his way to you or has changed positions. Knowing his location before you setup is crucial.

Chapter 3

South Dakota

With my college schedule all figured out and my make-up work for classes completed I was ready for my trip to the Black Hills. Hunting South Dakota meant flying, which was something new. Taking a gun aboard, finding the right gate at the airport; these things were all foreign to me. Unfortunately, I didn't book the flight in the best manner. I flew out of Charleston, West Virginia, and had two layovers before arriving in South Dakota. Later on I realized I could have probably flown directly from Pittsburgh right to Rapid City. Like they say, you live and you learn. This experience better prepared me for future flights while traveling to hunt turkeys.

I didn't own a gun case, so I had to borrow one from Bob Moran, the same fellow who had called in my first turkey. He loaned me his old plastic gun case with a key pad on it, which I'm surprised survived the flight. When you fly, your gun case has to have so many locks on it, and this particular one satisfied that requirement. Also, I didn't have any luggage. I flew only with a duffel bag, which Kenny got a laugh out of. Up to that point he had been traveling for about 15 years so he had it down to a science. Looking back, it was comical and since then I've improved my packing skills.

When I landed in the Black Hills I was in awe by the sheer beauty of the area. Kenny and I ended up renting a really nice cabin in the national forest. Later that day after unpacking, we headed out to roost some birds. The subspecies we were after were Merriam's turkeys, which I had never hunted and had no idea how much different they were to hunt. What quickly separates Merriams from Easterns is they like to gobble a lot, especially during the evenings. One thing worth mentioning is that on these out-of-state turkey hunts, oftentimes Kenny and I would split up. This allowed me to make mistakes, which I could learn from on future turkey hunts. I would come back to camp and discuss them with Kenny who would offer little hints here and there to help me out. Kenny had been hunting the Black Hills for around 10 years so he knew of a lot of good areas. That evening he dropped me off at one of his familiar spots and told me where I should hear turkeys. I sat in this particular location until dark, not hearing a single gobble. About a half hour after dark, Kenny pulled up to give me a ride back to camp. He had a big grin on his face, asking me if I had heard any gobbles. After explaining to him how quiet the evening had been during my sit he said, "Would you like to hear one?"

I laughed and said, "What do you mean? It's almost an hour after dark." With a grin still on his face, Kenny told me there was a turkey just down the road gobbling its head off. So, I jumped in the truck and we took off down the road a few miles. After a few minutes, Kenny stopped his truck and told me to jump out and grab a beer out of the cooler in the back. As I reached into the ice to grab a cold one, the turkey gobbled on a ridge across from us. I couldn't believe it! The ice sloshing around in the cooler had caused him to shock-gobble. This was the first time I had heard a Merriam's gobble. Their gobble is totally different from the Easterns I was familiar with. It was more high-pitched and really hard to describe until you've heard one for yourself. I absolutely love their gobble and was captivated by it that evening when I heard one for the first time. To this day, those mountain Merriam's are my favorite turkeys to hunt.

After that gobble, Kenny came unglued and started howling and laughing. We probably sat there for 10 or 15 minutes listening to the turkey gobble. Finally, Kenny told me I could go after him in the morning while he hunted down the road. "He's yours if you want him!" he said generously.

I told him he didn't have to do that, but he insisted I go hunt this bird because I had never shot a Merriam's before. I joke with him now about how he knew there wasn't going to be a chance in hell I was going to kill that bird. To this day he denies it and says he was just trying to be nice. Kenny never told me any strategies on how to hunt this particular turkey, which I'm glad for.

The next morning I got there early, around 45 minutes before daylight. Instead of approaching the turkey from above, which I would have done now, I went right directly beneath him. I finally approached within 50 yards below where he was roosting. When daylight broke he started gobbling like crazy. I bet he gobbled at least 200 times. I heard another turkey gobble in the distance, but not close enough to mess with. While the bird I was on continued to gobble, I soon realized that he had of hens with him. Finally they pitched out over to the uphill side, which could have been game over if I had been there when they flew down. One thing I quickly learned about Merriam's that day is, when they hit the ground they do not stay put. As soon as they flew down they started moving, covering 200 yards in a matter of minutes. Another silly mistake I made was trying to call to him. With Merriam's the gobbler will oftentimes gobble and cause the hens to drag him in the opposite direction of your setup. They don't want another hen stealing their man. I soon realized I needed to put the call away and try to get in front of them. Or take drastic measures. The gobbler, along with the hens, ended up crossing the national forest road and the last time I heard them they were gobbling about 400 yards away. Soon the gobbling stopped and I was afraid to call because they kept going in the opposite direction. Eventually, I decided to go back to the road where I saw them cross and began walking down an old national forest road. To my surprise, just before I walked up into a clearing I saw a fresh turkey dropping, which looked like it belonged to a hen. It was so fresh it was warm to the touch. I thought it had to be from those turkeys that just crossed the road. At that point I knew I was back tracking their route. All I needed was to hear them gobble.

I had a hawk call in my turkey vest. As you know, turkeys will shock gobble at a variety of unfamiliar sounds. The Merriam's seem to gobble even more so than Easterns at these random noises. I hit that hawk call and just up in the clearing ahead a gobble rang out. Had I been just five more steps ahead they would have surely seen me. Merriam's don't move all day even though it seems like they do. Eventually, they found a spot they liked to hang out. It just so happened that these birds chose this little clearing up above me, which was about a mile from where they roosted.

I was carrying a Remington 11-87, which my parents had bought me for Christmas that year. It was a turkey edition with a thumbhole stock and all camouflage. I was hoping I would be able to just pop up over the ridge before me and shoot him. I slowly dropped down to my knees and after crawling five yards I peeked over the ridge and there he was with a whole bunch of hens. They instantly saw me, however without hesitation I took a quick shot with just a tiny window of opportunity when he stretched his neck to see what danger had just approached him. His feathers were beautiful with snow white tips on his tail fan. I was so excited I just sat there in that clearing with him for almost three hours, soaking it all in. I was instantly addicted to hunting Merriam's from that point on.

I had killed the gobbler around ten o'clock with plans to meet up with Kenny around 1 p.m., so I began to walk to where he had parked the rental vehicle and waited for him. He had hidden a key so I could wait in the vehicle if I had gotten done hunting before him. Soon Kenny came strolling down the road so I got out of the vehicle and pulled out the gobbler from the back hatch of the vehicle, holding it up for him to see. Kenny started to fist pump, then came up and gave me a big hug. It was a special moment for both of us.

Kenny ended up getting sick on this particular trip and struggled to kill a turkey. He had seen them, but couldn't get a shot. There was a one bird per hunter limit in the Black Hills, so after

May 10, 2013

killing my bird on the first day I was on a mission to help him fill his tag. About three days later I went into a spot and roosted a turkey while Kenny was hunting another location. By roosted, I don't just mean the general direction he was. I knew the exact location. Once it had gotten dark I snuck in there and actually picked out the exact limb he was roosted on. There was an old road bed that I had walked when I had found this turkey, and I laid a big rock on the road so I knew the exact spot to cut in. Kenny was a little surprised I had roosted this gobbler because of my lack of turkey hunting experience at the time. The next morning we walked in there and I set up behind Kenny about 50 yards and let Kenny do his thing. The gobbler flew down and I don't think Kenny even had to call to him. The bird ended up working towards him and he was able to finally fill his tag. It was very rewarding to find a bird for Kenny since he had been gracious enough to invite me on the trip and also find the turkey I inevitably ended up killing. ↓

LESSONS LEARNED

Always be on the lookout for turkey droppings. Had I not noticed the fresh sign in the road I wouldn't have been compelled to use my locator call, which helped me figure out where to set up based on his gobbles. Where you find the sign you find the turkeys.

Chapter 4

Kentucky

During the fall of 2013 I began teaching full-time in West Virginia, which made my schedule a little more challenging for turkey hunting because I had to finagle my out-of-state hunts. Fortunately, though, I was able to periodically add personal days to my weekends, allowing me extra time to hunt. I also took advantage of spring break, which gave me a full week. Oftentimes throughout the Slam, this was necessary when trying to fit in numerous states in a short period of time.

Meanwhile, the spring of 2014 found me kicking off turkey season in South Dakota with the crew once again after getting home from Alabama. A friend of mine, Ryan Bennett had invited me to hunt in Kentucky.

I had been hunting with Kenny for a couple of years now and I was starting to figure out how to hunt turkeys. I was by no means an expert, but I was slowly starting to understand how to hunt them and be successful.

Ryan and I grew up playing baseball against each other. Both of us share a deep passion for turkey hunting. He was the first person my age I had met who also loved to turkey hunt. As this book is written he is closing in on his completion of the Super Slam with just a few states left.

After making a connection through some mutual friends and prior to our trip to Kentucky, Ryan and I traveled to Nashville, Tennessee to the National Wild Turkey Federation's (NWTF) Annual convention in February. During this trip we talked about our upcoming Kentucky hunt. Because Kentucky's spring season opened before West Virginia's and the place we were hunting was only about a four hour drive, it made this location the perfect place to start turkey season.

Ryan's Dad worked for the United States Department of Agriculture (USDA), having connections in a variety of states with multiple landowners. One of these connections was with a man who owned property in east Kentucky and also worked for the USDA. He gave us permission to hunt his property for turkey.

As Ryan and I were gathering up our turkey hunting gear, he informed me that we needed to be at McDonald's at 4 a.m. to meet this guy. Despite being a little skeptical of this situation, I still agreed and tried to remain optimistic that he would show up. As we sat there in our vehicle waiting, 4 a.m. came and went. With the clock ticking and shooting light approaching fast, Ryan tried calling the guy, who like an elusive gobbler had yet to be seen. Finally, 5 a.m. arrived and I began getting really perturbed that he hadn't showed up yet. The thought of missing the opening morning hunt was starting to become a reality.

I knew of some public land nearby and told Ryan we should just leave and go hunt. Fortunately, Ryan convinced me to be patient and wait for him. Finally, over an hour late, the man drove into the McDonald's parking lot. He was a pleasant old man, which made my negative thoughts quickly disappear.

Once we arrived at his property, he insisted on showing us the boundaries via his side by side. We didn't want to be rude, but we really didn't want to drive this at shooting light right on the opening morning of our turkey hunt for fear it would scare the turkeys. However, we didn't say anything because it was his property and after all, he was nice enough to give us permission to hunt. After the short ride, he dropped us off towards the back of his property to hunt. At this point it was well past fly down time and we figured most of the turkeys were probably on the ground.

Shortly after he took off, the turkeys began to gobble all around us in multiple directions. It was as though we were sitting in the middle of surround sound speakers. At this point, even after spending lots of time in the turkey woods with Kenny, I was still messing a lot of my turkey hunts up. Throughout this entire weekend we had at least two or three different opportunities to kill a gobbler, but things didn't go as planned.

On one particular hunt a gobbler was coming towards me, but the neighbor shot it first. However, around 4 p.m. with temperatures high, our luck began to change. After numerous obstacles, we finally got a turkey to gobble on the opposite ridge in front of us. This was a welcome sound and brought us out of our slump. Because Ryan's Dad had put this hunt together for us he was first on the gun. Up to this point I wasn't even thinking about the Super Slam. For me it was just a new state to hunt and a weekend where I was available to go hunting.

We headed over toward the area where we heard the bird and eventually Ryan connected, placing his tag on the bird. The gobbler had come in silent, surprising both of us. This wrapped up our opening day. We only had one more day to hunt and had to leave Sunday evening for home, so the clock was ticking.

On the final day of our hunt, we drove back from the campground we stayed at to the same location with the song, "Talladega" by Eric Church blasting through the speakers. To this day whenever I hear this song it takes me back to Kentucky. After parking, we began walking to the same area where we hunted the day before. No sooner had we reached the spot when we heard a couple of gobblers off in the distance. Ryan and I decided to split up and chase both turkeys.

The morning proved uneventful for me except for an encounter with a trespasser walking onto the property. This created another challenge, causing me to go home empty handed. However, Ryan continued to be on fire, filling his second Kentucky tag.

On the ride back home, we decided to make another trip back to

April 18, 2014

Kentucky the following weekend. We had learned enough about the land in the previous two days and my hopes had improved of killing my first Kentucky gobbler.

The following weekend found us back on the property at dawn, and like clockwork we heard some gobbles across from us on a ridge. We walked to this area and began calling to the bird with gobbles immediately ringing out. Thinking fast, Ryan decided to set up behind me about 30 yards in case he had to coax the bird a little further. The turkey came in swiftly, which caused me to set up in a poor position. I was on my belly in a very uncomfortable prone position and could hardly move. There were also very few shooting lanes and it looked like a recipe for disaster. The turkey continued to come closer and eventually reached 75 yards on top of the ridge, strutting back and forth and gobbling periodically. The turkey was looking in our direction and probably figured he should have seen a hen by now so he hung up. During the 15 minutes I watched this bird I remember distinctly hearing him drumming and spitting. The turkey hunt in Kentucky is the first time I remember hearing a turkey do this and my ears got really in tune to it helping me to recognize this sound throughout future hunts.

Ryan, who was still about 30 yards behind me, also quickly realized this bird had hung up. He began to do some soft hen calling and scratching in the leaves to imitate a feeding hen. Shortly afterwards, the bird's demeanor totally changed and his feathers folded up and he began walking off the ridge, quickly closing the distance. He was flanking me to the hard right and within shotgun range. Granted, I was still in a very awkward position on my belly, a terrible setup that, looking back, I should have never gotten into.

There was only one opening to my right that I could shoot through, so I would have to swing hard to my right in order to pull the shot off, which as you know is very difficult for a right-handed shooter. Thank goodness, though, the 11-87 that my parent's had bought me came with a thumb hole stock on it, which would allow me to shoot one-handed if necessary.

The gobbler continued to walk to my right and as soon as it cleared a large tree and reached the opening I put my red dot scope on his head and fired without bothering to stop the turkey. Finally, I had a bird down in Kentucky.

Between the two of us, Ryan and I had taken three gobblers in the four days we hunted on that piece of private property. The following year we returned and had another successful hunt. I haven't been back there since, but hope to return once again to hunt turkeys in this area of Kentucky. ↓

LESSONS LEARNED

When you have a buddy, use the float calling tactic. Had Ryan not been behind me calling and scratching in the leaves I doubt the gobbler would have ever broke from his knob. It's a deadly tactic that gets many gobblers killed every year.

Also, the spitting and drumming sound that a gobbler makes can be just the ticket if you can recognize the sound. There is no magic recipe to get your ears in tune with drumming. It just comes from spending time with gobblers at close range.

Chapter 5

Ohio

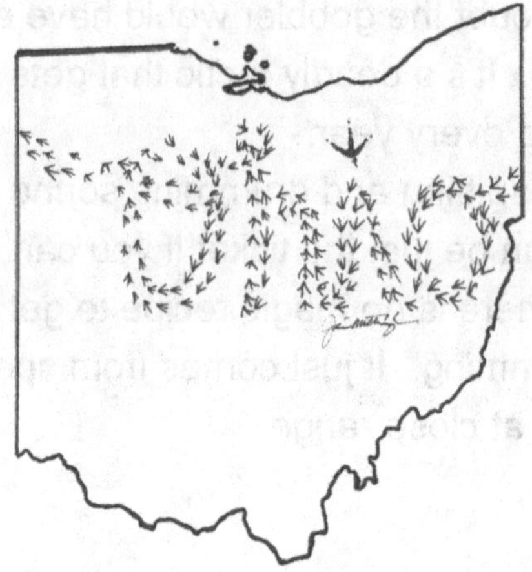

After traveling to Kentucky in 2014, I was off to the Buck-eye State. At this point I wanted to continue to expand my hunting opportunities outside my home state any time I had a free weekend. This same year Kenny, decided to begin his turkey hunting Super Slam quest. Because he enjoyed traveling so much to hunt turkeys, he was already 20 or 30 states in. At the time, only a couple of people had accomplished the U.S. Turkey Super Slam. He first heard about the Super Slam from Dave Owens, who is widely known in the turkey hunting community as the creator of *The Pinhoti Project*, along with winning the 2018 NWTF Grand National Senior Open Division turkey calling championship in Nashville, Tennessee.

Kenny met Dave at one of these turkey calling contests. Both being like-minded and having a passion for turkey hunting, they conversed at the show and that's when Kenny found out about the quest Dave was on. Dave had been one of the first people to attempt the Super Slam, which he completed in 2017. Kenny became captivated by the notion of such a journey and decided to start the Slam himself. Dave and Kenny ended up going on a turkey hunt together later that year, which began a lasting friendship.

One of the states Kenny hadn't harvested a turkey in yet was Ohio. Up to this point, both of us continued to stay in touch calling and texting about turkey hunting. One day, he expressed interest in hunting this state. Because I was relatively new at being a traveling turkey hunter, Ohio was also unfamiliar to me. Without putting boots on the ground I knew nothing. However, I had joined a deer lease this particular year from a customer who visited my taxidermy shop. Unfortunately, I didn't know anyone else that was on the lease and hadn't been there before to gather any information. All I knew was, I was paid up and had permission to hunt the property. Ironically, I got the lease to hunt deer and not turkeys.

I mentioned the lease to Kenny and without hesitating he agreed to hunt this location. After the trip was finalized, Kenny flew to Columbus, Ohio so I drove there and picked him up. From there the lease was about a three hour drive. Because we had arrived late in the day we weren't able to scout that evening and roost any birds or even get an idea of the lay of the land. At this point we weren't sure what we were getting in to. Kenny was up to bat first, since this was his trip and I hadn't even begun to think about working towards a Super Slam. Besides that, I wanted to help him get a bird since he had been so gracious to me on past trips to South Dakota and Alabama and teaching me how to hunt turkeys in general. It was now my opportunity to return the favor, and I was excited to help him check one more state off of his list.

Once we arrived at the lease, we studied a map and came up with a game plan on how to hunt this particular property. The lease we would be hunting was divided into several different sections, so we chose the section on the map that looked like it might hold turkeys based on the terrain features. Back then I had an old Honda Civic, which isn't the best turkey hunting vehicle, but it was good on gas. During those years I had to roll with whatever vehicle I could. I still get a laugh picturing Kenny and me driving down the Ohio dirt roads with our turkey hunting gear shoved in the back of that small car.

Opening day found us parked in front of a gate leading to the lease, drinking coffee as the sun began peeking over the horizon. My gut told me we should already be walking to our setup. However, Kenny, being the turkey guru, suggested we stay put for a while and I wasn't about to question him. He ended up dozing off in the passenger seat for about 10 minutes. When he woke up it was really getting daylight and Kenny became flustered because it was so light out.

We quickly put our turkey hunting gear on and began walking down a narrow road towards the spot we had picked out on the map. As I shined my light out onto the road it was literally polluted with turkey tracks. Probably more turkey tracks than I had ever seen in my lifetime. We looked at each other and instantly knew we were in the thick of things.

After reaching the spot we had picked out, we listened and heard one bird that gobbled close and the rest were off in the distance. After we set up about 40 yards back in the woods, the turkey flew down in the field in front of us.

He had some hens with him so we continued to send some calling his way in hopes of drawing him closer. Unfortunately, the terrain provided little cover for us to crawl closer to the birds, which left us with no option but to let the situation play out. At one point it looked as though the gobbler was going to break off from the hens and come towards us, however he decided to make a huge loop in the field and move to our right out of the picture. Kenny, having all of the experience, knew he was going to flank us and come into our setup from behind. It wasn't five minutes when the turkey let out a gobble 180 degrees from where we first laid eyes on him. Sure enough, Kenny was right. I remember thinking if Kenny hadn't been there I would've never anticipated the tom's direction of travel to the right. After the bird gobbled, it wasn't more than a couple of seconds when the bird came into sight and Kenny swung the barrel of his shotgun around and shot it as it poked its head up. To both of our surprise, he missed the 30 yard shot and the bird flew off. Typically, this wasn't a difficult shot for Kenny.

Missing a turkey is something that happens to all of us at one point or another if you spend enough time in the turkey woods. Finally, Kenny calmed down, but this bird had gotten under his skin as elusive birds often do. However, I knew he would kill this bird eventually. It was just a matter of time. The rest of that day was uneventful and we didn't get on any other turkeys.

The following morning Kenny decided to go back where he had missed the bird while I opted to hunt an area that I believed was an old strip mine where I had spotted some turkeys the evening before. That morning I called in some jakes, but was unable to entice the gobbler to come into my setup.

Kenny ended up killing the old gobbler that he had missed the day before. With Kenny's mission accomplished, we decided to drive around and check out the various fields on the lease to see if we could spot any turkeys. Sure enough as we pulled up to one of the last remaining tracts we located four jakes and a strutter along with some hens out in a field. It was around 10 a.m. and we instantly thought it was game time. Kenny pulled the car out of sight and parked it, instructing me to get out and try to use the terrain to crawl in and kill the gobbler. I had eyes on the direction that I needed to take. A little knob stuck out in the middle of a field like a beacon where the turkeys were hanging out, allowing me to keep tabs on them while crawling in for a shot.

Because of the company the gobbler was in, I decided not to do any calling. This was going to be purely a crawl mission. As I begin inching closer to the knob I encountered a little stand of trees in the field. It worked out perfect because where these trees were located the turkeys could not see me. I finally crawled to within about 100 yards of where I thought the turkeys were. As I slowly closed the distance towards the knob I periodically looked up to check on the bird's whereabouts. Eventually, I encountered another island of trees and realized I must be getting real close to the birds. Unfortunately, this group of trees had a bunch of dry leaves underneath them that were going to be impossible to cross without making any noise. However, as I crunched through the nearly 10 yards of leaves, sounding like a bag of chips, the hens heard me and started heading my direction. Looking back, I realize the turkeys mistook me for another walking turkey.

Soon the jakes joined in, and they closed the distance around 10 yards from me. And soon, I realized something was out of place. They began to head the opposite direction, leaving the field. Earlier we had confirmed there was only one gobbler in this group of birds. Finally, I spotted the longbeard I was after up close and personal at a mere 20 yards. Here I was again in another situation where I knew I would have to out draw him like a western gun fight. It seems like every turkey I kill is just inches from going wrong.

By then I had risen up on my knees with my shotgun on the ground beside me. All I had to do was reach down, grab it and try and out draw him before he high tailed it out of there. Usually the outcome is different when trying to out draw a turkey, but at this point with all of the effort I had put into this hunt it was worth trying. For some reason things have always seemed to work in my favor. As I shouldered my shotgun I quickly realized that I made a huge mistake. In the midst of the jakes and hens throwing me off guard I had forgotten to turn the red dot on my scope to the on position. The gobbler saw me, so I decided to put his head in the center of the scope, figuring I should be able to kill him anyway. Looking back, this wasn't the most ethical thing to do, but at the time I still had little experience in the turkey woods. As the turkey's head reached the center of my scope I shot and he rolled over on the ground. However, he got back up and flew off. I thought to myself, *I should've never taken the shot.* Hindsight is 20/20 I've always heard.

I got up and walked out to the spot in the field where I shot him and there were some feathers on the ground. Feeling dejected like all turkey hunters after a miss, I concluded I must have just blown out some of his tail feathers. I called Kenny and told him I had blown a shot and to come and pick me up. After Kenny had arrived I told him the whole story as he was driving down the road. About five minutes into the drive Kenny turned to me and explained that he was going to turn around, instructing me to go and look for the turkey, which I had thought was a goner. I told him, "What do you mean, it flew off!?"

Kenny said he had the same situation happen before. "When

April 22, 2014

a turkey is up on a high point they can be mortally wounded and
still be able to get their wings under them to fly away. This higher
elevation can allow them to fly off if they have enough energy left
and look for a hiding spot. Typically, they will fly off and look for
a hiding spot. It's worth going to look. After all, you owe it to the
bird to put in an effort and try to find it."

I was a little skeptical, but I listened to Kenny and decided to
go back and search for the bird. The bird had glided down into the
thick bottom beneath the knob. I began searching in brush piles
and looking around everywhere throughout this thick and tangled
area. Suddenly, there was one particular brush pile near a pond
that caught my eye. I thought this area looked like it would be a
good place to hide. To my surprise as I approached the brush pile
I discovered a red head sticking out of there. I thought to myself,

that SOB was right! He was tucked in there pretty good. About the same time I saw the gobbler he saw me. He tried to run out of there, but I could tell that he was wounded bad. As he made his move I was able to take one last shot at him and kill my first Ohio bird.

I couldn't believe how fortunate I was to get that turkey after the events that had occurred leading up to this. I called Kenny and we celebrated. It was one more lesson that will always stick in my memory bank while in the turkey woods. ↓

LESSONS LEARNED

If you feel like you hit a turkey, do your due diligence and look for him. Lots of times they will hide in a brush pile or thick cover. Search for them thoroughly and many times you will find the wounded gobbler.

Chapter 6

New Mexico

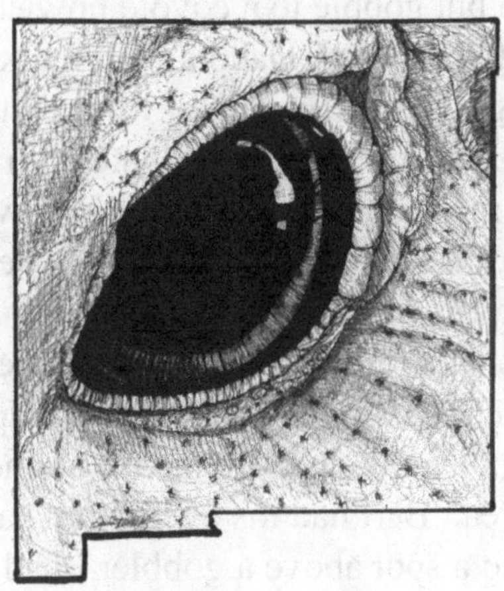

Following the Ohio trip in May of 2014, Kenny and I made plans to go on a trip out west to turkey hunt. Every year he traveled out west, but since he was on a mission to complete the U.S. Super Slam he wanted to check off some new states.

The two states we decided to hunt this particular spring were New Mexico and Colorado. We allowed ourselves a week to hunt both states. We decided that we would fly into El Paso, Texas and drive a rental car to New Mexico and then Colorado.

A couple of hours into New Mexico I noticed the terrain went from flat to mountainous and full of ponderosa pines. The area we were hunting was some of the most beautiful country I've ever seen. Once we reached our destination, we decided to split the cost of a rental cabin. A college friend of Kenny's named Bart had also joined us on this trip. Due to Bart having a medical issue from an accident he had in the winter, he wasn't going to be able to climb the steep terrain with us.

We arrived just in time to roost a few birds that evening before our hunt the following morning. All the roads in this entire area were down in the bottom and the turkeys were living higher up on the mountainsides. The combination of elevation and the rugged terrain made for more of a challenging hunt than other hunts I'd been on in the past. As we drove these roads we stopped occasionally, trying to get a response using a coyote call. The turkeys out west can't help but gobble to a coyote howler, just like the Merriam's we hunted in South Dakota. We marked waypoints on about 10 different gobblers. Back then we used the app GIA prior to OnX Hunt, which allowed us to navigate with no service along with downloading maps and marking locations with turkeys.

Once we arrived back at the cabin we reviewed all of the pins and tried to brainstorm which gobbler was the easiest to set up on in lower terrain, considering that most birds were half-way up out of the canyon. After devising a plan, we woke up optimistic the following morning. Kenny dropped me off at one location and drove to another area. Bart had his own rental car and hunted elsewhere. I climbed to a spot above a gobbler I had roosted the evening before. As it started breaking daylight I had nailed it perfect. I was set up just 40 yards above this gobbler on the limb, which I could clearly see. Soon, he began gobbling and to my surprise some hunters down below started calling to him also.

Not knowing any better at the time, I made a huge mistake by calling to him too close while he was on the roost. After softly calling to him, the gobbler stuck his head up, looking over in my direction, and flew off to probably the next county knowing full well there was no hen. It was an unfortunate situation and in hindsight I should have just stayed quiet and the bird probably would have ended up landing somewhere close enough for a shot. That was the extent of my first morning. Fortunately, Kenny ended up killing the bird he was after, calling it in from a long distance and filling his first New Mexico tag. Like so many other future turkey hunts, Kenny was tagged out first and waiting on me to fill my tag, while offering different strategies to help me succeed.

Later on at the cabin, we celebrated and then went out that evening to roost birds. My favorite thing about turkey hunting out west is being able to drive around and enjoying the beautiful scenery while putting them to bed with a call. Eventually, that evening we were able to roost a few more birds and once again came up with a game plan for the following morning. The plan was for Kenny to hunt with Bart, and they would drop me off at one location along the road and pick me up three miles down the canyon where the other two had parked at the end of the day. This would work out perfect because I could just hunt my way down the slope to the vehicle. With a pin marked on the GIS app I felt confident in hunting this stretch.

As I walked across the rugged terrain the wind began to pick up, making it extremely difficult to hear. However, as I continued to press on I decided to give my glass call a try. Surprisingly, even with the high winds I was able to make out a faint gobble, which sounded like it was far off. I figured I needed to get at least another 75 yards closer before setting up on this particular turkey. This is when I made mistake number two of the trip. Little did I know that unlike Eastern birds, the Merriam's subspecies will travel a long way to get to your calling if it is interested enough. When calling to the Eastern subspecies, you almost need to get inside their bubble in order to get their attention. So, unbeknownst to me as I'm trying to cut the distance between me and the bird, he's traveling directly towards me after the first call. As I finally reached an area where I decided to sit down, I looked up and there he was, standing right in front of me. This bird didn't fly off like the last one, but instead ran off leaving me with a feeling of dejection.

Even though it was only day two, I felt sour knowing that I had just screwed up two good opportunities on gobblers, especially when Kenny had already filled his tag and was waiting on me before we traveled on to Colorado. As we arrived back at the cabin my sour mood carried over into our evening roosting session and Kenny picked up on it. He was concerned and asked what was going on with me. I told him I was kicking myself for coming on this trip when I could be hunting turkeys in West Virginia right now. I knew where there were a lot of turkeys and I kind of wished I had just stayed home.

Kenny fired back, "Yeah, stay home and hunt West Virginia. Something we can do every year and we've been doing forever.

May 5, 2014

Don't you want to see new country? Anyone can kill a turkey in the same state and the same place each year. If you want to be a good turkey hunter and get better you need to go to these new places and figure out how to kill them. That's what is going to set you apart from other turkey hunters and take you to the next level of turkey hunting."

Being a competitive person, I really took to heart what Kenny said. Anything I do, I want to be the best at it. So when he said this, from there on out and during the rest of the Slam I always had a grit when I heard, saw, or knew there were turkeys in the area. I was not about to give up or take no for an answer. Whatever it took, I was going to get within shotgun range of a gobbler. And if it didn't work out I was going to come out swinging that evening or the next morning. Quitting was not an option. This is something that can't be taught, but comes from within each of us, and in my opinion it's what separates good turkey hunters from great ones.

After the dust settled and Kenny gave me a boost of motivation, I decided to go out on an evening hunt. I figured I would go back to the last spot where I had spooked a bird and see if I could get him roosted.

Kenny dropped me off at one of the national forest gates and then drove off to try and roost other birds for me. At this point there were about three hours of daylight left. Shortly after exiting the vehicle and walking down into the canyon, I heard a gobbler. Mind you, these canyons are so steep that on the map they actually fooled us into thinking we could just walk up to where we had roosted a bird in 20 or 30 minutes. Well, these 20 or 30 minutes in the early morning darkness turned into about an hour or hour and a half. The terrain was extremely rough on us and we were hiking a long way in the dark to reach these turkeys we had roosted the night before. To get to this particular bird, I had almost an hour walk, which left me with just a couple of hours before fly up. He teased me with yet another gobble and I knew it had to be the same bird I had spooked because he was still hanging out in the same area.

As I reached the area I quickly set up and called to him. Right away he was responsive with several gobbles. By the sound of his gobbles he wasn't gaining any ground and was staying in the same spot. I felt as though I was in a good spot, but for whatever reason he didn't want to come closer. I decided to look at a map and noticed that according to the terrain features he was down on a bench and there was a big hill above him. I decided to make a complete loop around the turkey and try and get directly above him. Once again I walked another hour and reached a spot where I had him pinned down. I took out my glass call and boom, he gobbled from the same spot. After he gobbled two or three times I decided to shut up and see what happened. Ten minutes later I decided to call again and quickly realized he had cut the distance in half. I quickly put my glass call away and shouldered my shotgun.

Those moments in turkey hunting when you know the turkey is moving in fast because his gobbles are getting louder is what I love the most about turkey hunting. The minutes leading up to when you see him and the anticipation is the ultimate for me in turkey hunting. This is one of those moments where time is suspended and I know I'm going to see him at any second.

Suddenly, I spotted a red head pop up in front of me at about 25 yards. I didn't even see his full body. I just put the red dot on his head and fired. He was a nice solid two year old Merriam's. With a few hours left of daylight and no cell phone service to call Kenny, I just sat there on this beautiful ridge with the bird, soaking in the memories of the hunt.

As darkness started to approach I decided it was time to head back down the mountain with my bird in tow towards where Kenny would pick me up. As I reached the road I sat there with my back against a tree in the dark waiting on him. When Kenny pulled up he didn't realize I was there already, so he decided to let out a coyote howl because we had heard the turkey that I killed gobble a few nights in a row.

Just before Kenny blew the coyote howler I said, "He aint gonna gobble tonight, big daddy!" Kenny put the howler down and paused for a second.

"Are you shitting me?!" He said in disbelief. I stood up from where I was sitting and Kenny came over and put his arms around me, giving me a great big bear hug. ↓

LESSONS LEARNED

Try working a gobbler with your calls from a different position. You never know if there is an obstacle between you and the bird or if the bird just doesn't feel comfortable coming from that direction. Backing up and making a circle to a new setup can get a gobbler to break.

Chapter 7

Colorado

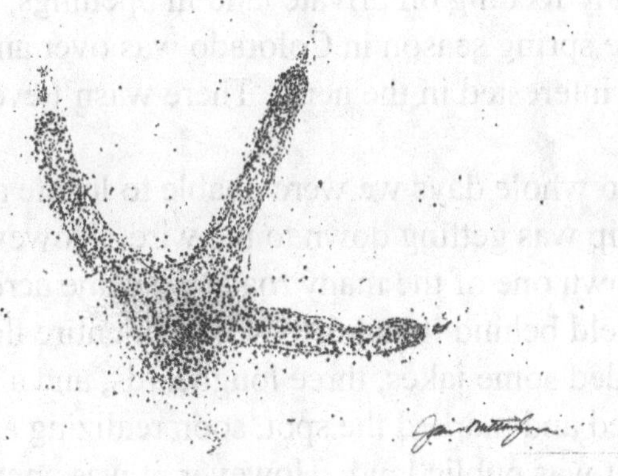

With my New Mexico tag filled on day three of our week-long trip, we still had time to fit in one more state before heading back East. We threw a dart and the following morning we were Colorado bound. Unfortunately, we didn't have any information whatsoever on the location of turkeys in this particular state and weren't sure what to expect. The only place where we had any remote idea of where to hunt them was in the foothills of one of the national forest lands. It seems that most of the turkeys out West live near the border where national forest meets private land. Kenny had gathered some information about turkeys in New Mexico from an online forum, but we knew nothing about Colorado.

We arrived in Colorado mid-morning and immediately began driving around looking for turkeys, but with no luck. We didn't even see any along the roads on private land. At this point things weren't looking very promising in the area we planned on hunting. Evening arrived and we decided to continue driving along the national forest roads in an attempt to roost some birds with a coyote howler like we did in New Mexico. Finally, at last light we were able to get a turkey to gobble along one of the forest roads. The following morning Kenny went in after this particular gobbler, once again filling his tag first thing, while I traveled to another area where we had found some tracks the previous evening. Unfortunately, we noticed that the breeding season appeared to be almost done. The turkeys we finally began spotting from the road were just casually feeding on private land in openings, but it looked as though the spring season in Colorado was over and the toms were no longer interested in the hens. There wasn't even any gobbling going on.

For two whole days we were unable to locate any gobblers and our trip was getting down to the wire. However, as we were driving down one of the many roads we came across a river with an open field behind it and discovered an entire flock of turkeys that included some jakes, three longbeards, and a bunch of hens. We stopped and marked the spot, soon realizing after looking at a map that it was public land. However, it was an ungodly area and these birds were going to be tricky to hunt. In order to access these birds we would have to walk in four miles. Besides that, the field was surrounded by huge high walls so you would basically have to slide down it order to reach the field where the turkeys were. Numerous canyons and other rugged terrain features were also included in this obstacle course, which would have to be conquered before even reaching the high walls that surrounded this field.

As I looked at the map I'm thinking, *man, this is going to be tough to get in there!* But they were the only game in town so we decided to give it a shot. Kenny dropped me off at an access gate where I began navigating towards the field with my GPS. Kenny had a great idea to keep tabs on the turkeys while I made the trek and communicated the turkey's whereabouts via text messaging in case they moved. We figured it would take me at least a couple of hours to access the field. However, his idea was short lived when we realized there was no cell phone service in this location. The plan consisted of Kenny meeting me at the gate after sundown to pick me up.

As I began the long journey to the field, I quickly realized how challenging it was going to be. There were all sorts of obstacles such as creeks, blowdowns, gnarly timber, and a couple of different canyons that I encountered along the way. Finally, after a few hours of walking, I reached one of the high walls that surrounded the field we had seen. From my position in the hollow on the right of the field, I was unable to see the turkeys. There was way too much brush and trees to look through. Carefully, I slid down the high wall on my butt, trying not to kill myself in the process. When I reached the bottom near the river I was probably 200 yards from where we had seen the turkeys a few hours ago. Because we had seen very few turkeys on this trip, I was taking zero chances of the turkeys spotting me at this point. So I decided to begin crawling on my hands and knees, even though I was still a long way from the turkeys. The last thing I wanted to do was spook them, because I had a really good feeling they would gobble that evening and I would be able to make a move on them in the morning.

Calling to them at this point wasn't an option because I knew there was only a slim chance they would come in, given there was a large flock of them. Also, with Merriam's I knew that oftentimes if you call to them they will travel in the opposite direction. After crawling for about a 100 yards, I realized I was getting close to the brushy field. Suddenly I caught movement out in front of me. It was a hen. This caught me off guard because I didn't expect the turkeys to still be there at this point. As she clucked and went about her business I thought, *Was she a lone hen in the field or had she strayed from the flock?*

Finally, she was joined by a few other hens and then I realized if the flock followed the same course along the river they were going to walk within shotgun range. As is always the case it seems, the hens were leading and the gobblers hung back about 100 yards. Soon the hens walked by me, left to right, and I started to get real nervous they might bust me because I didn't have a lot of cover to hide behind. Fortunately, they didn't see me as they passed by. Meanwhile, I kept an eye on the gobblers, which were in full strut the entire time as they kept cutting the distance. 60, 50, 40 – *Alright that's close enough*, I thought. The toms were following a road bed, but for whatever reason the hens had stayed below it. I

May 7, 2014

had to raise my shotgun quickly because the hens had started to get nervous. As the gobblers got within range they caught my movement and briefly came out of strut. Seizing the moment, I pulled the trigger and completely missed the bird I was aiming at. As luck would have it the entire flock flew off except for one of the three gobblers. He just stood there, unsure of what had just happened. I used this window of opportunity to swing my semi-automatic shotgun over and kill this bird.

I remember thinking, *how am I going to climb back up the high wall and carry this bird out of here?* I followed the river down to an area where there was a crevasse that wasn't quite as steep as the other areas and managed to climb out of there. As I began climbing I can remember sliding repeatedly. I would take three or four steps then slide and keep making my way up. This hunt was extremely tough, but worth every minute of it.

By the time I reached the gate where Kenny had dropped me off it was well after dark. I was still without cell phone service so Kenny knew nothing about my success yet. Once he pulled up though, a celebration was in order. This completed our western swing for the 2014 turkey season. ↓

LESSONS LEARNED

Study your online maps. Had we not had online maps and studied them after spotting the gobbler we would have never figured out a route into the area. Also, take advantage of new technology. It's getting more and more gobblers killed every year even though I'm a little conflicted with the ethics of its use.

Chapter 8

Mississippi

In the spring of 2015, with seven states under my belt, I officially decided it was time to attempt the turkey Super Slam. Honestly, I wasn't sure how fast I would accomplish it, but it was something I wanted to pursue. Kenny was already on his journey to complete it and I figured with all the states that we were adding up each spring, I might as well begin my journey as well.

In the off-season, Kenny and I discussed our plans for the 2015 spring season regarding which states we wanted to hunt on our western trip. I had planned on hunting in Alabama first, which through the years became a tradition for me each spring. Afterwards, Kenny wanted to hunt Mississippi because he needed this state to help him reach his goal. During the off season we decided to put in for a particular Mississippi area, which required a lottery draw.

Our plan was to hunt Alabama for about four days and then drive to Mississippi. We ended up both being successful in drawing the area that we wanted. The challenging part was that our permit was only good for three days and then we had to hunt on national forest lands the rest of the time.

I traveled to Alabama alone for my first ever opener there and ended up killing a turkey on the first day. This was also the first time I hunted with a 20 gauge during turkey season and I would continue using this gun for the rest of the slam.

On the second day of the Alabama season Kenny killed his gobbler, which was a switch considering he always seemed to kill one before I did. Then it was time for us to begin the journey to Mississippi. Because we arrived a day before our permit hunt began, we had to hunt on national forest land. Unfortunately, we didn't hear a single gobble that day and only cut one single turkey track. I remember biking into an area several miles along flat terrain which made for easy travel. Ironically, both of the tires on Kenny's bike went flat. As I followed him I couldn't help, but start laughing because he was Mr. Prepared all of the time and this type of thing never happened to him. I don't think he realized it, but I was able to sneak in a photo as I followed behind him.

The following day we were finally able to begin our hunt in the area we had drawn a tag for. Because neither of us knew the area that well, we decided to hunt together. To our surprise a turkey gobbled about a 100 yards away from our first set up. We looked at each other and were dumbfounded because Mississippi doesn't have many turkeys and to hear one gobble right away surprised us. There are a lot of good turkey hunters that have taken years to kill a turkey in this state while working on their slam, so the fact that we heard one was amazing.

Kenny was up to bat first this time. I decided to hang back at our initial set up while he moved about 30 yards closer to the roost to get in a better position. This had to be one of the most textbook roost hunts you could imagine. The turkey continued to gobble as Kenny called to him a few times. The gobbler cut off his calls with gobbles and finally hit the ground and marched straight to Kenny, allowing him to fill his tag early. I didn't get to see the actual kill shot, but heard the entire hunt unfold from where I was seated. While Kenny was working his turkey, a different longbeard started gobbling another 100 yards away from us. I thought, *man, are we about to kill two turkeys in Mississippi on opening day?!*

Unfortunately, the gobbler hung up and continued to gobble, but didn't want to come any closer because he had some hens with him – a typical scenario in the turkey woods. He was located deep in a beautiful swamp surrounded by standing timber. Eventually the turkey stopped gobbling, preventing us from gaining any ground on him.

March 19, 2015

We decided to be patient and not push this turkey out of the area in hopes of killing him off the roost the following morning. This was one of the few times we decided not to be super aggressive and back out because we didn't want to bump him, knowing that this might be the only other turkey in the area to kill.

We continued to hunt most of the day and decided to go back to this spot and roost the gobbler in the evening so we could pinpoint him when he flew up for the night. About two hours before dark we approached the gate where we had walked in the previous morning, right before a storm started to roll in. However, another vehicle was already parked there.

We left this spot and checked out some other areas for about a half hour, and when we drove by the original gate the vehicle was gone. This gave us the green light to go in there after that gobbler. We threw our gear on and walked in close to the area where Kenny

Kenny's fly up cackle the evening before my hunt helped me close the deal.

had killed his bird, leaving the bikes behind. As we sat there and listened for any gobbles it continued to thunder and lightning all round us and looked as though it was getting ready to storm once again.

Kenny turned to me and said, "Do you think I should do a fly up cackle?"

Not knowing any better I said, "Sure go for it!" He attempted the first fly up cackle and all we heard were crickets. Kenny decided to do just one more cackle a little bit louder than the first and the turkey hammered out a gobble from his roost, allowing us to know exactly where he was spending the night. We were pumped to say the least. I dropped a pin on him, figuring he was about 150 yards from us. After leaving the area we came up with a game plan to hunt him early the next morning.

The next morning arrived and we returned to the location two hours before daylight, trying to get within 40 yards of the tree where he roosted. As daylight came I thought to myself, *this definitely looks like a spot where a turkey would live.* I began seeing some hens in a tree out in front of me and one over to my left fairly close, which I didn't see until she started yelping. The gobbler only let out two gobbles. The last one was half-assed, almost as if he didn't really want to gobble, but did. I couldn't quite see him on the limb yet, but I knew he was real close judging by the sound. We couldn't call to him because we figured there were at least

Flat tires in Mississippi for Kenny.

three or four hens surrounding him.

To my advantage, the hen on my left flew off the roost and landed behind us, which meant that we were now between the gobbler and his hen. The gobbler followed suit, but landed in front of me. Kenny and I were separated by about 30 yards because when we first arrived in the dark I wanted to cover the last remaining yards alone to minimize movement and noise. After hearing him hit the ground and working his way towards us through the swamp it was super early, like six or six thirty and I could barely see him. As he slipped behind a large tree I made my final move to adjust the position of my shotgun. He finally stepped out and I took the shot, killing the gobbler.

At the time it hadn't sunk in yet just how lucky Kenny and I really were. To kill two birds on public land in Mississippi in two days was unheard of. Like I mentioned before, it takes some turkey hunters years to fill their tag in this state. Both of our birds had inch and a quarter spurs and looked like they could be brothers. It was a special couple of days in this state to start out the 2015 spring turkey season. ↓

LESSONS LEARNED

An evening fly up cackle can be deadly. If you have the time or chance, go out in the evenings when you can. You never know when you'll get an answer. And if he does answer you, I promise you'll be on his mind the next morning.

Chapter 9

Georgia

A couple of weeks later I was onward to state number three of the 2015 turkey season, Georgia. Because it was during the school year and I was teaching, I decided to take some time off and have a four day weekend. My friend Ryan Bennett, who had already hunted Georgia earlier in the season, decided to join me. The area I planned on hunting was brought to my attention by a friend of mine who is also an excellent turkey hunter. The friend gave me some specific spots to try in this state. While looking at these areas on a map I liked what they had to offer, however one particular section caught my eye more so than the others. I noticed a road leading to a very small piece of public land that connected to another road where you could park and access this area, which led to more public land. Just that little sliver of a road connected to this piece making it accessible. Judging by the map it looked very steep and gnarly. I decided to start out my hunt in this location because I liked what the terrain had to offer. It did receive lots of hunting pressure, but I knew there were lots of turkeys in there also, which made it appealing.

On the first morning of my hunt, Ryan and I drove down the road that led to the small piece of public land that touched the road. As we arrived in the dark we pulled off the side of the road to park when I noticed a spot on the ground with feathers everywhere where someone had recently cleaned a turkey. I thought, *well, this isn't a good sign!* But at the same time we knew turkeys were in there, so we decided to hike up to the highest point on the public land and listen for turkeys. We heard absolutely nothing. And the sad part was we could hear for a long ways off. Ryan and I looked at each other and came to the conclusion that maybe we should try another area. After looking at the map we soon realized we were up too high and besides we hadn't found any turkey sign at this elevation.

We decided to descent to a lower elevation and start cutting some ridges to see if we could pick one up. As we climbed down around 100 feet, sure enough, we began seeing turkey sign. After continuing to scale over ridges, we finally reached a distance of about five miles out from where we parked when I took out my glass call and immediately struck a gobbler. Finally, we were in business. We advanced a couple hundred yards and I called to him once again. Boom! He hit it! I began working this turkey from a nice flat spot on the ridge. Suddenly, I got it in my head that the gobbler wouldn't come to me because it was so trashy with brush. There were way too many obstacles.

I told Ryan we needed to loop around the turkey and get on the knob he was on in order to be on the same level. At the same time I realized the gobbler had a hen or two with him and was probably not going to come over and join us. However, not only was the gobbler responding to my calls, but the hens were too. Looking back now, while I was working this bird I should have stayed put, but at this point I still didn't have a whole lot of turkey hunting experience to know any better.

As was the case so many times before in the turkey woods, we began to make our move on the turkey not realizing he was also making a move on us. Once we began sneaking our way toward the bird we reached about the halfway point when I realized the gobbler and his hens were standing right where we had just called minutes before. After proceeding to kick myself I remained optimistic they would come over to visit us. It's natural for a turkey to move so I figured we were still in the ball game. Because we had lost elevation we were below the turkeys, which created yet another problem. However, we had backtracked and regained about 100 yards, close to where our original position was. Because we were down the ridge from them we had the roll of the mountain allowing us to start working back towards them a little bit at a time.

Soon, we got 80 yards below the gobbler, which is never ideal when you're working a turkey. Also, there were absolutely no trees to set up so I had no choice, but to lay down flat on my belly. Ryan stayed behind me about 100 yards and began scratching in the leaves and calling for me. Fortunately, the gobbler answered, however he still held his ground for quite some time, not wanting to break away from the hens. It was obvious they didn't want to come down the hill towards us. At this point I hadn't called at all to avoid giving away my position.

As time went on I knew that we had to do something drastic to get this turkey. We inched forward to within about 60 yards of the turkeys. All I needed was for them to come towards me about 20 yards or so. I had my mouth call in and decided to join Ryan's calling with some really light hen yelps under my breath. Obviously I sounded much closer to the group of turkeys, which totally changed the demeanor of one of the hens. When I called, her head instantly popped up over the ridge in front of us and she began working her way towards me.

I could tell my calling agitated this bird, which was absolutely perfect. As she closed in on 15 yards to investigate, I could see the gobbler's tail fan when he broke the crest. He strutted and continued to inch his way closer as well. At this point I couldn't see his head yet, even though they were around 45 yards away. Finally, after patiently waiting in a prone position, he stuck his red head up from behind a deadfall, offering me a shot. I put the red dot on his head and touched off a round. A lone hen flew off, which baffled me because I thought there was more than just the one hen up to this point. I quickly got up from my position running up to where I had shot at the bird and there he was a two year old Georgia mountain gobbler.

This was one of the most exhausting days of my life. Even though Ryan had already filled his Georgia tag he had two tags left so we decided to start cutting ridges again, stashing my turkey to

April 2, 2015

go after yet another gobbler we had heard. At this point we were around seven miles from my car. Then another gobbler popped up and by the time we finished messing around with this turkey it was midday – 1 p.m. and we were another mile or so away. This wasn't a flat eight miles either. It was a mountainous eight miles through valleys, over ridges, and side hilling it. It was definitely rugged country.

After picking up my stashed turkey we walked back to the vehicle. Ryan checked his GPS, which read that we had gone a total of 15 miles on foot the first day of turkey hunting in Georgia. I remember it was the most tired I had ever been during a day of turkey hunting. My feet were sore and my body ached all over. It was a very long day to say the least.

We ended up spending three more days in Georgia, allowing Ryan to fill his tag.

When I took Ryan along on this trip I didn't clear it with my friend after he had given me some intel on this trip. I learned that when someone gives you information about an area where gobblers are located – even though I didn't kill my bird right where my friend had told me to hunt – you should just keep it to yourself. It's disrespectful to the person that provided the information by bringing someone else along with you to the area. When someone tells you about an area, keep it to yourself. Kenny told me this and it's something I will always remember. I was young enough that I didn't know any better at the time. ↓

LESSONS LEARNED

A gobbler with a single hen is usually very susceptible to calling. Whether he leaves the hen or the hen comes with him. These gobblers can be called into gun range much easier than a gobbler with multiple hens.

Chapter 10

Montana

My 2015 quest continued and soon I found myself in Montana, preparing to check one more state off my bucket list for the Super Slam. By this time I'd started to figure out how to hunt turkeys on my own and felt as though my turkey hunting skills had improved.

With Mississippi and Georgia in the rearview mirror it was time to keep the momentum going. I had also hunted in a few repeat states, Alabama, Ohio, Kentucky, and my home State of West Virginia. Kentucky and Ohio were very good to Ryan and me. We killed two birds each in each state two weekends in a row. We were off to a banner year and I was hoping my luck would continue out West.

Kenny and I were going to head out West together again on a turkey hunting adventure and decided our first state would be Montana. I was familiar with this state because I had completed taxidermy school there and did some exploring in my free time on weekends. I had discovered a little valley where quite a few turkeys frequented so Kenny and I agreed we would start the trip hunting this location. For a backup plan, we also had some walk in areas on private property where we had permission to hunt after making calls prior to the trip. It's a good thing we lined up these places, because I had seen turkeys during taxidermy school in the summer and not in the spring when their pattern would be entirely different.

This was one of the worst travel experiences of my life. I had missed my connection to Minneapolis to get to Montana and had to wait at the airport about 14 hours until the next flight, which was later that night. It was a miserable experience. I wasn't going to make Kenny wait for me in the Montana airport, so I explained the situation and told him not to wait for me. He rented a vehicle and ended up roosting some birds that evening.

When I finally arrived in Montana I rented another vehicle and drove to the area where Kenny and I would hunt. Once I arrived at the motel I walked in and asked Kenny if he roosted anything. He told me to go over and check out the videos on his phone and see what thought. I liked what I saw. Kenny had roosted what sounded like two to three birds. The following morning when we arrived back at the area where he had roosted birds, what he had thought were gobblers were in reality just a bunch of jakes. It was hard to tell at first because they sounded like gobblers. We were a little discouraged, but soon our hopes lifted when we heard a gobbler off in the distance, probably about a mile away. Once we realized this was a longbeard we shifted our focus to this turkey. As we got closer to him, we discovered he was living right behind someone's house. However, national forest land butted right up against their property so we walked into this area and tried calling and working the bird. At first the gobbler was responsive, but soon he refused to break his position, like so many other stubborn birds I've hunted before. This went on for about 40 minutes when Kenny decided to inch a little closer to try and get a little farther into the gobbler's bubble. After crawling almost 200 yards closer to the gobbler he gave us the silent treatment. Meanwhile, Kenny didn't realize it, but from up on a knob I could see the turkey breaking as he continued crawling. While watching all of this unfold I could see that the turkey hooked to the left. Because the bird went silent Kenny had no idea he had changed positions. Unfortunately, I couldn't get his attention, and I also didn't want to risk the turkey seeing my movement.

Eventually, Kenny decided to call to the bird and soon realized the turkey was within shotgun range to his hard left instead of out in front of him. Finally, he was able to swing to his left and kill the gobbler.

Now I was up to bat. We didn't want to continue to hunt this area because we were pretty sure Kenny had killed the only gobbler in this spot. We had listened all morning without hearing any other gobbles, so it was time to move on. Around mid-day we decided to drive through some national forest roads and came upon a valley with a bunch of turkeys. However, the land at the bottom was all private property and there was no access. We didn't do any door knocking, but we should have. Soon, we realized that if we parked three miles away we could come up from behind the private property 200 yards from the valley on national forest lands where the turkeys were living. After covering almost 14 miles of terrain in Georgia, I felt I could handle it.

Down to my underwear before crossing a glacier stream in Montana.

We decided to drive near the valley towards evening and do some howling when we discovered turkeys everywhere gobbling throughout the valley. Most of the gobbling came from public land.

Going into the next day both of us felt pretty confident about this area. After parking, we figured it would take us an hour to complete the three mile hike in order to reach the valley where these turkeys were spending time. However, our calculation was wrong. It took us at least two hours in the dark to climb up the mountain to get above the turkeys and walk the public to where they were. Once we arrived at the top it was already beginning to break daylight and the turkeys were gobbling. From this location we still had another mile of walking left in order to set up on the birds. I was thinking we should have set the alarm earlier and started at 1 a.m.

To our dismay, after a couple of hours navigating the steep terrain we realized the turkeys were on the ground. Our miscalculation had cost us some time, but eventually we arrived at the location where we had dropped some pins the day before. From that location, which was on the boundary where public meets private, we could see the birds down on private a few hundred yards away and gobbling their heads off. The hill we were standing on was almost vertical. So now we had two challenges before us. It left us with no choice but to set up where we were.

As we started calling to these birds they gobbled back, but held their ground with the hens down in the valley. We figured there were at least five gobblers in this group. Our goal was to try to get one satellite bird to break off, which seemed impossible after trying for an hour. Our last ditch effort was to mimic an entire flock of turkeys. Kenny and I put our mouth calls in while also calling on glass calls. The turkeys went completely nuts and practically choked themselves calling back to us. Where we were sitting on that mountain, it was so steep you had to dig your heels in just to keep from falling. Not to mention all of the thick underbrush, vegetation, and trashy woods that we had to contend with. However, it was the only option we had to set up on these birds. If the turkeys did decide to come to us it was going to have to be a 15 yard shot.

After the chaos the woods fell silent, but within a few minutes we heard a nearby gobble. Finally, we had gotten two gobblers to break off and come in to our setup. As they inched their way up the hill I whispered to Kenny, "Is he coming up here?"

We were thinking there was no way in hell. You would have to shoot these turkeys after they flew down from their roost because they're not going to come up off of private, we concluded. The gobbling got closer and closer, and we realized these turkeys meant business and it sounded like two of them were coming in. Soon, I heard leaves crunching, mixed with the continued gobbling, when suddenly at 15 yards one of them stuck his head out. That was the only thing I needed to see because I knew he was a longbeard based on the way he gobbled. I took the shot and he flopped down the hill. I had to retrieve him fast because if I didn't he would have likely flopped all the way to the bottom of the mountain. To my recollection, it was the steepest terrain that I have ever killed a turkey in. The blast from my shotgun was so loud it echoed across the scenic valley for what seemed like a minute.

After picking up my bird, we had to walk back down the rugged terrain, which was equally miserable because we had to climb back up the mountain where it flattened out so we weren't side hilling it the entire way back to the vehicle. It took us a brutal three hours to walk out of there, but having a nice Merriam's turkey draped over my back made it all worthwhile. With my tag filled on the second day we were off to hunt turkeys in Idaho. ↓

May 3, 2015

LESSONS LEARNED

Western Merriam's live in steep terrain. When we made our initial setup on this bird I never would have dreamed he would come up that steep face to our calling. Unfortunately, we didn't have any other choice. In this situation all you can do is try and hope for the best.

Chapter 11

Idaho

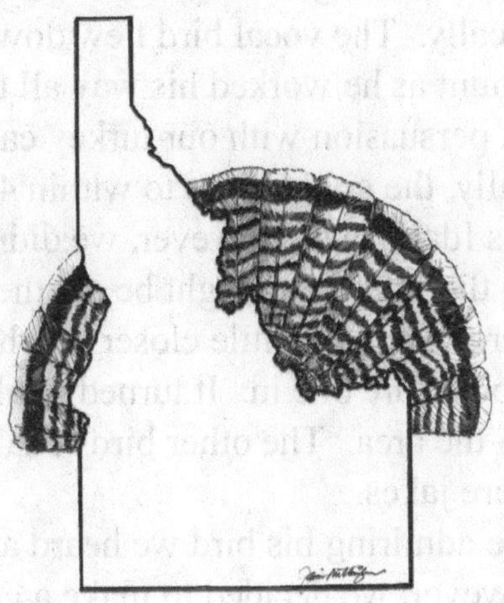

Because my flight had been delayed and I rented my own vehicle, Kenny and I drove all the way back to the airport to drop the rental off before traveling to Idaho. This cost us almost eight hours of lost time towards our next turkey hunt. After finally getting all squared away with the vehicle we left for Idaho and arrived in the evening. We had just enough time to drop all our gear off where we were staying and head out to roost some birds. Previously we had picked out a few spots on the map that appeared to be likely areas.

We drove the national forest roads in this area and did some coyote howling so it was business as usual and we were right on track. The birds were pretty quiet as we drove around. However, when we stopped for the last time that evening and hit the coyote howler we heard a couple of gobblers off in the distance. We marked this location and decided to come back and hunt there in the morning.

Once we parked the vehicle, daylight began to break and instantly we heard gobbling. The part of Idaho we were hunting is some of the prettiest country I've ever seen. I felt very fortunate to be hunting turkeys in such a beautiful location.

We decided to set up near the national forest road because the turkeys were only about 100 yards below us. One turkey in particular was doing most of the gobbling while the other one was calling more sporadically. The vocal bird flew down and it appeared to be a textbook hunt as he worked his way all the way up the road with a little bit of persuasion with our turkey calls as we coaxed them along. Finally, the gobbler got to within 40 yards and Kenny was able to fill his Idaho tag. However, we didn't jump up right away because we thought there might be another longbeard coming in. I decided to crawl down a little closer to where we had heard them to see if I could lure one in. It turned out Kenny had shot the only longbeard in the area. The other birds I saw after crawling down the road were jakes.

As we sat there admiring his bird we heard a gobble far off in the distance. However, we decided to make a go of it and spent about an hour walking in the direction where we thought we heard the gobbling. Approaching the area, we discovered a nice green field with a little dip in the middle of it, which looked promising. About that time I heard a hen call and as I looked off over the rise, 15 turkeys stuck their heads up. It was game over. We had gotten too close and busted the entire flock, which consisted of a mixture of jakes, longbeards, and hens. They flew off, scattering in every direction.

Because we hadn't called to them at all, we stood a pretty good chance to be able to work them in an hour or so. We set up in a group of towering trees and then waited for something to happen. Suddenly, I noticed something that looked out of place at about 500 yards across from the green field. I had forgotten my binoculars so I asked Kenny for his. He had been looking at the same thing I was, so before handing them over he took a look and finally noticed two gobblers bedded down under a tree in the shade. As we sat there thinking of a strategy, Kenny asked me if I thought they could hear a call that far away. Honestly, I didn't think there

May 4, 2015

was any chance of them hearing it, but it was worth a shot so
Kenny handed me the binoculars and I watched them as he let out
a call. He put in his mouth call and yelped, but they didn't even
flinch. He tried a second time, calling a little bit louder, but still
no reaction. Kenny decided to put the mouth call away and take
out his glass call. He called out a few times as loud as he could,
and through the binoculars I could see their heads perk right up.
Then I saw one of their heads move forward and because we were
so far away there was a delay in the sound of the gobble. When
they answered, Kenny started calling even more to them. They
gobbled a few more times and then stood up. I told Kenny, "Dude
you're not going to believe this, but they're fixing to come over
here." After they stood up, both gobblers started marching across
the field towards us. At this point we had all of our gloves, masks,

and turkey vests off. Thank goodness there was the little dip in the field 100 yards out, and when they vanished into it, that allowed us to quickly get situated and ready for a shot. It wasn't more than a couple of minutes when they appeared out of the dip and marched straight toward us within shotgun range, allowing me to kill one of them.

This was one of the craziest encounters I had run into thus far, for a turkey to come in from that far away and walk within shooting range. It seems like the western turkeys do things that you would never expect. We figured those turkeys were part of the flock we had seen earlier and were still anxious to get back together. I suspect that's why they were so eager to come in like they did.

Both Kenny and I had tagged out in Idaho on the first day. This gave us the opportunity to enjoy the remainder of the day in this state. We ended up finding some morel mushrooms in the woods, which we later cooked up along with the wild turkey and capped it off with a few cold ones. Dave Owens and Mark Heffron, aka "Squirrel", had also been hunting in Idaho, both filling their tags that morning. These guys joined us in the hotel room for a celebration later on. ↓

LESSONS LEARNED

Merriam's turkeys can cover some serious ground when they're in the mood, much further than an eastern can. In some cases, they will also cross fields and even main roads to get to your calling. If you hear a Merriam's gobbling getting closer, forget about cutting the distance like you would on an Eastern and just let him come to you.

Chapter 12

Washington

After the celebratory dinner with Dave and Squirrel, all of us were off to Washington to finish off our week-long trip, except we had planned on hunting in different areas. Kenny and I basically threw a dart at the map, picking out a spot we thought looked promising and then drove two hours to reach this location. Unfortunately, we didn't arrive until the following morning, which prevented us from roosting birds the evening before. However, we did hear a gobbler, but it was in someone's yard and not even close to any available public land. There wasn't much we could do about this, but it was nice knowing that turkeys were in the area.

Later that morning we spotted a gobbler along the road and after looking at our maps we noticed some public land 100 yards or so above the turkey. The last time we caught a glimpse of him he was starting to head in that direction. We decided to go after him and found out that it would be a three-mile hike from the closest access point in order to get in front of him. By the time we reached the location where we thought we would see him he was nowhere to be found and had gone completely silent. It seemed we had spent the majority of the first morning chasing our tails and quickly realized we needed to figure something out soon. About midday we decided to stop by a national forest ranger office in order to gather some information on some areas where we could find turkeys. The employees there were super helpful. One of the guys told us about a creek south of us where he had seen a bunch of turkeys. There was a mixture of private and public land in this spot, but he figured we should have good luck on getting permission there. Towards evening, we followed the creek and knocked on a couple's door that owned a large farm. They didn't give us permission, but they gave us the name of some friends of theirs who lived further down the creek. We knocked on his door and he gave us the name of yet another guy to try. This guy gave us permission to hunt his property, which bordered national forest land. He mentioned there were a few turkeys hanging around. Because it didn't seem all that promising, we still wanted to give the other guy he had mentioned a try, who supposedly had more turkeys on his farm and no other hunters to compete against. We pulled up to this old shack, which looked like something off of the movie, *Deliverance*, except no one was playing a banjo on the porch. No joke, the sound of me knocking on the door caused a turkey to gobble in the field behind this guy's house. Kenny and I just stood there looking at each other in disbelief, thinking *we've got to get permission here*. Unfortunately, though, no one was home.

As we went back to the gate where we had parked and got into our vehicle, the owner pulled in and looked at us suspiciously. I explained to him where we had gotten his name and after asking if we could turkey hunt he had no problem with it. He just asked that we be careful of his cows. By this time it was too late to hunt so we called it a day and that concluded our first day in Washington.

We went into day two with lots of optimism based on the activity from the day before. We decided it was best to split up in the morning and hunt the two separate pieces of private ground. I arrived on the private property the following morning not really knowing what to expect, however I did hear a turkey that was still on its roost. I soon realized the gobbler was roosted on the border of public and the neighboring property, which I didn't have permission to hunt. I decided to get relatively close to the roost so I could make a play on him and find out if he had some hens with him. I was really hoping he would land on public. However, he flew square into the neighbor's yard and instantly began strutting with the hens there. I knew if I waited him out he would eventually work his way onto public. In the meantime I heard a gobbler a long ways up on a mountain on national forest land. Once this bird started gobbling he didn't stop. I frantically looked at a map trying to figure out how hard it was going to be trying to get to his location. I figured it was going to take me at least an hour or two to get to this turkey.

After standing there contemplating for a few minutes I told myself, *Screw it, I'm going after him.* I wanted to come in from above and behind him so I made a big loop to arrive at this location. While in route every time I would stop to see if he was still there he would gobble his head off. Finally, I arrived above where he was gobbling and noticed he was in a thicket. It almost seemed like he was lost up there and trying to find company. As I walked down into the middle of the thick brush, I found a road leading out to him and soon realized he was on the same road probably about 100 yards out. I

May 8, 2015

thought, *Man, if he stays on the road I've got a chance of killing him.* So as I stood in the middle of the road I let out a call and no sooner did I get the sound out of my mouth when he hammered out a gobble. I continued to work him from the road there, and then walked up above the road to set up and wait for him. It wasn't more than a couple of minutes when I could hear him drumming just around the curve in the road. I shouldered my gun and flipped the safety off and watched as a beautiful white tipped Merriam's rounded the corner. After watching him for only a second or so I took the shot. Kenny wasn't supposed to pick me up until around one o'clock and it was currently 10 a.m. I knew the walk down was definitely going to be a lot easier than the walk up, so I decided to take my time and enjoy the morning.

Kenny didn't kill one that day, but had been on turkeys. However, on day two he ended up killing one on the private land he hunted. To this day we still hunt on this property. It is one of those lifelong connections we made during the Slam.

This state concluded the 2015 season for me; Five new states – Georgia, Mississippi, Montana, Idaho, and Washington, along with four repeat states – West Virginia, Kentucky, Ohio, and Alabama. I remember thinking what a leap it was for me to hunt in this many states during one season. ↓

LESSONS LEARNED

If you can find a road through the thick stuff, use it to call from and set up on a gobbler. This turkey was gobbling on a road surrounded by trashy woods. I realized the road gave him access to the east of me. Bank on a gobbler using a road or a path if you notice one between him and where you're calling from.

Chapter 13

Virginia

After my annual week-long trip to Alabama in 2016, where Kenny and I both had success in tagging a few birds, I was off to Virginia. Once again I had picked up a few tips and continued to learn from Kenny.

My dad had a guy that worked for him who owned around 80 acres, which was only about an hour from my parents' house. This worked out perfect because I could stay at their house and drive over to the property in the morning. When the Virginia season rolled around, Dad took me over to the farm to meet the landowner. I didn't really have high hopes for this area because where my parents live there isn't a good population of turkeys. However, my attitude changed when we pulled into the owner's driveway and saw a hen feeding in his field. He gave us the usual, "They're everywhere!" speech that seems common among landowners.

After meeting the landowner he showed me the boundaries. I was going to be hunting with my friend Ryan Bennett, who didn't live far from this property. Both of us had a three-day weekend to get the job done in Virginia.

When Ryan and I arrived the next morning the weather was cold, but surprisingly the turkeys were gobbling pretty good. We were finally able to get a turkey to gobble down below us about 150 yards away. I sat along the woodline and started to work him with a glass call. About the time the turkey started to come in, I went to sit down and realized that it was too thick for a shot and for the gobbler to navigate through. Racking my brain on what to do, I noticed a field directly behind me consisting of some saplings and good cover so I figured I would try to call to him from this location in hopes that he would think that the hen naturally moved from the thick stuff to the open field. I got up and took off running after making a decision to set up in the saplings. Because it was so cold and dry I could hear the gobbler walking. After only a few minutes in the new spot I heard him gobble, and he was literally standing on top of where I had just been sitting near the thicket. I thought, *Man, why didn't I just stay put in that spot?* This still haunts me to this day. Apparently it wasn't too thick for him not to walk through. However, I knew it wasn't over and I was still in the game. Unfortunately, though he never did pop out into the field. About that time 300 yards below, Ryan and I heard a hen yelping. We figured the gobbler must have heard her too because he made a beeline to her. Eventually, we determined that he and another gobbler had gotten with those hens below us. I kicked myself for this bonehead move and knew I should have stayed put in the first spot.

The following day we saw these two gobblers in the field along with a bunch of hens, and then a snow squall came in. The visibility was so bad we could hardly see. Fortunately, however, the turkeys remained in the field. There was a large brush pile in the field which would make excellent cover and hopefully allow us to get to within shotgun range of these gobblers. I was getting ready to make a mad dash out to the brush pile when my buddy talked me out of it because he thought I would just bump the birds. This was another decision I soon regretted making on this hunt. I shouldn't have let him talk me out of this move. Anytime you have inclement weather like that coming in and you can make a move, take it. With the combination of the snow and the brush pile, I could have snuck in and taken a shot. Instead of making a move, though, we stayed about 200 yards out and the flock eventually moved out of the field.

On Sunday, the final day, we heard a turkey across a little road that was on the owner's property. This bird gobbled every single morning we were there, yet we hadn't made a move on him. I told Ryan, "You stay here and hunt the ridge, I'm going to cross the road and go after him." Because I roosted this turkey the night before, I knew where to set up. I got in there close to the bird, which had roosted on the side of a hill. Because it was still so dry, every leaf that I stepped on in the dark sounded like I was shattering glass, which kept me from getting into the position I wanted to.

When the turkey flew down he landed to the right and just down the hill from me, which prevented me from taking a shot when he hit the ground. But then he gobbled and once again he was in the field. I had this little hump I had to crawl over and I knew that once I did he would be within border-line shotgun range. Once I reached the top and his head was stretched out, I took the shot. However I underestimated the range and completely missed. The gobbler was clueless though, which was a good thing, and the entire flock flew away as a result. That was my first weekend in Virginia, which turned out to be heat breaking. Ryan and I had a lot of action, but we were unable to make it happen.

Even though there were birds on the 80 acres, we still didn't have a lot of confidence in this location. The following weekend, Ryan's dad set us up with two properties closer to where he lived. We got out there on a Friday afternoon and because we weren't allowed to hunt afternoons we went out to roost some birds. Ryan went to one farm and I traveled to the other. As soon as I arrived there was a turkey gobbling real good. He gobbled every couple of minutes the entire evening. *This was very encouraging*, I thought. Finally, I laid my eyes on the turkeys and saw there were three gobblers in this group. I watched as they flew up and roosted. I love roosting almost as much as I do hunting. Sticking with them and the anticipation for the next morning's hunt is one of my favorite aspects of turkey hunting. You don't have the pressure to kill them.

I knew exactly which tree they were roosted in, so I was prepared for the morning hunt. Ryan had heard some turkeys too, but these birds sounded like a better option and with three gobblers together we figured we could try and get two of them. The next morning we found ourselves set up near the roost on the wood line near the edge of the field. It was a beautiful crisp morning for the most textbook hunt you could imagine in the turkey woods. All three of them were gobbling good on the limb. We gave them just a little tree yelping, which they cut off. Calling probably wasn't necessary, but when daylight arrived we had set up a little bit further down from the turkeys than we wanted, so we thought they might pass by out of range going to the field. However, we needn't have worried. All three gobblers marched right to us. The bad thing, though, Ryan had set up a little behind me in an awkward position because the birds were above where we anticipated them being. The first gobbler walked right out onto the road. However, as he reached the opening he immediately acted as though he

April 17, 2016

smelled a rat and was fixing to get out of there while the other two were still behind Ryan, covered by brush and not offering him a shot. It was now or never. I clicked the safety off and fired a shot ending the grueling four day chase. It wasn't as celebratory as it usually is for a new state because we were both disappointed that we didn't pull off the double. It was a beautiful turkey with inch and a quarter spurs.

Later on, while looking at a map of the farm where I shot my bird, Ryan and I realized that I was only 80 yards from the West

Virginia border when I killed this turkey. Thankfully, the gobbler was on Virginia soil. Talk about cutting it close. ↓

LESSONS LEARNED

Use all your resources. Ryan's dad knew the farmer that got us on the land we hunted. If you know someone in a state you're headed to, make the call and see if they can help you out. It's worth a shot.

Chapter 14

Maryland

The first week of May in 2016, Ryan Bennett and I decided to hunt turkeys in Maryland. This was another state that we had no information on from anyone else. It was a convenient place that I could drive to from my house, since West Virginia borders Maryland and it was only a couple of hours away. As Ryan and I started driving, we didn't know what we were getting into on that first night. Upon arrival at an area where we planned to hunt, we set up camp at a campground we had found, but unfortunately we didn't have enough daylight to roost any birds that evening.

The following morning found both of us splitting up and walking into different areas in hopes of finding some birds. I ended up hearing a gobbler across the way and got relatively close within about 100 yards of the roost. I didn't anticipate hearing any gobbles so this was very encouraging, since I didn't know anything about this place. The gobbler must have been roosting on an old dead limb, because when he put his weight on it to fly down the limb broke off, creating a heck of a commotion. I was afraid this might cause him to be scared and fly away, but shortly afterwards he began to gobble again. Fortunately, he had been roosting with a bunch of hens that evening and stayed with them, so I decided to mess with him for a bit after daylight trying to call him into shooting range, but nothing happened so I moved on. I looked at the map and the next ridge over looked promising. It bordered a large private field and appeared as though it should hold some turkeys.

It took me 45 minutes to reach the ridge, but it was worth it. Along the way I found some fresh scratching made the previous evening or first thing in the morning in the wood line bordering the field. At that point I decided to try my glass call to see if I could get any responses. As soon as I hit it, boom! Two turkeys answered from the field. I continued to call to them and they were instantly hooked and coming towards me. This rarely happens to me on day one of a turkey hunt. I decided to back off the field edge around 40 yards so the birds could get onto public in order for me to take the shot. There was a road bordering the field and I was expecting them to follow it along the border. However, in the back of my mind I knew this wasn't a good situation. Any time you're asking gobblers to leave a field and walk into the woods it generally doesn't work out, so I had my doubts. Therefore, after I knew they were committed, I stopped calling.

After about five or 10 minutes of silence I thought, *All right, it's time to give them another call.* On my first call they instantly gobbled and to my surprise were already in the woods. They had flanked me from above and were moving in a circle so I knew I was in a bad spot. A couple of minutes had passed since my last call when I spotted both of them hanging up just out of range. At that point I was afraid to call to them because the woods were pretty open. I was fearful they would see there was no hen nearby. They continued to strut about 60 yards out and eventually lost interest, fading back over the hill in the direction they came from. As soon as they disappeared I got back on my glass call and called pretty hard at them, cutting and yelping. They gobbled three or four times and apparently became convinced that a hen was nearby and came back. But instead of coming straight back they continued to walk in a big circle. I have no idea why they did this. I guess because they're turkeys and that's what turkeys do. Then, they began making another circle towards my left and were still out of shooting range as they were working their way in. However, I knew that once they reached my hard left they would be in borderline shotgun range, within 40 or 50 yards of my 20 gauge.

I found a nearby tree to support my gun on and spun around, making one last move to get into position for a shot. I thought, *As soon as the lead gobbler reaches the opening I'm going to shoot him.* With my red dot pointed at the opening in anticipation, the first gobbler walked in, allowing me to squeeze off a shot. It knocked him down. However, the bird quickly pulled himself back together and flew away. I thought I had made a lethal shot, but unfortunately, I spent the remainder of the day searching for him with no success. I checked every brush pile, behind logs, you name it, with no sign of him. I figured he would be hiding in these spots, but he never showed up. I started questioning my shot and figured I didn't hit him as good as I thought.

Later that day Ryan and I arrived back at camp to find all our gear scattered across the ground. It appeared we had been robbed, but then I found a plastic container where chips had been eaten and soon realized that a black bear had helped himself during the day while we were out hunting. Fortunately, that's the first and last time a black bear has ever come into camp.

I was feeling pretty dejected after the miss as we sat around camp that evening, and was looking forward to redeeming myself the following day. However, day two came and went with little action. On day three I decided to hunt on the other end of the property, which was a couple of miles down the road on public land. The morning left us empty-handed, but around mid-day I struck up a conversation with a gobbler who liked what he heard. I wasn't exactly sure how the public land was laid out in this particular area, but I knew that I was right on the border where public meets private.

After calling to him for a while, he soon hung up about 100 yards out for about an hour. I'd call to him again and he would go silent. 20 minutes later it was the same thing. He would be in the same spot. Eventually, he lost interest and moved away. I could tell by his gobble he was traveling down the hill in front of me. Then things started making sense to me as to why he was not coming towards me. The turkey was in a private field and there was a large fence separating the private from the public. Apparently he couldn't find a way to get through the fence onto public land. Finally, I was able to get a good vantage point from a hill on the public side of the field. Come to find out there was a quartet of longbeards down there. There was still hope. The woods that surrounded the field were public land. As I watched them I knew they would eventually come over to roost. However, in Maryland you can only hunt until midday, so I had to take my shotgun back to the truck and put it in its case. Afterwards, I returned to the spot and stayed until dark to see if they would roost in this woodline.

Sure enough, when I returned they were out in the field along with a couple of hens. After waiting until daylight was fading, I watched as they started walking directly towards me. I thought to myself, *If I bust them I'm really going to hate myself.* However, they ended up taking a route that was about 100 yards above me to the steepest part of the ridge that lay next to the field. They walked so far up the steep ridge I couldn't even see them, but heard the flapping of their wings as they flew up to roost. I liked my chances, though. There were multiple targets in there and I was itching to fill my Maryland tag.

Later that evening it began to pour. However, with the conclusion of day three I was optimistic for the area where I had roosted the birds. We ended up breaking camp and getting a motel because everything was completely soaked. I knew I had to get a good night's rest and have my stuff together if I was going to kill a gobbler.

It was game time! The following morning I hiked back to the same location and once again climbed to the steepest part of the ridge above where the gobblers had roosted. Originally, I didn't think the hill was that steep, but it felt as though it took forever in the dark, especially since I kept my flashlight off and also made a large loop to avoid walking up on them. I was extremely cautious and everything I did on my approach to the roost was considered. Once I closed in on the top of the ridge I decided to settle in about 50 yards downhill from where it sounded like they were located.

Hopefully a gobbler would land in front of me and not fly down into the valley. To my surprise, as it began to get daylight I could see one of the gobblers across even with me on the next ridge and straight down my gun barrel. Apparently, I hadn't dropped down too far from the ridge. Finally, four gobblers flew down, but instead of heading towards the field like I had anticipated and side hilling it towards me they walked farther up the hill and started to gobble. It was very foggy because of the rain, which worked to my advantage. Once they reached the top of the ridge I figured I could use the lip of the ridge to sneak in and kill one. At that point they hadn't found any hens so I decided to start calling. However, as I let out a few yelps on my glass call a nearby hen, which was still roosted, decided to start calling. The four gobblers must have recognized her calling because all of them made a beeline to the uphill side of her tree, where they continued to gobble their heads off and wait for her to fly down. The entire time I called to them I also used the fog to my advantage by slowly crawling in closer, gaining ground to within about 100 yards of the gobblers. Every time the hen called I called, which caused her to become agitated. However, the longbeards still refused to break away and come towards me. Suddenly, though, I caught a break. Instead of the hen flying down towards the gobblers she flew down towards me. At this point I wasn't quite on top of the hill, but I could still take a shot from the side of the hill. That's all that I needed. Suddenly, the hen walked by me on the downhill side of my setup. This was perfect! Of course, when the gobblers saw her they started traveling in that direction on the top of the hill, walking right towards me. As the four gobblers reached shooting range I shot at the lead gobbler, knocking him down. However, like earlier in the hunt, he got back up so I took a couple of more shots with my semi-automatic 20 gauge. Afterwards, I saw him lay down in a brush pile about 60 yards in front of me. With only three shells in my gun that was it. Fortunately, I had one more shell in my pocket. As I snuck up to the brush pile where he lay I could see he was still alive and his head was sticking up. At that point I wasn't sure if he could fly or not. If so, it wouldn't take much for him to get off of that mountain and fly away to safety. After loading my final shell,

I snuck in around him and he got up one last time, but it was too late. I took one final shot and anchored him for good. Afterwards, I was convinced I had a malfunction in my shotgun, but it made no difference at that point. I had filled my Maryland tag.

The fog coupled with calling helped me close the distance on the four gobblers. May 10, 2016.

Once I got back home I shot my gun and found nothing was wrong with it. I figured that I had done some poor shooting in Maryland. Day four after a miss was sure a fiasco, but to witness those longbeards coming across that ridge in the fog created a memory in the turkey woods that I will never forget. ↓

LESSONS LEARNED

Keep after it when you miss. It would have been easy for me to pack up shop and pout or go home after my miss on the first day. However, it just made me want it that much more. Stay focused after a blown opportunity.

Chapter 15

North Dakota

With a gobbler down in Maryland and a week off from teaching for spring break, it was time to do a western swing and head out to North Dakota. Our plan was to fly into North Dakota and then hunt Wyoming and Utah during this trip. We had good information in North Dakota, zero in Wyoming, and a little bit of intel in Utah. I would be hunting with Kenny once again. In true Kenny fashion he arrived in North Dakota one day before me. He said that he would find some birds before I arrived and have one waiting for me when I got there. The location we were going to hunt was kind of a hidden gem at the time. However, since then it's received more pressure from hunters.

Throughout the entire flight I kept wondering if Kenny had gotten on any birds. The problem was I couldn't get in touch with him on his cell phone via texting. I figured he must be in an area with no service. However, before my flight left I tried calling him and finally got through. He answered and was very short with me saying that he couldn't talk right at the moment and asked me what time I will be arriving so he would be there to pick me up when my plane lands. The conversation only lasted a minute. I figured he must have been on turkeys or something and was unable to talk.

After my plane landed in Bismark, I had several text messages from Kenny telling me to call him once I landed. I could tell he was in a great mood once I called him. He seemed extra bubbly so I knew he must have found turkeys earlier. I asked him, "So, did you find some? What happened?"

Kenny said, "There's too much to talk about. I'll tell you once I get in the vehicle."

After arriving at the baggage claim I grabbed my gun and luggage and walked in front of the airport to meet Kenny. As he popped the hatch of the vehicle and I went to throw my gear in and to my surprise there were two dead gobblers in the trunk of the rental. I started laughing and told him he should have saved one for me. He said, "There's a lot more where those came from."

Fortunately, with the tag we had you could kill two turkeys in the same day. I knew it was a good sign when Kenny said, "You're going to love this place." With Kenny tagged out I would be up to bat the following day.

Because my plane landed at four o'clock we had about three hours to drop my stuff off at the motel and head out to roost some birds. As we were driving to where we were going to hunt, Kenny said he had heard at least six more gobblers in this spot. Feeling a little guilty, he said he wouldn't have shot the two birds if he didn't think we could kill more. It didn't bother me, though. I was happy he filled his tag first thing.

Once we turned onto the road we saw two strutters with a hen in a field about 300 yards away, and they were in an area we could hunt. As we sat there for a minute watching them, I began to plan my approach for the following morning. I noticed there was a U shaped creek and an electrical pole that looked like it was within shotgun range of where the turkeys were strutting. This would be a great place to set up, I thought. Kenny and I discussed the plan and we both figured the best way would be to walk the creek bottom and pop up where the pole was for an ambush on the gobblers.

There I was in North Dakota for two hours and already had some birds located. Things were going great! Kenny dropped me off, allowing me to follow through with my plan while he left to go roost more birds. If I wasn't able to pull a shot off I would at least be able to roost them for the following morning.

As I approached the creek I soon realized I wouldn't be able to walk the edge of the creek bank because it was too steep and almost vertical. Therefore, I dropped down into the creek, which I soon found out was waist deep. *At least the current isn't moving too fast*, I thought to myself. Fortunately, I had removed my turkey vest and emptied all my pockets before entering the creek. At one point on my journey down to the creek I came to a section that was chest deep, forcing me to raise my shotgun over my head. It probably took me an hour of walking through the waist to chest deep water until I finally reached the light pole. Unfortunately, as I walked down the creek I lost track of where the gobblers were. I wasn't sure if they moved on or switched directions. The first challenge of walking down the creek was over, but now I had to figure out how to get up and out of the creek bed. I basically had to dig my fingers and toes into the steep bank and climb up to the pole. Much to my relief, when I popped up the gobblers were in the exact same spot with the hen, without a care in the world. At this point they were in borderline gun range, around 60 yards out. It was windy so I figured I could get a little bit closer without being detected. However, I decided it would be best to go back into the creek and walk an additional 20 yards, which would put me closer to the gobblers.

I crept up the bank once again and they were still clueless, which made for an ideal stalking scenario. I slipped my gun up on the edge of the creek, preparing to take a shot. I tried using my mouth call for a bit, but they still didn't come out of strut. Eventually, one of them turned around facing me and I killed it. It was so windy the shot was muffled and it sounded like a little pop gun went off. Judging by the way he acted, it didn't appear as though the other gobbler knew his buddy had gotten killed.

As I sat on the edge of the creek enjoying the moment I thought to myself, *I've only been off of the plane for three hours and I already filled my tag*. What a great way to start the trip. North

Dakota had been kind to us so far. While sitting there soaking in the hunt I looked further on up the creek at least 500 yards and there were more gobblers along the edge of it. I reached in and got my binoculars out and noticed at least four more gobblers. Now, I usually don't like to kill two gobblers at once because it makes me feel greedy, but I figured since it was a separate hunt that I would go after them.

With my first bird tagged I decided to leave it behind and start making my way up the creek towards the location where I had spotted the other birds. Eventually, the creek turned into a ditch, which I continued to follow. Once I reached the location where the gobblers were I peeked up and noticed just one gobbler with a couple of hens. After sneaking in and getting into position I was able to shoot the lone gobbler. I was officially tagged out in North Dakota.

Without any service, I had no way of getting in touch with Kenny, so I took some pictures and just sat there once again,

May 13, 2016

soaking in the hunt of these two gobblers. The following day Kenny and I took photos of the two of us with our four longbeards.

By the time I gathered my turkey vest and the rest of my gear it was almost dark, so I began my journey along the creek bed back to the spot where Kenny was going to pick me up. As Kenny began pulling up in the vehicle I was sitting on the edge of the road and decided to pull the same trick that he did at the airport when I arrived in North Dakota. When he finally reached the spot where I was sitting I played it off like I didn't get anything, but then pointed to them and the celebration began.

Even though we were both tagged out, we decided to get up early the following morning and just listen to the amount of gobblers that were in the area where Kenny had roosted some the evening before.

With North Dakota out of the way we were left with about nine days to focus on filling our tags in Wyoming and Utah. ⤓

LESSONS LEARNED

Use the terrain in open country. Out west you will encounter many areas without trees or cover for you to make your move on a turkey that won't gobble or come to calling because of the presence of hens. Take advantage of dips and rolls in the topography to get within shotgun range.

Chapter 16

Wyoming

Kenny and I decided to hunt in Wyoming, which wasn't too far from the area I had previously hunted in South Dakota. We had absolutely no information whatsoever on where to find turkeys in Wyoming, but we were both excited about the new territory. We arrived to the area from North Dakota just in time to try to roost some gobblers, but unfortunately we were unable to locate any. Looking at some maps, we finally figured out an area that we would hunt in the morning. Judging by the map it looked like a pretty good climb to get into the area, but once you made it past the steep part it flattened off and looked like good turkey country.

The following morning we found out the climb took a lot longer than we thought. It turned out the steep part we saw on the map were sheer cliffs. However, we ended up finding a little pass to make it up to the top, but it put us way past gobble/fly down time. Once we reached the top it was beautiful turkey country, but we didn't hear any gobbles. We did find some dried-up turkey droppings and scratchings, but it looked like it was done during the winter months. It left Kenny and me wondering if there were turkeys in the area, but they just didn't feel like gobbling on that particular morning. Even though it was silent up there, we still spent the majority of the day trying to get on some gobblers because we were confident there were some in the area. However, we never ended up finding any birds.

That evening, though, we roosted a gobbler close to a road. This would be the bird Kenny would go after the following morning. I decided to try a new area and ended up hearing a gobbler, which I spent all day chasing. However, he had hens with him and every time I called he would gobble, but of course the hens would drag him in the opposite direction. He was vocal enough to help me keep tabs on him, but it felt like a lost cause. He'd call and be on a ridge over, then I would chase him and repeat the process. However, at one point I laid eyes on him in a little clearing and he had a beautiful white-tipped tail fan, which I still remember as plain as day. Eventually, the gobbler walked out of the clearing and disappeared beneath a little lip. I seized this opportunity to quickly run over to the lip while he was out of sight, fully expecting to be able to kill him there. However, when I got on my knees and peered over the edge he vanished. After attempting to call I soon realized the gobbler stood just outside of shotgun range. Upon crawling even closer I estimated wrong and he was actually 100 yards away. I could never quite catch up to this gobbler on day number two.

The following morning I decided to go after him again while Kenny decided on his same area also and ended up killing his bird. I was a glutton for punishment, which is common practice in the world of turkey hunting. It felt like the movie, *Groundhog Day.* The same scenario kept happening again and again. Unfortunately, this gobbler was the only bird I heard, but just like the previous day I could never get close.

Kenny and I met for lunch and had a good laugh after noticing that the gobbler he killed looked like it had gone a few rounds with Connor McGregor. Its feathers were all disheveled. After taking some pictures we dedicated the remainder of the day to trying to get my tag filled.

That evening I went into the same location while Kenny searched out some new ground and howled from the road in hopes of locating some gobblers for me to chase. I was able to roost a gobbler, but he flew across a canyon. I figured it was going to be at least a two-hour walk to reach him the following morning, but I knew the exact area where he had flown up so I felt confident I would be able to kill my turkey. In the meantime Kenny also had roosted a bird and placed a pin on its location. We had a serious debate about which bird we were going after, but finally I decided I would go after the gobbler Kenny had roosted. From the pin it looked like the bird had flown up next to a flat area which had been timbered off. Both of us felt confident the gobbler would land in this opening come morning.

We devised a plan, which to this day is one of the most bad-ass turkey moves we've ever done. In order to get in the perfect position on this turkey before he flew down I was going to walk over to where Kenny had dropped the pin, while he climbed the opposite mountain to howl from there. Because this turkey gobbled at the howler every time the evening before, Kenny thought he would do the same thing in the early morning hours way before he should, which would allow me to find his location and get into the perfect position in the dark.

There was a road that led to this skid flat, which would allow me easy access to the area. Kenny said he would wait 45 minutes before hitting the howler. This would give me enough time to reach the area Kenny had pinned. I figured this was kind of a shot in the dark, but it was worth a try.

When early morning arrived I began my journey to the location without the aid of a flashlight. The walk wasn't too bad in the dark because I stayed on the road most of the time. Once I arrived close to the location, I veered off of the road a short way and set up. It hadn't been more than 10 minutes when Kenny let out a howl from his spot on the mountain. The timing was perfect. The gobbler nearby didn't let out a full gobble, but instead a half-assed gobble.

May 16, 2016

I was in a pretty good position where I was and only had to move an additional 20 yards in the dark to get in the perfect spot. It was super cold, probably in the 20s that morning, and I still had about two more hours to wait until the turkeys flew down. I've never been that cold before in my life. I figured I was only about 20 yards from where this turkey was roosted, and I wanted to kill him as soon as his feet hit the ground.

As daylight started to break and the turkeys began to get vocal, I could tell he had several hens with him. As luck would have it they were behind me, along with some jakes, and I was between them and the gobbler. Soon, he began gobbling in the tree right in front of me. *This is perfect*, I thought. *I'm in a position where I can shoot the skid flat and into the woods if necessary.* It was an ideal set up, but it was difficult to keep from shaking because I was so cold. I got a visual of him dancing around the limb all morning and then suddenly he flew off his roost. Upon landing he hit the ground 30 yards in front of me. I should have shot him as soon as he landed, but brush had obscured the roost and I thought there might be other birds with him. I wanted to make sure that it was a gobbler. Also, I had a difficult time seeing his beard. He started to walk by me just out of range while the other turkeys slowed down a bit. To my left on the skid flat all of the turkeys eventually bunched up, making it difficult for a shot because of how close together they were. However, I could see the gobbler and some jakes strutting around there also. I finally swung my gun over to the left where all of them were, waiting for the gobbler to separate. Eventually, he came into shotgun range and stuck his head up offering me a shot. It was a beautiful white-tipped Merriam's. One of the prettiest white tails you've ever seen. Kenny, who was still across the road up on the mountain, let out a celebration howl letting me know he heard the shot. I walked out of the area, meeting Kenny at the truck, and we began celebrating. ↓

LESSONS LEARNED

A locator call is deadly out west. If you're hunting with a buddy have them continue to use the locator call while you move in on a gobbler to track his exact location on the roost. It will set you up well for your morning hunt.

Chapter 17

Utah

With Wyoming in the books, the last stop of our 2016 western tour was Utah. Of the three states we hunted this spring, Utah was probably the best. Kenny had a connection with a gentleman who owned some land, and we had permission to hunt. He was also going to allow us to stay in his house. It was one of those setups almost too good to be true.

After driving over to meet him, we quickly found out how nice of a guy he was. However, once we entered his house with all of our gear, we felt like we were imposing on him and his family. We ended up sleeping in the basement the first night. I could tell Kenny was ready for a hotel after the first evening. This guy had gotten us permission to hunt a piece of land only five minutes from his house and supposedly there were turkeys on it.

After meeting the landowner we drove through his property and spotted a lone gobbler, which made us both confident in the area. It was close to fly up time when we watched the turkey cross the road and go up into some thick brush. We figured the gobbler would probably roost somewhere in there.

As we drove a little further, two turkey hunters came down the hill, one of them toting a beautiful gobbler on his back. I remember glancing over at Kenny and seeing his smile instantly fade away because someone was hunting the piece we had gotten permission to hunt. Usually it's not a good thing, however, we stopped anyway and talked to the hunters. We found out they had been hunting since the beginning of the season, which was two weeks prior. We asked them if we could hunt in there the following morning and they said it was fine because you can only shoot one bird in Utah anyway. They also informed us that there were some other gobblers in the area. They wished us luck since we only had a couple of days to get the job done. At this point we weren't feeling as optimistic as before. However, despite the curve ball thrown at us we still formulated a game plan for the following morning.

After speaking with the hunters we hung around the area for a bit and ended up hearing two other turkeys gobble. We also didn't forget about the turkey that had crossed the road earlier. Our plan was that I would go after the two gobblers up high and Kenny would hunt the one we saw cross the road.

The following morning I walked up the hill, trying to get above the turkeys we had located. I hadn't pinpointed their exact location the evening before, but I had a general idea of where they were roosted. We also didn't hear the bird that crossed the road, but we knew he was up there.

As daylight approached I was unable to get the turkeys to come to me off the roost. There were two gobblers and some hens in the group. They started to go in the opposite direction, towards the bottom of the hill where we had talked to the hunters earlier. They stayed in the thicket too, in an area I would have never imagined them to enter, and refused to walk out into the open. I'm not sure if it was the pressure from the hunters the day before or what, but after it became apparent they weren't coming out of there I decided to belly crawl into the thicket after them. Eventually, I got within shotgun range of one of them when all of a sudden I saw a bunch of red heads poke up. I had my shotgun raised and ready to shoot, however I couldn't verify if they were gobblers or jakes. Shortly after, they disappeared below a small knoll a mere 25 yards away. This left me frustrated, thinking I might have missed my opportunity.

As I turned my eyes to the left, here came a beautiful white-tipped gobbler coming up the hill in full strut. About the same time I spotted him he saw me and came out of strut, high tailing it in the opposite direction. But I was too quick for him. I already had my gun raised for a shot and dropped him.

I didn't have any cell phone service to call Kenny so I decided to climb to the top of the hill to see if I could get a signal. About the time I reached the top I heard a turkey gobble and soon I realized he was in the field. Unfortunately, the gobbler saw me at the same time and vanished. Once I got cell phone service I realized that Kenny was out in the same field in the corner and I had just scared away the gobbler he was after. He was mad at me to say the least, but it didn't last very long. Old Kenny wasn't used to me shooting a turkey before him on a trip. This was the first time this had ever happened. However, he was very panicky and wanted to shoot one badly. I finally calmed him down by telling him about the other gobblers I had seen accompanying the one I shot. I reassured him the other gobblers running for cover were probably clueless as to what happened. I told him, "Chill out, you're going to kill one!"

May 18, 2016

Just about the time I got him calmed down another turkey gobbled out from the hill. I was going to stay there, but I had already been in the thicket and knew the lay of the land. At this point I wasn't sure if Kenny wanted me to go or not, but he did. I started to crawl basically the same route I had taken before, and by the time we worked our way down into the thicket, the turkey was on fire gobbling his head off. I figured we could probably call this turkey in but we were hesitant to call to him for fear of how he would react. Sometimes after birds have been messed with it's easier to try and get to within shotgun range of them without calling. The gobbler we were after was pacing back and forth within the thicket and we thought it might have gotten separated from the other turkeys. We weren't entirely certain, though. I think he heard us crawl to the last position we were in because he started to long-neck around the corner, which allowed Kenny to kill him. It had only been about two hours between the time I shot my turkey and Kenny got his.

With North Dakota, Wyoming, and Utah in the books we were out of tags and had some extra time to kill, so we drove to Salt Lake City the following night. All in all it was a great Western trip. We had a few beers and went to a nice restaurant and said our goodbyes until the next spring. It was always kind of bittersweet when it came to the end of turkey season because we both knew we wouldn't be able to hang out until the following year. ↓

LESSONS LEARNED

Always be aware of your target and beyond. I was glad I used patience to correctly identify the gobbler without fear of shooting a jake. If there is any doubt whatsoever don't pull the trigger until you can correctly identify the bird is a tom.

Chapter 18

Florida

In 2017, seven new states were on the travel list. I decided I would kick off the season in Florida. The Osceola subspecies can only be found in the Sunshine State and it just so happened I needed one in order to complete my Grand Slam. Finding public ground here can be challenging, but as luck would have it a customer who dropped a deer off at my taxidermy shop in November 2016 had Florida plates. I seized the opportunity and asked him if he knew of anyone that had land where I could hunt. Without hesitating, he said a friend had a few acres and would probably let me hunt for a small trespass fee. I didn't waste any time and called him, explaining my situation and securing permission to hunt his property in March.

The property was in the central zone, about 100 miles below where the easterns and Osceolas start getting blended together.

After thinking it over I decided to take someone on the hunt with me. I figured I would ask a gentleman from Missouri I met in the Black Hills of South Dakota, Joe Diestal. He also needed the Osceola for his grand slam. I also spoke with another man, Eric Warlick, from the Pinhoti Project. Kenny knew Eric also, but I decided to reach out to him via Facebook trying to get some information on North Carolina. I thought about adding this state to my list this spring and Eric lived there. I had an uncle who also lived in North Carolina along the coast. Eric said if I didn't have any luck on my uncle's property, he would help point me in the right direction on some public ground near the western side of the state. In the process of reaching out to him I told him I was heading to Florida to hunt in mid-March and extended an invite to him. At this point I had two buddies accompanying me on my hunt. I picked up Eric at his place in North Carolina and then drove 12 hours down to Florida. Eric and I hit it off and I quickly realized what kind of a hunter and person he was as we exchanged hunting stories. After the long ride I knew we would become friends.

We arrived at the property on a Friday and had just one day to scout before the season began the following day. We ended up sleeping in my truck in his driveway and woke up about 4 a.m. When we woke up we saw lights on in the house. Eventually he came out and we talked turkey over a cup of coffee and he explained how he usually hears them gobble first thing in the morning. Sure enough we heard a couple turkeys gobble back in the woods on his property. After driving to another portion of his property we also heard more turkeys. Eric and I were both excited to say the least.

Still waiting on Joe to arrive, I decided to hunt close to the house the following morning.

When opening morning arrived it was cold for Florida, hovering around 40 degrees, and the weather turned really nasty in a hurry. However, we remained optimistic because the night before we had found a lone gobbler. Because Eric had killed a couple birds previously in Florida we were going to hunt together and I was going to be up to bat. As soon as it started breaking day there was a lot of noise on the neighboring property – side by sides, four-wheeler traffic. We figured it had messed with the birds because we had heard three or four birds the evening before and now we only heard one turkey gobble two times. As we started to slip into the swamp near the location where we heard this gobbler our calls went unanswered.

About nine o'clock we heard some hens get into a fight in the palmettos. Lots of fight purring going on. Eric and I realized this was our opportunity to cut the distance on them since they were occupied. We got down on all fours and started to crawl through the palmettos towards the fighting purrs. We kept slipping closer as they continued to purr, thankful they were pre-occupied.

Fortunately, there is a ton of cover in Florida so if you're able to get down on the ground or you stand a good chance of remaining undetected. As we slipped closer and closer we eventually laid eyes on the turkeys, which were probably about 50 yards away. Finally, we spotted the tail fan of the gobbler through the brush. Eric was to my left and I finally raised my gun while the gobbler strutted back and forth, clueless we were even there. Eric and I noticed a small hole in the vegetation where I could shoot. The gobbler was about 10 yards from walking through this opening for

A narrow window gave me the shot I needed to complete my Grand Slam and state number 18 of the Super Slam. March 18, 2017.

a shot. Eric whispered, "Take the shot when he passes through the opening. I'll cut to try and stop him. With any luck he'll stick his head up." I thought man, this is a 50-50 shot kind of thing.

Finally, the gobbler reached the hole and was moving so fast Eric didn't even have a chance to cut. I took a shot and the gobbler folded right up, and I had my first Osceola. He sported one and a quarter inch spurs. He was an absolutely beautiful turkey. Since this hunt Eric and I have done a lot of turkey hunts together. This was a special first hunt together.

Joe was able to fill his tag on the other piece of property. Unfortunately, Eric left empty- handed after our three-day hunt, but I'm glad he was there when I shot my first Osceola. ↓

LESSONS LEARNED

When a turkey is preoccupied, whether fighting or strutting, it's time to carefully make your move and get into position for a shot. This hunt was a prime example of this. When those hens were fighting we made our move to crawl to within gun range.

Chapter 19

Tennessee

After the Sunshine State I had to sit on the bench for a few weeks until it was time to hunt turkeys in Tennessee around the first of April. This was the second state I would be traveling to during the spring of 2017.

On our trip to Florida Eric had given me some intel on a public area to hunt, which allowed me to spend the next couple of weeks checking out some maps prior to leaving. My plan was to leave after work on Friday and hunt Saturday and Sunday, since West Virginia is so close to Tennessee.

When I left Friday evening I had to drive through Nashville, which ended up being an absolute disaster. Because of getting hung up in traffic I didn't arrive to my hunting destination until around eleven o'clock. I was prepared to stay at a campground there and had brought all of my gear, however it was so late I decided on staying at a hotel. My taxidermy business was producing supplemental income so I had extra money to splurge. Kenny always stayed in hotels and said you hunt better when you stay in one opposed to a campground. You can get a hot shower and a good night's rest in preparation for the next day's hunt. I thought about that a lot and any time I had the extra money I would opt to stay in a hotel. However, when I arrived I couldn't find one with a vacancy. The town where I wanted to stay had some type of festival going on, forcing me to stay at one of the campgrounds nearby. Fortunately, it was only 10 minutes from the area I would be hunting.

After setting up camp I decided to drive out to the spot, just to make sure I didn't run in to any unforeseen obstacles such as locked gates. I also wanted to check the availability of parking because the access point wasn't well marked. However, it turned out I was able to pull into a power line there and easily park.

The next morning, opening day in Tennessee, I woke up super early in order to beat other turkey hunters. Because this area had a good population of turkeys it was a popular area and got lots of pressure. Accordingly, I made a point to get there early in order to beat the competition. After parking I hiked back to a ridge bordering a field, which I had located on a map prior to arriving. I had to sit in the dark for about an hour before daylight when I looked right above me and spotted some turkeys, which I had walked under earlier not even realizing it. As daylight increased I noticed there were about three or four of them. I thought to myself, *there's got to be a gobbler in here somewhere.* However, to my disappointment all the turkeys I had spotted were hens.

Fortunately, a turkey did begin to gobble behind me around 200 yards. I was pinned down by the hens above me and I couldn't move on this gobbler, so I had to wait for the hens to fly down. This is when I realized there was no gobbler with them. By the time this transpired, the only gobbler I heard in the area ended up smack dab in the middle of the field with some hens, making it impossible to sneak up on him. I walked over to a little knoll, which allowed me to watch this group of birds. He gobbled repeatedly from all of the attention he was getting from the hens. Most importantly, this allowed me to keep tabs on him. About nine o'clock the gobbler began drifting toward the edge of the field. However, the woods there were open, making it impossible to approach him.

As I continued to scan the terrain around the field, I noticed a little creek bed that ran pretty close to the edge of the field. I thought this might give me a chance to lie down and sneak up close to the gobbler. In order to reach the creek and remain hidden

I had to double back from where I was set up. I knew there was no point in calling to this turkey since he had five hens with him. Also, I wasn't using decoys and didn't have any to set out to try and lure him over. The only option in this circumstance was to use the terrain and that's exactly what I did.

Finally, after I reached the creek about 200 yards from him, I started to work my way up the creek on all fours. It wasn't really a creek, but a small depression with standing water. As I moved in closer to the gobbler I thought, *this might actually work*. My clothes were getting soaked, but I didn't care at this point. It was the best plan and I was sticking with it.

The entire crawl took about an hour. I would slowly inch my way along, occasionally lifting my head to keep tabs on the gobbler. I repeated this process several times in order to make sure he was still there and hadn't moved on. Before I knew it I was almost within shotgun range of him. It was closing in on ten o'clock and he was still out in the field strutting. The depression I crawled in eventually took a bend and the field edge got really steep. This shift in the terrain was perfect, I thought, because it would allow me to slide up above the steep edge and lay my gun up on the bank, hopefully within shotgun range. However, when the field edge got steep I lost track of him and I was going to have to roll the dice and take a guess where I wanted to pop up. The last time I had spotted him he was around 60 yards away.

I opted to crawl 15 more yards and pop up over the edge. I figured he should be in range at that point. Still positioned on all fours, I slowly climbed the bank and slid my shotgun up on the edge. As I peered up they were about 50 yards in front of me, but with my 20 gauge I felt comfortable taking the shot. As I squeezed off a shot the gobbler jumped straight up in the air. I fully expected him to fold up once he hit the ground. However, when the bird landed he instantly took off running in the opposite direction. Looking back, I believe he just jumped up because he was scared. As he was running away I squeezed off a second shot and plowed him in the back of the head, which rolled him over. I was in utter disbelief that I had actually hit the gobbler.

After walking out to the field I carried him over to a little knoll,

soaking in the mo-
ment, and gave Eric a
call thanking him for
pointing me in the di-
rection of the WMA.
I carried him over to a
little knoll, soaking in
the moment, and gave
Eric a call thanking
him for pointing me
in the direction of the
WMA. Afterwards, a
game warden checked
out my turkey. He

April 1, 2017

was a real friendly and professional guy, congratulating me, and
then I was on my way.

I went back to camp and hunted the next morning. But as I was
trying to close the deal on a gobbler, two other turkey hunters shot
the bird out from under me. The turkeys had been gobbling consistently at about 100 yards and I didn't even realize they were set
up there. I had been in the process of making a move on them and
trying to close the deal, but they beat me to it. This was my last
hunt for Easterns in Tennessee.

What I remember most about this experience, other than killing
this turkey is when I arrived back in West Virginia I discovered I
had left my right boot at the campground. Prior to the trip I had
just bought a pair of Kentetrek boots, which run around
$400-$500. I wasn't about to drive eight hours back to the campground to retrieve it. I thought about calling the game warden I
had met, but I ended up just ordering another right boot. So, the
$500 pair of boots turned into about a $750 pair of boots. Yeah,
that sucked! ↓

LESSONS LEARNED

The lesson learned in Tennessee is to keep track of your expensive boots. Besides that, another lesson was if you have gobblers out in a field and calling isn't working, which nine times out of 10 it won't if they're with hens find a piece of terrain that will allow you to get closer. There is usually some type of terrain which should allow you to sneak in for a shot on a gobbler. Even though this gobbler had five hens, and there were 12 eyeballs that could see danger, if you can't see them they can't see you. That's why in this situation the little creek bed along the field edge was all I needed to get within shotgun range of him.

Lastly, an automatic shotgun is best for turkey hunting because it will allow you to keep your sights on him for a follow-up shot if you miss like I did during this particular hunt. When you pump a shotgun you can lose your line of sight. I remember following that gobbler with my red dot after I missed and he hit the ground running. This allowed me to pull off a second shot and fill my Tennessee tag. My gun also has very little recoil helping me to stay on target when the moment of truth arrives.

Chapter 20

North Carolina

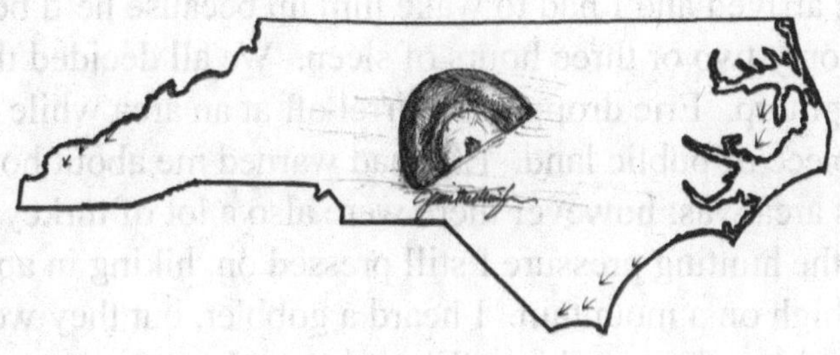

The third state I would be heading to in 2017 was North Carolina. I had an uncle who lived on the coast, so I messaged my friend Eric to see if he thought the area would be a good spot to hunt turkeys. He said I should head over to his area and not worry about hunting the coast, because he had been hearing quite a few turkeys. I told him I would return the favor by helping him fill his tag when he decided to hunt West Virginia.

This particular spring I had two consecutive weeks off. One week was spring break from the school where I taught and thankfully, I was able to take an additional week off using personal leave time. With a total of two weeks off, my plan was to hunt four different states, which was going to be a tall order.

I arrived at Eric's property in North Carolina a day early, which allowed me to do some scouting and spend some time listening for birds in different locations. I rode with Eric on the first morning to a section of national forest and heard a hen, but no gobblers. However, as we drove around during mid-morning we spotted several turkeys and began hearing gobbles as we continued to stop and listen. Both of us felt optimistic going into the opener.

Towards evening we tried to roost some gobblers, but unfortunately neither of us were able to locate any.

Another friend of ours we nicknamed, Squirrel was supposed to arrive the night before the opener; however he ended up arriving later that evening, driving up from Florida. Eric had set up a camper in his yard so we didn't inconvenience him in his house, which worked out perfect. Because Squirrel pulled in so late he decided to sleep in his vehicle so he didn't wake me up.

Morning arrived and I had to wake him up because he'd been running on only two or three hours of sleep. We all decided that we would split up. Eric dropped Squirrel off at an area while I drove to a piece of public land. Eric had warned me about how popular this area was; however there were also a lot of turkeys.

Despite the hunting pressure I still pressed on, hiking in about an hour up high on a mountain. I heard a gobbler, but they were down low and I was up too high. Even though I was an hour away from the gate it didn't matter – there were still other hunters nearby. The gobbler I heard was probably a 30 minute walk away. Despite this, I decided to go after him. As I made one of my final moves on him a shotgun blast from another hunter sealed the gobbler's fate, forcing me to start searching for another.

As the morning wore on I was able to locate another turkey. Once I got to a spot where I thought I could shoot him, however I messed up. He was in the corner of a field and I was in some open hardwoods. When I called to the gobbler it was an invitation, but he didn't RSVP. I was asking too much of him. There was a large expanse of ground separating us and the woods were too open for his taste. I could tell he wanted to see a hen, but without a decoy he wasn't interested. Fortunately, he did come out of the field and enter the hardwoods, but hung up at around 80 yards in the open woods. I had called to him with a less than desirable setup. If I could do it all over again I would have closed the distance another 50 yards. There was a little ditch I could have crossed and snuck in on him. Maybe if I called from that spot I could have killed him. Hind sight is 20/20 though.

Even after that turkey walked off, he was still gobbling. I continued to mess with him for two hours but he was stubborn and refused to come in. It was mid-afternoon when I decided to call it a morning. When I arrived back at Eric's house everyone had already filled their tags, which included Squirrel, Eric, and his wife. As I walked into the camper all three of their gobblers were hanging inside. They were trying to get a laugh out of me. I was happy for them and all, but I felt like the odd man in the group coming back to camp empty-handed. I thought to myself, *Okay, now I definitely need to kill a gobbler.*

I hung out with them and celebrated for a little bit and then hit the woods again around four o'clock. I opted to try a different area this time. In North Carolina you can hunt in the afternoon, which gave me more time. As I reached my destination I decided not to do any calling and just sit there and try to roost some turkeys. As it closed in on the end of legal shooting time, I remained in the same spot with no action at all. However, I began hearing something walking down the road. It sounded to me like a man walking. At this point I'm 20 yards off the edge of the road watching a large stand of hardwoods on a ridge. I'm thinking, *Man this dude is walking all the way back here again.* Shortly after, I saw a red head poke up and a big old beard. I was in disbelief. Because I didn't anticipate the sound to be a turkey, I didn't have my gun raised. The gobbler didn't booger terribly bad, but he saw enough to skedaddle out of there. I felt discouraged. It was a hard lesson learned.

45 minutes before fly up a turkey gobbled out in front of me about 150 yards, grabbing my attention and giving me a boost of encouragement. At this point I was debating on whether or not to call to the turkey. *Should I wait until morning?* I pondered. Not wanting to mess things up, I elected not to call and just put him to bed for the night. After hearing a gobble I located him out towards the end of the woods. Eventually, three other lone gobblers joined him. At this point I felt very optimistic about the morning hunt. I was able to watch all four turkeys fly up before dark. I wanted to close the distance even more and pick my setup out for the morning hunt, so I waited until dark and took the road beside me, which ran right up to them. The road followed the top of the ridge and they were just down off the steep side.

As I walked down the road I could still see the turkeys against the skylight. I stopped and placed a large stick in the road to mark the spot where I needed to turn in order to start cutting down the hill to where I wanted to set up come morning. Even though I had the spot marked on my navigation system, it's always nice to mark the location for peace of mind. Then I crawled towards them in the dark and picked out the tree I wanted to set up on. I wanted to be about 60 yards on the high side of them so when they flew in this direction they would be within shotgun range. With four gobblers in the mix I stood a good chance of killing one if they didn't spot me.

By the time I started walking out of this area it was well after dark. Once I arrived back at the camper I filled the guys in about the roosting area I had found. They were all telling me that I already had one of those gobblers killed. I was optimistic, but any time I roost a gobbler I never think the turkey is dead. I never like to get that cocky. Up until the time I pull the trigger I'm thinking about what's about to happen and what could go wrong.

The next morning arrived and I walked into the roosting area about two hours before daylight. Without using a flashlight I walked down the same gravel road that I had used the previous day and finally reach the stick that I had laid down in the middle of the road which marked the location to cut right. From the time I left the road I only had about 150 yards until I reached my setup. Even though it was a shorter distance it took me almost an hour to cover this ground. Because it was so dry I took it slow – one step at a time so that I didn't spook any turkeys. Finally, I reached the tree I had picked out the night before. I thought, *Now it's just a waiting game*. Once again, I decided to refrain from calling and just let them fly down.

When the birds finally woke up they were lonesome and on fire – hammering out their calls like crazy. I'm certain if I had set up further away and called they would have come right in. It was a beautiful crisp morning as I watched the turkeys gobble their heads off. I had gobblers directly in front of me and to the right and left of me. As I had eyes on the gobbler in front of me up on a limb at 60 yards he became antsy and turned towards me. From my setup

I was actually above him. At this point I figured they hadn't seen me yet. I could tell he was getting ready to fly down so I flipped my safety off. It's a good thing, too because he flew directly at me off his roost. When he flew down his feet landed a mere 10 yards downhill from me.

His feet had touched the ground for only a couple of seconds before I decided to let him have it. At the shot the other two gobblers flew off into the distance. I quickly ran over and picked up my North Carolina gobbler.

April 9, 2017

Without calling or using any decoys, I attribute woodsman-ship skills to tagging this gobbler. ↓

LESSONS LEARNED

Asking a turkey to cross open woods without decoys is not recommended. Use some kind of terrain feature such as a bend in the hill to your advantage before the gobbler pinpoints you within shotgun range and realizes there isn't a hen present.

Another helpful tactic is marking a roost location with an object like I did by placing a stick in the road or pick out a landmark where you can easily find your way to the roost that you located the evening before. It's important to mark a trail or easily accessible area, which will allow you to access the tree or setup you pick out without making too much noise when you walk in. Don't just rely solely on marking the area with a pin on a hunt application. These objects will provide you with a visual or reference point that will grab your attention and remind you to turn and head in a specific direction towards the roosting location.

Another lesson I learned from this trip is a turkey and a man sound very similar when they're walking through the woods. A turkey is loud having those big club feet. I should have known it wasn't a man because I had seen him go the opposite way. However, it's always important to properly identify your target first. I've always made sure of that. Any time you're in the turkey woods and hear something walking like a man, nine times out of 10 it's usually a turkey.

Chapter 21

South Carolina

The fourth state I would be hunting in 2017 was South Carolina. This state would mark the halfway point in my two week trip. Even though I was already in North Carolina it still was quite a drive South to reach my turkey hunting destination. Like most of the states I hunted, I did some advance research. I contacted some wildlife biologists who provided some helpful information about the turkey population in the area where I hunted. This eased my mind, considering that I didn't know much about turkeys in this state.

However, my friend Ryan Bennett, who had visited the area the previous year to do some turkey scouting, explained how promising the turkey habitat looked in the particular WMA I was interested in. My other friend, Eric, had also hunted South Carolina quite a few times and pointed me to an area he had seen before. The area once had a decent turkey population, but it had declined in recent years. So, I was between a rock and a hard place; I had to decide if I was going to hunt an area I had never seen before, or the area Eric had mentioned. I opted to hunt the area I had never been before.

In order to hunt this WMA, hunters are required to check in with a game warden very early in the morning, which I had read in the regulations prior to the hunt. This was similar to other WMAs I had hunted in the past.

I drove all through the night to South Carolina, arriving just in time to hunt. When I arrived at the WMA check station, I asked one of the employees if she knew of any areas where I would be able to hear a turkey. Without hesitation she pointed me to a road where she had seen a strutting turkey not too long ago. I wasn't sure whether to believe her or not, but I really didn't have any other choices so I figured I would give it a try. Without wasting any time I drove to the exact road where she had spotted the gobbler.

As I followed a map to the location I discovered a gate, which prevented entry. However, it was unlocked. This was concerning along with the truck I found parked there. I decided to keep on driving and blew past it through the gate. Once I passed the vehicle there was a guy in the truck and he flashed his high beams at me a bunch of times. At first I thought he was trying to signal me that this was his spot and he had arrived there first. Reluctantly, I turned around and rolled my window down to talk with this guy. He informed me that the gate is normally closed and there was a good chance I might get locked in if I drove any further. I thought, *Well I don't want that to happen.*

I thanked the guy and turned my truck around parking a couple hundred yards behind him. With my plans to hunt in this area derailed and daylight breaking fast I decided to go to the right of where I was parked a few hundred yards and listen for turkeys. As the sun rose over the horizon my confidence was zilch. The area that I was in didn't look promising. My gut feeling told me there were no turkeys in the area.

Eventually, to my surprise, I heard a couple of turkeys in the distance. I began walking towards them. As I got closer, I figured someone else was probably already on them by the luck I was having. When I reached the turkeys, they had already flown down. After a few failed attempts at calling the turkeys I decided to start crawling towards them in hopes of getting as close as I could. As I closed the distance I realized the birds were in this beautiful swampy area filled with palmettos. It reminded me a lot of my time hunting turkeys while in central Florida.

Eventually, I saw them, two gobblers strutting in the gorgeous palmetto flat. The sun danced off their feathers, displaying their remarkable iridescent colors. Another reminder of why I'm a taxidermist. I ceased crawling for fear of getting spotted. They had two hens with them, which as usual complicated things. Staring at the two longbeards, I was in disbelief that I was in the game right off of the bat. As you know, the world of turkey hunting can flip upside down in a hurry.

At this point I was only about 50 yards off the gravel road when suddenly the turkeys eased off of the flat and disappeared. In an attempt to stay with them I began walking towards the road trying to put a loop on the turkeys. I thought that the turkeys were going to cross the road, but I couldn't see any movement. As I closed the distance I looked down the road towards where I had last seen the turkeys and realized they were walking right at me. Obviously, I wasn't going to use a call because they were coming, so I just froze in my tracks and waited. It was the perfect ambush. As one of the gobblers reached an opening I took the shot and he fell right on the gravel road. I really wasn't far from the gate either. I texted Eric and the others about the turkey hunt. I figured they would never believe me since South Carolina is notoriously a tough state to kill a bird in. After all, it had taken Kenny two years to kill a gobbler even while having numerous encounters. The turkeys are extremely difficult to hunt there. It was evident that luck played a huge part in this particular hunt.

This was day three and with two states down and two weeks remaining to hunt in four states total I wasn't sure what to do. There were no other states at that time with open turkey seasons that I needed in order to continue to reach my goal. Finally, I made a decision to hunt South Carolina for a few more days in this area and then head back to North Carolina and hunt with Eric before traveling west to hunt Iowa and Missouri. Long story short, that morning I heard another turkey gobble in the distance where I had previously dropped a pin. I had decided earlier that if I stuck around I was going to deal with him.

On the second morning I got on this turkey, but I wasn't as close as I needed to be. He flew down, joining up with some hens. I messed with him for awhile, but failed to kill him. Towards evening I knew this turkey had roosted in the same location twice so I decided to set up on the edge of a swamp. There was standing water for as far as the eye could see. As I looked around for sign I noticed some turkey scratchings right on the edge of the swamp. I knew this son of a gun was hanging out here so I decided to set up until dark and try to catch him going to roost. After sitting until dark with no action, I decided to do a fly up cackle. To my surprise a turkey gobbled out in the middle of that swamp. I thought, *How crazy is this that he is roosting out there.* I figured there had to be a piece of dry ground out there that the turkey flew up from, or else I would have seen him fly across the open water from the hardwoods where I had been set up.

Eventually I convinced myself there was a piece of dry ground that the turkey was hanging out on. I estimated he was about 100 yards out so I dropped a pin on him. As crazy as it sounds, my plan was to wade out there through the water and find whatever piece of dry ground he was on. Well, this wasn't one of my brighter ideas.

I arrived two hours before daylight and began wading through the swamp. At one point the water reached my waist as I pushed on. Not wanting to spook the gobbler, I waded in total darkness. Eventually, I reached the area where I had dropped the pin. Most of the water was up to my knees, but still it was very scary doing this in the dark. I thought to myself, *I must be a lunatic!* To my dismay, I soon realized there is no piece of dry ground in this swamp. At that point I knew the best thing to do was head back to the hardwoods. All I could think of is that he must have flown up from the opposite side. However, I wasn't entirely sure. Gradually, I managed to maneuver my way back to where I had hunted the previous evening, at least 45 minutes before daylight, which tells you just how early I got out there to wade through the swamp.

Sure enough, the turkey gobbled twice that morning without

me calling. Suddenly, I looked up and watched the gobbler sail through the air across the swamp, landing a few yards from where I did the fly-up cackle the night before. As soon as his feet hit the ground the longbeard went into strut. Keep in mind that I hadn't done any calling except for a fly up cackle hours before. You can't tell me this was a coincidence. I believe that turkey knew exactly where I had made that cackle from and he was bound and determined to land there to check on the hen.

April 10, 2017

I was about 30 yards from the spot where he landed, and shortly after he landed I got a clear shot and drilled him. I'll have that image buried in my mind of him sailing over that water for the rest of my life. This is one of my favorite hunts of all time. I feel the first bird in this state was luck, but I definitely earned the second one.

After filling my second tag I drove back up to North Carolina and shot another gobbler a couple of days later. ↓

LESSONS LEARNED

Any little nugget of intel you can collect from someone, hang on to for future hunts. The information the DNR employee gave me at the check station put me in the area where the turkeys were.

Another thing is, don't underestimate the power of the fly up cackle in the evening. Not only will it locate the bird, but it will help draw the gobblers in to your setup like it did for me on my second hunt in this state. That bird knew exactly where I had made a fly up cackle the night before.

Chapter 22

Iowa

Filling my tags earlier than anticipated in North and South Carolina put me ahead of schedule. With no other seasons open yet, in the states I needed for the Super Slam, I opted to travel to Iowa a couple of days before the opener to do some scouting. I'm probably the only person in the history of turkey hunting to go to Iowa early to scout because of their reputation for having an excellent turkey population.

My tag for this state allowed me four days to hunt, so the extra time gave me the opportunity to listen for gobblers during the early morning hours and pinpoint some locations to hunt. Iowa's reputation for turkeys rang true; during these morning sessions I heard lots of turkeys. I also spent some time during the day walking through wooded areas and having to duck and hide from turkeys due to their abundance. It was a very productive two days of scouting. The turkeys I encountered intensified my anticipation for the Iowa season to begin.

The evening before the opener, I saw four gobblers in a field. However, about two hours before fly-up time they moved out

116

of area. I knew they traveled quite a distance before fly up time because I hadn't heard them gobble for awhile. Then suddenly, just before dark a lone turkey to my left flew up along the field edge. I suspected it to be a gobbler, but I wasn't for certain.

Once it grew completely dark I crawled along the edge of the field to try and identify it. Upon fly-up I could tell this turkey was extremely wary, based on how it approached the roost. I suspect the four gobblers I saw earlier ran the field and kept this turkey at bay.

At 50 yards from the tree, I used the skylight in my binoculars to see if I could pick out his profile to determine if the turkey had a beard, but the angle I had made it very difficult. Unfortunately, he caught my movement and turned from an overly wary gobbler to being completely switched on and flew off just after I spotted his beard.

Being disappointed in myself was an understatement. I had gone from having a gobbler in my lap to messing it up completely. However, there were still lots of turkeys around and even though I had scared the gobbler away I elected to return there in the morning and sit along the edge of the field where I had spotted the four gobblers.

As I nestled against a tree an hour before daylight an owl called. A turkey let out a half-assed gobble a few hundred yards away, before a turkey should even think about gobbling. I thought, *this is perfect; I'm going to close the distance before sun up.* Without any lights I began walking through the woods, trying to get as close to the gobbler as possible. Because it took me such a long time to set up near the roost, I was dangerously close to gobble time. I began hearing drumming as I reached the 50-yard line from his roost just at first light. Suddenly, a chorus of gobbles surrounded me.

I soon realized these gobblers had hens with them, based on all the yelps that chimed in. Trying to remain optimistic, I had hopes they would fly towards me. They flew down, but in the opposite direction. Two other gobblers I had been hearing while amidst the chorus earlier decided to join the gobbler. Unfortunately, they eluded me and headed out into the field.

I kicked myself for leaving the field edge, but it was too late.

It was time for another game plan. Soon, I figured the best action would be to make a huge loop and try to pinpoint their location. I crawled to the edge of the field and spotted the birds about 200 yards out. A terrain feature in the field allowed me to keep tabs on them while I crawled back into the woods in order to make my move. Luckily, there was a dip running across the edge and down into the woods. I figured this was the best chance I had to close the distance. Because the gobblers were henned up it was pointless to call so I continued to crawl, stopping periodically. Suddenly, I heard the crunch of leaves nearby, in the familiar cadence of a turkey walking. I looked up from crawling and realized it was indeed a turkey.

April 17, 2017

Out from the woods opposite of the field was a lone gobbler extremely cautious. Even though I was in the middle of stalking the other gobblers in the field, this was a welcome interruption. I remained on my belly like a fallen statue, watching him close the distance and finally disappear behind a tree. This was my cue to raise my shotgun and get into position for a shot. As the gobbler slowly walked out into the open I tipped him over, filling my Iowa tag.

I walked over and lifted the mysterious nomad gobbler. As I caressed its beautiful feathers, I was in disbelief that once again I had finished my hunt on the first day like in North and South Carolina. When I picked up the gobbler to carry it out of the woods I could tell it was a very heavy two year old, which was characteristic of Iowa. ↓

LESSONS LEARNED

One of the lessons that was reinforced during this particular hunt is that footsteps made by a turkey and those made by man sound very similar. Usually you can tell the difference between a deer and a turkey based on the cadence and rhythm they make.

Although seeing plays a huge part of turkey hunting, hearing will serve you well in situations where the turkey comes in from an unexpected location. Especially, during afternoon hunts, when gobblers are less vocal.

Chapter 23

Missouri

Because I had filled my tag so early in Iowa, I was able to pack up and leave the same day for Missouri. Up to this point I was about nine days into my trip and wasn't expecting to arrive in Missouri until the end of my two-week vacation. I had allowed about four days per state, but once again the cards were in my favor and I had ample time, which is often necessary in the turkey woods. I'd rather be lucky than good any day. I mean, who crawls through the woods and has a random gobbler walk up on you like it happened in Iowa?

A buddy of mine got me in touch with a gentleman from West Virginia who owned property in southern Missouri near the Arkansas border in the Ozarks. After getting his phone number, I gave him a call to ask if I could hunt his property. He was one of the nicest guys I've ever met. While working towards my Super Slam I met so many great people, and he was definitely one of them. He even allowed me to return and hunt deer, which I've done a few times. On the phone he explained how he had a cabin on his property where I could stay while I hunted. Up to this point I hadn't even met the guy and he had already offered a place to sleep. Like other situations during this journey, it was almost too good to be true.

After a long drive I arrived at his cabin and unloaded my gear. It was too late to roost any birds, so I hung out at the cabin by myself, in amazement of how cool this place was. The gentleman didn't expect any payment, but I felt I should pay him for being so generous, and it was also the right thing to do. On one wall was a large topographical map of the property I would be hunting. After looking it over carefully I spotted the highest point on the property. I knew instantly this would be where I would go first thing in the morning to begin my hunt. My buddy said there were a few turkeys on this property, but I was a little concerned because of the population decline.

As soon as I reached that high point the next morning, I heard a few gobbles in the distance. And then, suddenly, boom! Right beneath me about 100 yards a gobble thundered through the morning air. Luck had found a path to me once again. I was in a perfect position above him and decided to close the distance. As I've mentioned before, I like to get tight to them on the limb if at all possible.

I found a good set-up spot within 60 yards of him. By that point his gobbles had toned down and weren't as frequent, but he gobbled enough for me to keep tabs on him. I soon learned he had hens with him, a haunting scenario for all of us. I anticipated him flying to the uphill side of the ridge, but there was a pasture below him so I had a 50/50 chance of him flying in my direction. Of course, in turkey fashion he decided to fly straight down to the pasture. However, during my set-up while I was focused on this bird another turkey had gobbled twice to my right. He was also within 100 yards. Because the first gobbler I had pursued was down in the pasture with his hens, I decided to abort the mission and go after the second gobbler. Once I relocated to the edge of the steep hill I was on I reached a fairly open spot that looked promising.

After I threw some calls his way, he quickly answered a couple of times and continued to be responsive, but failed to come any closer. I ceased calling to the stubborn bird and waited patiently to see if he would budge. Unfortunately, he wasn't gobbling on his own, so the chances of sneaking up on him were slim to none. I decided to go silent for about 20 minutes in hopes of tickling his curiosity.

Ten minutes into my silence, I heard the familiar sound, *pfffft vooom*. He had broken his position and was drumming, however I still hadn't laid eyes on him. It seems that most of the time when I hear drumming they're close enough to shoot. This was an exception though. I had been focusing all of my calls down the hill to the left, hoping he would think the hen was down there and would come straight to me or at least just above me on the steep slope.

It doesn't happen very often, but he followed the script and walked right to me. As he approached I waited for him to clear some brush and fired a 20 yard shot. He was a sneaky little two year old, the way he moseyed in trying to take advantage of the hen while the boss gobbler was down in the pasture occupied with all of the hens.

I gathered up the gobbler and walked back to the highest point where I had first listened for gobbles at dawn. I remember sitting there for a

April 18, 2017

few hours, reflecting on the hunt and how fortunate I had been for things to work out like they did during the four-state run and hoping my lucky streak would continue. This was one of my favorite trips of the entire Slam, as I had killed a gobbler on the first day in each of the four states. I figured in extra days for scouting and filling a second tag, but physically it took only four days.

The West Virginia turkey season had kicked off just a day earlier, so with five days left in my vacation I decided to drive back and make it in time to hunt in the morning. I could have hunted Kansas because their season was open, but I elected to head back home. I packed my gear and arrived that evening in time to hunt with my buddy Ryan Bennett the following morning.

My lucky streak continued and I was able to fill my West Virginia tag also. This meant that I had shot a gobbler three days in a row in three different states – Iowa, Missouri, and West Virginia. It was a good three-day run. Not often are you successful in three states in three days, and even though West Virginia wasn't a new state it was a personal best. ↓

LESSONS LEARNED

When you've been calling to a gobbler that holds his ground, often times going silent will pique their curiosity, causing them to slip in to investigate.

Typically, they will come in either silent or, in my case, drumming, allowing you to keep tabs on them. Another important ingredient in this equation is staying above the turkey you're calling to because they will naturally want to get above you. This is the reason I purposely turned my head and threw all of my calls down the hill. This created an illusion that I, meaning the hen, was further down the hill than I actually was. It worked, and he walked directly to me.

If you can't get to the high ground because of an obstacle such as brush, get into a position where you can at least cover the travel routes to the elevation change.

Gaining permission to turkey hunt has become more difficult in recent years, especially with the number of turkey hunters constantly growing. However, depending on what part of the country you're in, most land owners don't care about turkeys as much and will allow you to hunt their property. Therefore, when you're driving around and see turkeys on a farm, edge of the road, etc., it doesn't hurt to ask.

When knocking on a landowner's door, I prefer to wear street clothes and not camouflage. In my opinion it sends out a better vibe and is less intimidating. I want to look presentable, so on my trips I pack regular clothing in the event I need to ask for permission. Also, when approaching landowners it is essential to take a deep breath and be articulate when introducing yourself. Being well-spoken will help communicate effectively your desire to hunt on their property. I always start out the conversation with where I'm from and what I do for a living. This is a great icebreaker and sets the tone. Then I merge into asking them if they let anyone turkey hunt on their farm/property. Lastly, I always offer to pay them for permission to hunt, especially if they're a little hesitant or say no. I figure $200 to hunt a turkey is worth it to me.

Getting information or leads on where to hunt is a slippery slope. First, turkey hunters in general are secretive for the most part. Not as much now, but they used to be. I used to like trading spots in different states with turkey hunters. For example, I would provide them with the pinned location of some turkeys in one state if they gave me the same intel in a state I wanted to hunt. A lot of people look down on pin trading because they think it's not as pure because you're not finding these places on your own. However, trading pins and GPS points has never bothered me because it's not a guarantee that you're going to fill your tag, even though last year or five years ago the person that gave you the information shot one. Now, does it help that you know there were turkeys in these locations in prior years? You're darn right it does. It doesn't make you any less of a turkey hunter if you received some information from someone. Throughout my slam I received information, but not the entire time. I did some on my own, but also got help. You can't be on such a limited schedule without some help from other hunters. I try to avoid trading information now because of having been burned a couple of times by them sharing it with the wrong people and before you know it a spot is ruined. That's why I call it a slippery slope. Be careful who you share pins with. Make sure it's with someone that you know you can trust.

Chapter 24

Pennsylvania

After Ryan and I filled our tags in West Virginia in late April, we decided to travel to Pennsylvania and scout some public land within a couple of hours from home. If necessary, we also planned to knock on some doors to gain permission on private property if we ran across turkeys. After arriving we found some turkeys fairly close to public land and spent some time scouting, but nothing jumped out at us. Even though we kept getting turned down to hunt these private properties, our persistence eventually paid off. On one of our last stops that day, we knocked on the door of an older woman's farm and finally got permission. She explained where to park while hunting and we put this land in our back pocket. We didn't see any turkeys on her property while driving around, but after looking at her land Ryan and I had a gut feeling it held turkeys.

After leaving this area, I waited a couple of weeks before going back to hunt. I left my place one Friday evening, and once I arrived I looked for sign and tried to roost some turkeys, since Ryan and I hadn't walked it the day we got permission. After putting boots on the ground, I began looking for turkey tracks. After doing some glassing I spotted a few jakes out in her fields, but no gobblers. But, as I walked back to my truck in the dark a hellacious thunderstorm moved in. Right before it reached me, thunder and lightning ripped through the air. Every time it thundered a group of three turkeys started gobbling. They gobbled so much I was able to sneak in and locate them on the limb towards dark. This allowed me to figure out a game plan for my morning setup. When I initially heard the gobbles, I could have easily said I know where the turkeys are and left, knowing I had some turkeys to chase the next morning. However, pinpointing their exact location before the hunt puts you way ahead the following morning.

When I returned the next day under the cover of darkness, I soon realized the turkeys I had roosted, were actually off the field edge about 50 yards. I knew there was a strong chance those turkeys would travel to the field, especially since they were probably still wet and wanted to dry off in the open. So, I decided to play monkey in the middle and get between the turkeys and the field and hope for the best.

As turkey hunting goes, it didn't pan out like I anticipated. It was still thundering when I left my truck and the turkeys still responded to each crack of thunder. There was still two hours left before daylight and I was hoping to set up about 30 yards from them before they were awake and active on the limb, but they were already chatty. I was torn. I knew the sound of thunder and rain would help cover the noise of my footsteps and I would be able to approach without being detected, but at the same time it was risky.

Cold and wet, I opted to sit against a large tree I had picked out the night before, listening to them gobble. I waited two hours in darkness for them to fly down. When dawn approached they continued to stay on their limbs with some hens nearby. I decided not to call. This was purely a bushwhacking hunt and my ambush was perfect. Soon, I saw them get fidgety on the limb and I knew they were preparing to fly down. I figured they would land in the woods because it was quite a flight through the air to land in the field. However, in usual turkey fashion, the first turkey soared over my head landing on the field edge within shotgun range. Unfortunately, I had to do a complete 180 in order to get in position. Before I made my move, I wondered if I should wait for the other two gobblers. However, I elected to turn around and take a shot at the gobbler, anchoring him instantly while the other gobblers were still in the tree.

April 29, 2017

I remember thinking, *Man, this is my 24th state! I'm halfway done with my Super Slam.* I felt like it was a great accomplishment and was excited for the journey ahead and future gobblers that awaited me. What a ride it was. It makes you appreciate each moment in the turkey woods and each memory that's made grinding out those states and the challenge of trying to fill my tag with a limited amount of time.

Two weeks later I brought Kenny back to this same spot and he was able to shoot one of the other two gobblers I had chased. It felt good to be the one helping the old man out for a change. ↓

LESSONS LEARNED

Any time you have a spring thunderstorm close to daylight or dark it's a good thing. It seems as though a gobbler can't help but gobble at the thunder. If there is a turkey there I promise you he will gobble.

Any time you hear turkeys in the evening you need to find which limb he is on and know where to setup for the following morning's hunt. Just knowing their general direction isn't good enough to seal the deal.

The thunderstorm coupled with me sneaking in to survey the situation the evening before and finding the exact limb the turkey was on is what killed this gobbler in Pennsylvania.

Chapter 25

New York

After Pennsylvania I had every intention of my season being over. It was the second week in May, and I already had a successful run. However, after sitting on the bench for a few days I started getting the itch to hunt once again and started looking at places to hunt over Memorial Day Weekend. I decided to start researching where seasons were still open and the states that would be a reasonable drive, considering I was only going to have a couple days to hunt. Eventually, I chose New York even though I had zero knowledge on the state. However, after looking over maps of counties I found a place that looked promising and figured this was a great place to start. I was slightly skeptical because I wasn't sure how many birds I would find this late in the season considering how many turkey hunters had probably pressured the area.

I called ahead to get a room for this trip because there were no campgrounds in the area, and I also didn't feel like sleeping in my truck for three days. However, to my dismay, there was some type

of function going on in the area and everything was booked. Fortunately, the owners of one of the motels offered an apartment they
owned, which happened to be on a nearby farm. They charged me
the same as the nightly motel rate. It was definitely more than I
needed, but much appreciated for the weekend hunt. When they
had mentioned that the apartment was on a farm my ears instantly
perked up and I asked them if they had any turkeys. They said
there were turkeys all over the place.

Regardless of hunting pressure, this was going to be my starting
point. I figured I would hunt directly behind the apartment.

After school ended, my three-day weekend commenced. I
drove all night to New York in order to have time to hunt first thing
in the morning. After pulling the all-nighter I arrived at the apartment around 2 a.m.

When you picture New York you think city, but this was far
from it. It was down in the Catskills and was the type of mountainous country I was use to hunting. Once morning arrived I walked
back on the couple's farm and discovered a couple of ground
blinds. A tell-tale sign that someone had already been hunting
in the area. On a positive note, I called in a lone hen so I figured
there had to be gobblers there at some point. But the woods were
silent that morning and I didn't even hear any turkeys on the limb.
Because of the state regulations I could only hunt half a day and
had much more ground to cover.

This particular area had pieces of public land broken up into
various sections and I had about 20 different areas I was interested in hunting. I ended up traveling to each of these places, which
made for a long day. After putting boots on the ground, around
mid-morning I ended up bumping into some jakes on one of these
public pieces, but there were no longbeards in sight. I had spotted
them from the road and was able to make a large two-mile loop
on them while on public land, coming in from behind. This ate up
a couple of hours of my morning. Afterwards, I was off to other
pieces of public, walking them and looking for turkey sign. Soon,
it was about an hour before quitting time and I felt extremely exhausted. I'm not exactly sure how many miles I hiked that day, but
it was a fair amount.

Even though my legs were sore, I had just enough steam in me to check one last area, which consisted of 100 acres of public land. There was a big open field, but you had to hike up a large hill in order to reach it. Just before reaching the top, I peeked over the ridge and looked down into the field. To my surprise there was a gobbler with three hens. Unfortunately, the gobbler had spotted me and immediately stretched his head up, looking straight at me. I figured the game was over as I sat there like a statue expecting him to run off at any minute. He stared at me for what seemed like 10 minutes, which in reality was probably only a minute or two. Finally, he put his head down and began feeding. When he did this I instantly melted to the ground, which put me out of his line of sight.

The wind was whipping pretty fast, which worked to my advantage and probably threw them off a little as to what I was. Because I had little confidence in this area, I had left my gun in my truck, figuring I would just look for sign. As he put his head down to feed, I dipped below the ridge so he couldn't see me. The tiredness had left my body and I ran on a full sprint back to my truck. I had about 45 minutes before quitting time. I had to make it happen. Because the gobbler had hens, I knew there was no chance of pulling him away from them. I noticed to his right was a huge rock wall. I knew I had to get within shooting range of him and the rock wall was my only hope. I swung way wide from the field, crossing a creek near my truck. My plan was to reach an area 100-yards to the right of the rock wall, because the turkeys were on the left side. I had to gain more ground, so when I approached the 100-yard mark I got down on my belly and started crawling to the wall. Once I arrived, I positioned myself along the wall and crawled some more towards the field edge, cutting the distance to the gobbler, which had originally been 200 yards away. The wind helped cover any noise I made while cutting the distance, and I felt confident I could kill this longbeard.

The stalk had taken about 20 minutes and I kept checking the time to make sure I was still legal. Finally, I felt close enough to where I could pop up and see the gobbler, which I thought should be in shotgun range. The first time I looked the gobbler and hens were still out of range at 80 yards. They were still feeding with no care in the world. So far, everything was going as planned. I continued along the wall, knowing full well I needed to cut the distance another 40 yards before they would be in range. Eventually, I picked out a tree along the wall and figured I should be within shotgun range when I reached it. The anticipation was overwhelming and I felt tense, knowing the moment of truth could happen any time. Once I reached the tree I slowly raised my head and eased my shotgun over the wall. They were exactly 40 yards from me. Thankfully, the wind had made this stalk so much easier, helping to conceal any noise and movement.

At this point I was able to sit, because the wall hid everything except my head. It was perfect! Fortunately, they never noticed me getting my gun into position, so I was able to take my time preparing for the shot. The spot on the wall I set my shotgun on wedged my gun in tight, almost as if it was on a vice. As I looked through my red dot scope, the gobbler had his head down feeding and pecking. I thought, the next time he puts his head up I'm going to shoot him. As crazy as it sounds, it was so windy that when I shot the gobbler, the hens, which were 10 yards to the right

May 18, 2017

of him, had zero reaction to the shot. With 12 minutes of shooting time to spare, I had killed a New York gobbler on day one.

It was unbelievable. During the entire spring turkey season I had killed a gobbler on the very first day of each hunt. I attribute this to pure grit and luck. While on the hunt it meant pushing myself to walk many miles and checking "just one more" spot before calling it a day and being persistent and persevering. Most turkey hunters aren't willing to put in the miles necessary to be successful. I don't kill turkeys because I'm good. I kill turkeys because I'm gritty. ↓

LESSONS LEARNED

During this particular hunt I learned the wind can be your friend. While trying to put the stalk on a turkey the wind can help conceal your movement and cover up any unwanted noise. Use it to your advantage during situations where you need to reposition yourself in order to get within shotgun range of a gobbler.

Lastly, landforms such as the large rock wall I hid behind while getting into position can also help you close the deal on a gobbler. In the northeast there is lots of rocky terrain and hills that you can use to your advantage. Pay attention to the type of terrain features that will help you get close to turkeys.

I credit the wind and the rock wall to my success in New York.

Chapter 26

Texas

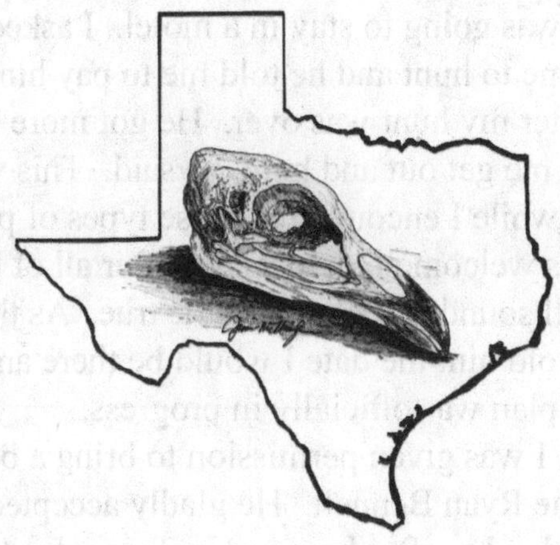

During the spring of 2018, I decided to hunt the Rio Grande subspecies in Texas. Because there is very little public land available in Texas, you either have to know someone that owns private land or pay an outfitter. I didn't know anyone in this state. Therefore, not long after the 2017 season ended I had researched what I needed to do in order to go on a hunt there.

I was free in mid-March, which was perfect because that's when turkey season opened in south Texas. I didn't want to go on a guided hunt, but I was willing to pay a trespass fee. I knew it was going to cost me some money, but there weren't too many other choices.

After striking out on several attempts to gain hunting permission, I was finally given an ounce of hope. While making calls I was given the number of a landowner, who explained that some years he had turkeys and other years he didn't. It was a 50/50 shot, but up to this point it was the best chance I had from all my phone calls. Not wanting to waste my time he told me to call back in a few months to see how the turkey activity was. In the meantime, I researched other places just in case things didn't pan out with this landowner.

Two months rolled around and I called him back. The landowner said he had been seeing tons of turkeys and told me to come on down. He even allowed me to stay in his ranch guest house after I told him that I was going to stay in a motel. I asked him how much he wanted for me to hunt and he told me to pay him whatever I felt it was worth after my hunt was over. He got more satisfaction seeing people like me get out and hunt, he said. This was my kind of guy. Once in awhile I encountered these types of people during the Slam and it was welcomed. Especially after all of the road blocks. However, it still sounded too good to be true. As the conversation wrapped up, I told him the date I would be there and he gave me his address. A plan was officially in progress.

Fortunately, I was given permission to bring a buddy along, so I decided to invite Ryan Bennett. He gladly accepted my invitation and joined me the day after I arrived in Texas due to our schedules conflicting. I gave Ryan the address and jokingly told him he might have to cancel his flight if this guy killed me. Once I arrived at the property I started to feel a little better about things. The landowner had a really nice house and the area looked promising. Once I met the guy he started talking like we'd known each other for years. Eventually, he drove me to the ranch house on his property and showed me where I'd be staying during the hunt. Things just kept getting better. As he drove me around on his property, there were four longbeards in strut about 200 yards from the ranch house. I thought to myself, *this is something out of a dream.*

After dropping me off at my sleeping quarters, he told me to have fun hunting and that he would come back tomorrow and check on me. After unloading my gear I stepped out onto the deck of the ranch house. Boom! I heard the same birds gobble and instantly knew where they ran off to. However, they had hens with them and I knew it would be hard for them to break away. I figured it would be another situation where I would have to try and get in front of them. And this is exactly what I did.

It was midday and I saw them hanging out in the shade of a mesquite tree while the hot sun was beating down. Some of them were in the tree and some were underneath. I noticed there were a couple of really big strutters mixed in there. Eventually, the gobblers started traveling down into a little dip in the terrain.

I learned pretty quickly that crawling in Texas is rough on the knees and elbows. As I inched towards the gobblers I started to get pricked by cactuses. It seemed like I spent the rest of the week pulling out the sharp quills. The Lone Star Sate isn't a friendly place to crawl, that's for sure. They have miniature cactuses you can hardly see and they let off a ton of quills all at once. Despite getting poked during the crawl from hell, I pushed on. It was a small price to pay for getting close to a gobbler.

As I closed the distance one of the satellite gobblers started to veer off to the right and I was able to shoot him. I hadn't been hunting for two hours. This left me dumbfounded. I thought to myself, *we've still got three more days of this.* I called Ryan and shared the exciting news and filled him in on the turkey activity on this property.

The next day we didn't waste any time and we started chasing turkeys for the next three days. Ryan ended up filling his tag and I added one more to the freezer. The whole trip I was thinking I needed to get Kenny down here to hunt this property. After all, he had taught me so much about turkey hunting and I wanted to return the favor. Eventually, he was able to find time to hunt Texas with me, and since then we've turned this into an annual trip, typically hunting around four days.

March 23, 2018

After the first year I hunted in Texas, the landowner came down to visit us at the ranch house every evening and we would cook turkey and drink beer. He took a liking to all three of us and we've become really good friends.

I'm really fortunate for finding this landowner connection. Out of the entire Slam, Texas is the best thing that's ever happened to me. ↓

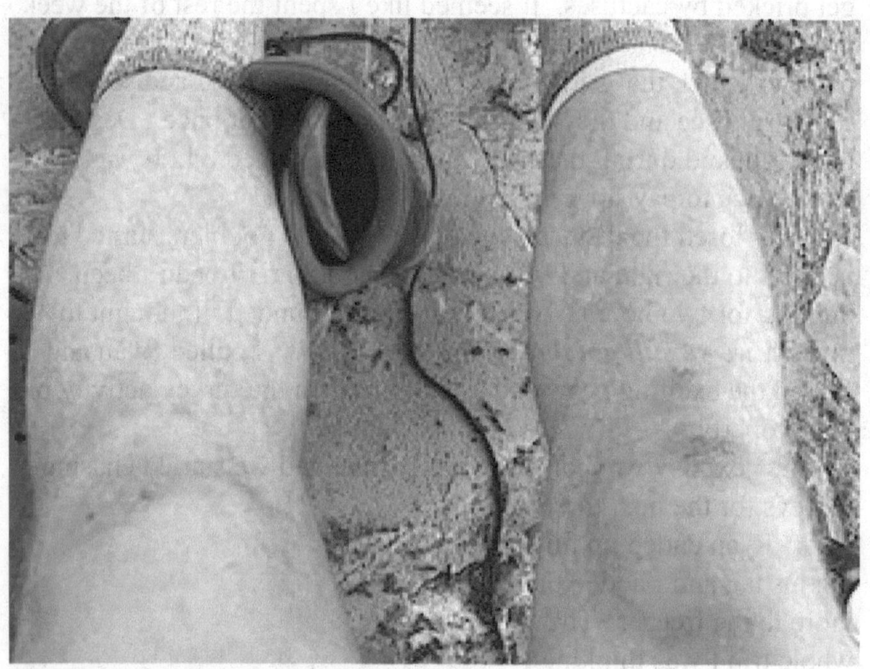

Crawling in Texas is rough on the knees.

LESSONS LEARNED

The Rio Grande turkey covers lots of ground throughout the day. When they're traveling in a large group, there is only one way to kill them and that is to get in front of them or figure out where they're likely to spend time loafing during the middle of the day and plan your approach. Calling them up in this type of situation is not impossible, but extremely difficult.

More than half the turkeys I have killed have been taken by being in the right position. Although I love calling turkeys and that is my favorite way to hunt them, turkeys cannot be killed like this at all times. Turkeys have to be in the right mood to be called, and if you want to consistently kill turkeys you need to learn to go to them and make things happen.

Chapter 27

Nevada

A couple of weeks after my Texas hunt, my plan was to take advantage of a four-day weekend and try to hammer out Nevada and California. Nevada was challenging because there were only two counties in the entire state that held a population of turkeys and just two non-resident tags per year were given out for public land. However, there was a loophole that allowed the landowner to sell you his turkey tag. Because my chances of drawing a permit were slim to none, I decided to go the route of contacting a landowner to try and secure a tag. Fortunately, through a friend I was able to contact a landowner who had some turkeys on his property along with a tag, which he was willing to sell me for $100.

A week before my plane landed in Reno, I gave the landowner a call to touch base with him one last time. This is when things got interesting. Because he hadn't heard from me he had sold three other resident tags to people in Nevada who were also going to be hunting on his farm. Unfortunately, this farm wasn't very big either, around 200 acres. Now there were a total of four of us hunting there. I thought, *Man, this isn't good at all, but maybe there are plenty of turkeys for all of us.* Besides this, safety was also a concern. Despite all of these last-minute curve balls, I kept Nevada on my radar and I was going, come hell or high water.

After my plane landed in Nevada, I drove a couple of hours before I finally reached the farm. Once I pulled up to the farm I met with the landowner who explained how the turkeys on his property were still in their winter flock. Afterwards, I drove down the road and ran into the other hunters who were all watching this flock of turkeys on his property which consisted of around 100 turkeys. There were about 20 gobblers and a mixture of hens and jakes. Because they hadn't broken up yet, it was going to be a challenging hunt. Plus, I was competing with the other hunters targeting the same flock.

At the time, I contemplated making the six-hour trip to California and returning once I filled my tag. However, after explaining my decision to the landowner he quickly talked me out of it, encouraging me to hunt on opening day. Even though I couldn't afford wasting a day, I figured I would give it a shot and treat it like I was hunting on public land. My plan was to beat the other hunters into this location and set up closer to the turkeys.

By the time I made up my mind that I was staying, there was about an hour of daylight left. A large bluff overlooked the farm, which I could see from the landowner's house. I asked him if it was okay if I took a pair of binoculars and climbed up on the bluff in order to watch the turkeys in hopes of watching them fly up. This wasn't going to be a huge mystery considering there were only about 10 trees on the property for them to roost in, so pinpointing them was easy. I continued to keep tabs on them while I watched the other hunters leave the area before the turkeys flew up for the night. Soon, they started approaching the trees and I watched as they flew up. I thought, *I've got to kill one of these gobblers as soon as their feet hit the ground, before any of these other hunters mess things up.*

Because it was wide open, it became apparent that I needed to get right under them. This was risky business, considering that I had to crawl and setup under 100 turkeys without getting detected. The chances of them seeing me and sailing on out of there were good. However, as I looked at the trees from the bluff, I noticed a root ball from a fallen tree. The root ball resembled a little fortress, which would conceal me from the turkeys overhead.

I quickly started devising a plan and figured if I crawled to the root ball underneath the tree and lay on my belly I might be able to pull off a shot when they landed. This would require me to begin crawling a couple of hours before daylight in order to arrive before the other hunters. I wasn't quite sure how serious the other hunters were, but I figured they wouldn't be as ambitious or as crazy as me to follow through with this type of plan.

Because I was in the middle of nowhere there were no hotels or campgrounds. However, there was a little town with three houses and one of them had a little apartment, which they allowed me to rent during my hunt. As I got settled in for the evening, I saw that the sunrise time was ridiculously early, pushing 5 a.m. However, I knew that I was going to have to wake up early in order to get underneath of the turkeys. I wanted to be in position at least an hour before they woke up, just to play it safe.

Morning arrived and found me back at the property in time to begin Operation Root Ball. Because it was still pitch dark, I was able to begin walking towards the trees where the turkeys were roosted. Without the aid of a flashlight, I continued walking until I got within 100 yards from the tree where I planned setting up. At this point I began crawling through the field to the root ball. I could see the silhouette of some of the turkeys in the tree against the horizon as I made my approach and kept tabs on them, which allowed me to determine how much distance I needed to cover. Moving at a snail's pace, it took me about 45 minutes to cover the remaining stretch until I finally reached the tree with the root ball. It exceeded my expectations and was a better set up than I could have ever imagined.

Because the trees were near a creek the ground was soft, which made for a very comfortable set up as I remained in a prone position with my back to all of the turkeys above me, hoping they would land in front of me. Once I settled in I remember thinking,

One of these turkeys is dying from this spot.

Between the 20-30 degree temperature and the fact that I had laid in this spot for so long, I began to get uncomfortable. As soon as the sun started rising the turkeys, which were perched on the second floor above me, began stirring and becoming vocal. It was the craziest amount of turkey sounds that I had ever heard while turkey hunting. My ears were filled with gobbling and drumming from the 20 or so gobblers roosting just above me, eager to fly down and greet the new day. This was definitely one of the most memorable hunts of the entire Slam. With a big smile on my face, there was no other place I wanted to be than underneath this tree in the root ball with turkeys hovering above me.

The headlights from the other hunters started rolling in, which made me a little nervous that they might try to walk across the field towards my setup. I noticed one hunter set up some decoys 500 yards away in a side field. *He needed to get a lot closer in order to kill one before me,* I joked to myself. I have to admit, I felt a little bad coming in before the other hunters and setting up right by the tree, but all of them were locals and I had very minimal time to get the job done.

All of a sudden, one by one the turkeys started flying and put their landing gear down fast. Fortunately, they landed perfect, just in front of me within shooting range like I had anticipated. I knew that I had to kill one of these gobblers quick because if I didn't they would bunch up. I certainly didn't want to risk shooting more than one bird with one shot.

March 31, 2018

Soon, I noticed one particular gobbler hit the ground and go into full strut. He had a beautiful white tipped tail fan. I thought they were supposed to be Rios, but this one looked like a Merriam instead. *This is the one!* I thought. I took the shot, tipping the bird over instantly. After shooting him it was like breaking up a flock of fall turkeys. Turkeys flew in every direction off the ground and out of the trees. To be honest, I probably did the other hunters a favor by scattering them.

Not wanting to disturb the other hunters, I grabbed the bird and walked back to the creek, lighting up a cigar, and thought about how thankful I was for the bird and this experience. Later on, as I walked back to my vehicle I ran into one of the other hunters who was baffled when I shot because he had no clue I was that close to the roost. He asked how I had gotten so close. I explained the entire process to him. A lot of hunters wouldn't think to hunt them like this, but I knew it was something that needed to get done in order to fill my tag with limited time.

After arriving at my truck, I drove to the landowner's house and thanked him for allowing me to hunt on his property. He was excited for me and extremely happy I had a successful hunt. ↓

Roost trees in Nevada. Look close and you can see the root ball I crawled into.

LESSONS LEARNED

While turkey hunting, especially on public ground or in this type of situation where you're competing with other turkey hunters and have a limited amount of time, I've learned the earlier the better. I've found that it's worth the small sacrifice of being uncomfortable for a short period in order to be rewarded later on. With turkey hunting, nothing is ever a guarantee, but it will help put the odds in your favor.

Chapter 28

California

The short hunt in Nevada gave me plenty of travel time to make the six-hour drive to California. Once again, I was driving solo, taking in all of the sights along the way and realizing how blessed I was to be able to travel through such scenic areas and to hunt turkeys in a new state. All of my hard work was paying off on my journey to complete the Slam, and the anticipation and excitement for seeing new territory was building with each mile I put in the rear view mirror.

The region in California I hunted had a river that meandered through it. Although I won't mention the name to protect the area, it probably won't make a difference because of how heavily pressured the location already was. Besides the research that I had done prior to the trip, I had zero intel on this location.

As I pulled into the parking area which accessed the public land around mid-day, I quickly realized how popular the location was by all the vehicles parked there. It looked like a used car lot. However, there was a hiking/bicycle trail, so I thought maybe some of these folks weren't going after turkeys like I was. I walked down the trail a few hundred yards and noticed some hunters coming towards me. One of them had a turkey draped over their shoulder. *Either that's a good sign or a bad sign,* I thought. Unfortunately, I had been mistaken. Not only did one of them have a turkey, but all three of them were packing out a gobbler. This was discouraging considering there would be three less birds in the equation. After talking to them I found out there were a decent amount of turkeys, however I questioned whether or not I should even attempt to hunt there since they had just removed three. Despite this, I decided to keep on going and walked about an hour to the furthest section of the area. Based on my observations along the hike, I soon realized this particular river bottom was made for turkeys. Even though there was turkey sign mixed with boot tracks.

A couple of hours into my hike, I finally saw some turkeys out in a field, which was encouraging. I didn't spot any gobblers, but I knew once nightfall came I would get one roosted. Sure enough, towards dark I heard a gobble, but this alone wasn't good enough for me. I wanted to find out which limb he was roosting on and where I should set up for the morning hunt. I began creeping up on him, getting closer and closer, and finally decided to get down and crawl. Soon, I saw a large clump of bushes and trees, which I used to hide behind as I picked out the limb the gobbler was perched on. I also tried to predict where he was going to land and find where I would setup for the morning.

His bright red head stood out like a beacon and every breath he took, a gobble rang out, penetrating the evening air. About 15 minutes later, I heard some other hunters using a crow locater call nearby. The gobbler went crazy every time they called. As the locater call got closer, I eventually spotted the hunters from behind a clump of brush. I found it peculiar that none of them were wearing any camouflage. To top it off one, of the guys was wearing a white t-shirt.

I continued to keep tabs on the gobbler while also watching the hunters as they continued to close the distance and walk into the open field. Eventually, when they got within eyesight of the gobbler his entire demeanor changed. After one of the hunters let out a call the gobbler flew out of the tree and sailed across the river in the opposite direction. I cussed him out under my breath. I was irate, but it comes with the territory when hunting on public land. There went my roosted gobbler for the evening. I didn't say anything to the hunters, I just sat there trying to think of a Plan B for the morning. I figured the best thing to do in this type of situation was to hike to the back corner of the property the next morning and hope for the best.

Although I was frustrated, I decided to call it a night and went back to the campground to recharge my batteries and focus on my plan of attack. When morning arrived, I returned two hours before daylight in order to beat the other hunters. This time I hiked further back than before and arrived at the corner I had picked out. It wasn't long until the early morning silence was broken by gobbling. It also wasn't long before I saw other hunters coming down the trail. I soon realized the turkeys were on private property, however I did hear a few sporadic gobbles that were on public so I worked those birds for awhile with no luck. Finally, around noon, I spotted some turkeys in what appeared to be a

Volleyball knee pads made crawling less painful.

public land food plot. There were two gobblers with a pair of hens. I knew that calling to this turkey was out of the question, considering how much hunting pressure the area was receiving. I didn't want them to gobble and risk alerting the other hunters.

I can't remember exactly how many days into the season it was, but I knew it had been long enough that the turkeys had definitely been messed with. I began watching them about 200 yards away as they started working their way in the opposite direction toward a little break, which they reached when they exited the field. I quickly decided that when they reached the break I would sprint as fast as I could and take a shot at one of the two gobblers as I popped up over the hill. Meanwhile, through my binoculars I kept close tabs on them until finally, they were out of sight. I removed my turkey vest to lighten the load and like a shot fired at a track

April 1, 2018

meet, I was out of the blocks on an all-out sprint with all the steam I had in me. I wasn't sure if they could see me, but I was willing to take the risk. After a minute or so of covering the distance, I momentarily caught my breath and didn't even bother crawling. I turned my red dot on and decided to make my move, popping up over the terrain change. There they stood, just milling around with one of the gobblers a mere 15 yards away from me. The gobbler smelled a rat and started running, but it was too late. I anchored him while he was trying to escape.

The following morning I was able to hunt until 10 a.m., which was the final hunt during my three-day weekend until I had to catch my flight back home. I had one final close encounter with a gobbler and almost killed him, but he ended up traveling into thick brush with some hens and busted me while I was crawling the final 60 yards. ↓

LESSONS LEARNED

An aggressive approach has helped me kill a lot of turkeys, and it paid off in this state. I have found when turkeys reach a change in the terrain and you can get to it in a minute or two of the turkeys being there, chances are that when you pop up over the break you will be able to take a shot.

More than half the turkeys I have killed were taken not by calling, but by using the terrain and woods to get into a position to kill a gobbler. However, if setting up and strictly calling to a turkey is your thing and the only way you want to turkey hunt, that's fine. But if you want to consistently kill turkeys, it doesn't always work out like that. Using the terrain and woods to get either in front or behind them in order to get within shotgun range can help you be more successful.

I don't believe that I'm naturally good at really anything in my life. However, I don't mean this to sound arrogant, but I'm good at having a two-second or less window to pull a shot off. I'm not sure if it's just instincts or from shooting with my Dad at a very young age. As a youngster I would often practice with a .22 in the backyard or go squirrel hunting with my Dad. Therefore, if there is one thing I feel I'm good at, it is shooting a gobbler with a very small window of opportunity. I don't think this is some-thing that can be taught. You have to be able to learn how to do this, mostly through trial and error. You can't teach the instincts required to be in the heat of the moment and being able to pop up and make a shot on a mature gobbler. Throughout the course of this Slam, I can't tell you how many times I had to make a snapshot within seconds of a turkey seeing me.

Being able to use the terrain and being a good woodsman is the way I was taught to hunt. Getting a turkey within shotgun range doesn't always mean calling to them. Often when you're calling to a turkey it can push him away like the gobblers I hunted in California. I knew there was zero chance of calling in this gobbler, because he had hens with him that would pull them in the other direction. Worse yet, he would gobble and alert other hunters in the area of his location. At 200 yards, there was no way I would pull him all the way across the wide open field to within shotgun range. There was a hell of a better chance of me going up over that break and killing him than there was of him leaving his three hens and crossing that wide open field. Would it have been awesome for him to do that? Of course! Are the chances of me getting hit by a meteorite just as good as that happening in that moment? Probably so. It took as much skill to sprint across that open field and take a half-second shot as anything you can equate that to in turkey hunting.

Chapter 29

Delaware

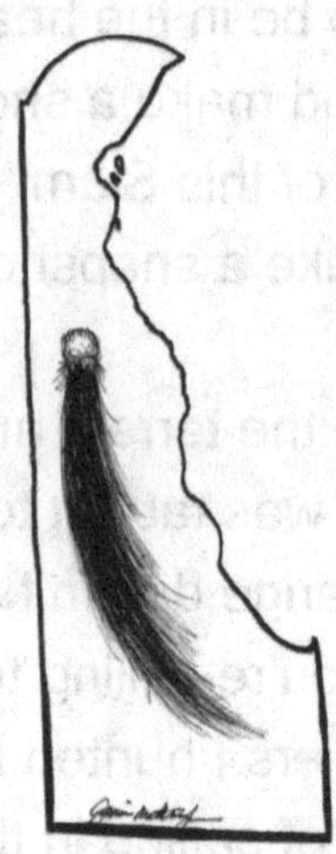

The third state into my 2018 spring turkey season was Delaware. Because I live close to this state, I figured I would be able to hunt there on a weekend. This is a unique place to hunt because you're required to take an online turkey hunting safety course before you even apply to hunt turkeys there. I decided to complete the course well in advance of the season since I needed this state for the Slam. This is the only state requiring this type of course in order to turkey hunt. Upon completion, you have to apply for the piece of public land you want to hunt, which is another $200. To top it off it is non- refundable if you don't draw. Most states will give your money back if you don't draw or at least give you a preference point, but Delaware is very strict about this. When I applied four years ago you had a pretty good chance of drawing, but I would imagine now with the popularity of the Slam and turkey hunting growing it is probably tougher to draw here.

As luck would have it, I drew opening weekend on the particular piece of property I had applied for. When I started coming up with a game plan, I figured I would either take a Friday or Monday off from school. However, after looking at the weather and seeing that high winds and rain were in the forecast, I elected to take Friday off to do some scouting the day before the season opened. This may sound like a dumb decision since I wouldn't be able to hunt until the following day but, I knew the nice weather would allow me to scout this particular piece of property and hopefully roost a gobbler near one of the fields in this area. Having an entire day to scout is sometimes extremely valuable, especially going in to a new area. I was putting all of my eggs in one basket, not in a cocky or arrogant way, but trying to be smart about this hunt with the limited amount of time I had.

After school on Thursday, I drove up to Delaware and didn't arrive until late in the evening. First thing Friday morning I drove to the area and didn't hear a single gobble. Disappointment instantly seeped into my mind. I thought, *Man, I could be in trouble*. However, as the day went on I drove the roads and finally located some turkeys around midday. They were in a field with just a little piece of timber that separated it from another field. I knew those turkeys would probably roost in that strip, so about 2 p.m. I made a large circle, taking at least an hour to complete, and got to where I could overlook this field. However, when I reached the field the turkeys had disappeared. I figured because it was the hottest time of day they had left the field to find shade, but would eventually come back later on.

I decided to sit down and continued to watch the field, and around 4 p.m. the same group of turkeys entered the field. There was a huge gobbler, a satellite gobbler, and a whole bunch of hens. Normally I don't check for spur size, but after three hours of sitting in this spot observing the turkeys, the largest turkey came in so close I looked through my binoculars and his spurs were at least an inch and a half. This was the only turkey I've ever hunted where I knew it had one of the best set of spurs that I've ever seen on a turkey. Not that this mattered, because I was willing to kill either one of these gobblers in the field.

About sundown that evening, all of the hens and the gobbler finally left the field for a second time. I didn't see the gobbler fly up, but I could hear his wings beat in the woods and knew he had roosted close by. I started to feel optimistic for the morning hunt.

I pinned his roost location and my plan was to return a couple of hours before daylight and set up right in the timber where I had seen the gobbler walk in the evening before. If he followed the script, I would try and kill him when he flew down in the timber and was on his way back to the field. I had a good feeling they would return to this field because they had spent most of the day there. The scouting I did the previous day had really paid off. It provided me with the necessary information that allowed me to find their core area. I was worried that someone might beat me to the gate on opening morning because there was only one way into this property.

I had gotten a cheap motel on Thursday night, but opted to sleep in my truck at the gate that evening because I didn't want anyone to park there and ruin my plan for the morning since I had spent so much time with these birds.

Morning arrived and I walked into the timber, as planned, two hours before daylight, picking out a nice-sized tree to lean against. I thought it was a good location; however I soon realized that I was sitting near a red fox den and could hear pups rummaging around and whining. The noise caused the turkey to gobble a couple of times while it was still dark. This was when I realized that I was set up too far down from where I needed to be and decided to crawl another 40 yards. I knew that I needed to be between the gobbler and the field. At this point I was feeling pretty good about my situation and thanked the fox pups for allowing me to hear him gobble early and make the necessary adjustments. If he hadn't gobbled until daybreak, I wouldn't have been able to move because he would have seen me.

Soon the old tom gobbled like crazy, but I never heard the satellite bird gobble once. I remember thinking, *I wonder what happened to that turkey?* It turned out that the big gobbler that I was after didn't fly down in the woods like I had anticipated. Instead, he sailed over me and landed in the field directly behind me and took all of the hens with him. Now that he was 60 yards behind me I was in a pickle. Because he was just outside shotgun range, I needed to cut the distance and inch my way up there a little further in order to get a shot. I began crawling, making microscopic movements on my belly while using trees and brush to help conceal me, and eventually reached the edge of the field. I knew that when I came up off of my belly the turkeys were going to see me, but I figured that I should be able to take the shot before anything bad happened. However, when I finally came up onto my knees to make the shot, all of the turkeys put their heads up. Fortunately, they didn't take off running. The gobbler I was targeting was by himself in the middle of the field, so I took the shot and completely missed him. As you can imagine, the entire flock scattered instantly, leaving me dejected after ruining the shot opportunity. Afterwards, I sat there for a few minutes gathering my thoughts and figuring out what exactly just happened. Suddenly, my mind clicked back to the satellite gobbler that I had seen the night before. I thought, *He's got to be around here somewhere.* When I took the shot he hadn't yet made it out to the field. No sooner did I look down the field edge a few hundred yards and there he stood. Obviously, the shot hadn't bothered him, nor had he seen all of the turkeys run. He just stood there alone, looking confused.

Because he hadn't run off I figured I might have a shot at killing him. However, I knew because he was on the edge it was going to be really challenging. For whatever reason, I could tell he wanted to be with the flock and was concerned about where they went. However, maybe he was used to flying solo. Whatever the reason was he began sneaking down the field edge coming directly towards me. I wasn't about to call to him at this point because I didn't want to screw anything up, so I just sat there like a statue waiting for him to come into shotgun range. Unfortunately though, when he got within 100 yards he left the field and disappeared into the woods. Anticipating that he would try to walk through the woods behind me, I got into position and bore down on my shotgun. Within a few minutes he appeared at 30 yards and I drilled him.

To first miss the turkey I was after and then have the other gobbler walk right to me a couple of minutes later was nothing but luck. *Someone was looking out for me that day.* I had thought as I was on my way to retrieve the two-year-old satellite gobbler.

As for the long-spurred turkey, I had a buddy who would be hunting this property the following weekend and I filled him in on

April 14, 2018

this particular old gobbler. I explained how I had missed him and the rest of the story behind my hunt.

When he arrived that weekend he saw the same big gobbler. The following morning he killed him. He sent me a picture. It had inch-and-three-quarter spurs. Spur-wise it would have been one of my biggest turkeys. My buddy had it weighed at the check station and it was around 25 pounds. It was a tank of a turkey.

I was happy for my buddy and fortunate I had gotten my long-beard after missing this old gobbler I was originally after. ↓

LESSONS LEARNED

On this particular hunt, I learned that having an entire day to scout a new area prior to hunting is invaluable. A lot of times when I arrive at a new place it's in the dark and I'm hunting the next day, so the extra day allows me to study the lay of the land and observe turkeys prior to the hunt. My gamble of taking Friday off instead of Monday paid off big.

Chapter 30

Arizona

The fourth state on deck for another three-day weekend was Arizona. My plan was to fly into Phoenix where I would meet up with Kenny. This was Kenny's 45th state towards his Super Slam and I was working on number 30. It was the master and his protege so to speak, grinding out another state on our list. The tags both of us had acquired for this particular area were in a very remote location. Because we both knew there wouldn't be any lodging in this area, we rented a Suburban in order to have enough room to sleep. This meant that we had to fly out with all of our camping gear so both of us had a lot more luggage than usual. We also had to buy some gas cans to fill up, because we were so far away from any gas stations. Even though this hunt started out with some challenges, I ranked this state high on my list of favorite places to turkey hunt.

As we drove the many miles of gravel roads towards our destination up in the mountains, we finally found what we decided was a good place to sleep. We wasted no time and used the remaining hour and a half of daylight to head out and try to roost some birds. Our plan was to focus on a canyon in the area that had a river flowing through it and also a few ponds that we had discovered on the map. We knew water was key in this state due to the dry environment. However, the river was going to be extremely difficult to access because of the steep terrain. It would definitely be a rough hike. That evening Kenny walked over to check things out by the river and do some listening in the canyon while I went to the ponds to see if I could roost some birds.

As we were walking down the dirt road we cut some fresh gobbler tracks in the sand, which was encouraging for both of us. It wasn't long after my evening sit when I heard a gobbler by the pond and roosted one just before dark. He was very vocal. Unfortunately, Kenny didn't hear any gobbles at all. When I approached him I could tell that he was a little discouraged. I told him, "Chill out big daddy! The young guy found you one. Don't worry." Even though I found the roosting spot, I let Kenny hunt it. After all, he had found the area and it was his trip. I was basically just tagging along.

When morning arrived we elected to climb above the turkey, however looking back we should have gotten between the turkey and the pond, but the pond was down low. After looking at a topography map the night before, we thought we would be able to call him to a little flat above his roost. Not the smartest plan, but it sounded good at the time. Nonetheless, we set up above the gobbler I had heard and he proceeded to gobble is head off. Unfortunately though, he flew down and stayed with some hens, right next to the pond. Both of us could tell he wanted to come up to the flat, but he held his ground. Eventually, he walked up the next ridge and out of sight. We decided to trail him and began slowly following, using his gobbles to keep tabs on him and allow us to make a move.

Taking it one step at a time, we began to hike up the ridge, trying our best not to spook him as we glassed the surrounding area. I stayed about 10 yards behind Kenny the entire hike. Periodically we would stop and call, listening for any response, but he never gobbled again. After a couple of hours of crossing over multiple ridges I watched Kenny come up over one of the peaks while I stayed behind, when suddenly he froze in his tracks. In one motion, he removed the gun from his back and took a shot. When Kenny had popped over the hill, all of the turkeys we had been following were mingling just below him. The gobbler was right there with the flock, allowing him to pull off a shot.

We didn't take no for an answer by giving up on him earlier, and it paid off. Luck was involved, but the combination of skill and perseverance also played a hand in getting the job done.

Around mid-morning, we decided to walk over to the canyon rim above the river. Shortly afterwards, we decided to descend the canyon and walk down to the river. There was turkey sign everywhere. Tracks, droppings, scratching-you-name-it. This was encouraging and it boosted our spirits for the next couple of days.

As we left the area and started walking back up the canyon, which was about a mile hike of very steep terrain, I walked over to a rock face that extended for as long as I could see and noticed a little black dot around a bend in the river. To my surprise, after raising up my binoculars to take a look, there stood two gobblers on the edge of the river. Excited, I called Kenny over and said, "You're not going to believe this!" We stood there looking at our maps and noticed a very distinct bend in the river, which allowed us to drop an accurate pin on them. Afterwards, we made a loop and dropped down into the canyon even with them where there were enough trees and foliage to conceal our approach. After about an hour of mostly sliding down on our butts along the steep canyon wall we reached a little sand flat along the river bank. I wasn't able to see where the turkeys were located, but it was the middle of the day and I figured they should still be mingling around the general area. Up to this point we continued to crawl to the river bank on the flat, hoping to lay eyes on them. I hadn't crawled 50 yards when feathers caught my eye. It was the back of a hen along the river bank. I thought to myself, *Wow, they're right here!* When I laid eyes on them they were a mere 15 yards. We had crawled in tight, almost on top of them. Well, it didn't take long and I spotted the gobbler. I got into position on my knees and it was time to make a move.

In the meantime the hens started to become squirrely and moved away fast knowing that something in the area wasn't right. Two gobblers soon reached an opening when I decided it was time for the shot. However, I failed to compensate for the drop off from the river bank to the sand flats and shot the dirt about six yards in front of me. Naturally, all of the turkeys flew away, leaving me heartbroken. I knew instantly this miss could cost me. After all, I only had three days to get the job done and usually only one opportunity will present itself. At that moment I thought I would have to return to Arizona. I was throwing and kicking stuff, pissed that I had blown the shot on a gobbler that had no clue I was there. Nonetheless, we pushed on and climbed back up the canyon once again before breaking for lunch. Afterwards, we got in the vehicle closer to the canyon where we would stay the night.

That evening I ended up hiking back down the canyon, once again roosting a turkey near the river. It wasn't one of the turkeys that I had missed, but a new gobbler with hens and jakes. Kenny checked out another area, but failed to roost any birds. With a promising area picked out, I hiked up the canyon for the second time that day, which meant I had completed four miles plus all of the other walking around we did that day. Kenny and I were once again feeling confident the turkeys would fly down along the river bank.

The next morning after descending the canyon we found some deadfall to set up behind and didn't do any calling. We were just hoping they would fly down within shotgun range. Plus, they had a bunch of hens with them. Of course, they didn't follow the playbook and instead of flying down on the river bank they flew directly over our heads. Therefore, we spent the better part of that morning chasing them around. They gobbled once in awhile, but we failed to catch up with them. Around mid-day I started to get a little nervous because all we had was that evening to hunt and a few hours the following morning before we had to head to the airport and catch our flight. We decided to take a quick nap under a shade tree to recharge our batteries, but I couldn't sleep a wink. My wheels were turning and I was still beating myself up from the gobbler I should have killed. Kenny woke up and must have noticed my wheels turning and said, "Alright man, let's go find one. We're going to hike until we either find one, scare one, miss one, or something."

This brief resting spot allowed us to put some wind back in our sails and soon we found ourselves hiking down the river. I took the lead, staying about five yards in front of Kenny. Once we came around a bend in the river I felt Kenny's hand touch my back and then he pushed me down to the ground. I said, "What?"

He whispered, "I just caught the sun gleaming off a turkey's back about 75 yards up on the edge of the river." At that point I still couldn't see it so I climbed up on the flat of the river bank and began crawling while Kenny stayed back. I hadn't crawled 30 or 40 yards when I reached the hens. There were four of them along the river bank, but no gobblers in sight. I thought to myself, *Man, there's got to be a gobbler here somewhere.* Unfortunately, the hens started drifting towards me and got within 15 yards on the flat as I laid there on my belly. The hens sensed something wasn't quite right and started alarm putting. As they slowly walked away I had my shotgun up tracking every bird that walked by. When they got past me a gobbler came up off the river bank and appeared very nervous and began trotting. I had my gun pointed towards the left and he of course came from the right so I shifted my gun to take a shot. When I did this he

April 29, 2018

started trotting faster, but it was too late. I was able to get my red dot in front of him and shoot, instantly anchoring him. I ran up to him and grabbed him. I was so excited I picked him up and started running over to the flats towards Kenny. Meanwhile, I spotted him running along the river bank towards me, long- necking it to see if I had made a killing shot because at that point I was still above him, out-of-sight. I whistled at him and he looked up while I stood there holding the turkey. Both of us instantly yelled out and gave each other a big hug ecstatic about the hunt.

We were living high on the hog, laughing about me missing the first gobbler. It was the student and the mentor sitting there by the river soaking in the moment. Life couldn't get any better. It was a special trip and I hope to make it back to this area some day.

We hiked up out of there for the umpteenth time and celebrated at the Suburban, drinking one too many beers that evening. Unfortunately, we were out of tags, so instead of sleeping in the same spot we decided to drive to a relative of Kenny's and spend the night there. It beat sleeping in the Suburban for yet another night. We did some sightseeing the next morning before we flew out. ⌄

LESSONS LEARNED

If I learned anything on this trip it is to never give up. If you miss a turkey, keep swinging the bat. Also, if a turkey isn't gobbling or you lose sight of him it's okay to slow play him like we did with Kenny's gobbler. Just keep creeping in the direction that they are traveling. A lot of times you'll be able to spot the turkey before they spot you and sometimes this will give you a shot opportunity.

Chapter 31

New Jersey

I was on a roll and feeling pumped about the Slam so I decided to drive east the following weekend and hunt the Garden State. Up to this point I wasn't married and didn't have any children, but I was dating my wife at the time so I could do this without any major repercussions. Therefore, I don't sound like a complete degenerate as you might think for traveling out-of-state almost every weekend.

With a tag in my pocket I was New Jersey bound, leaving on a Friday and making the six-hour drive to Philadelphia, where my sister lives. The place I planned on hunting was relatively close to the city so this worked out perfect. A friend of mine had helped me make a connection with a landowner that owned around 15 acres. Prior to the trip I had called the landowner who, said he saw turkeys all of the time and they were always hanging around his pool. He also told me where to park, that he would be asleep when I got there Saturday, and to go ahead and start hunting. At this point I hadn't met the guy, but he seemed pretty laid back.

My sister lived smack dab in the middle of the city. From there I would drive the remaining few hours to the private land where I would have a short walk to hunt.

As I arrived in Philadelphia and started passing skyscrapers, I felt a little funny driving through the city with my shotgun in the back and wondered if it was even legal to do so. *Well, it's in the case and I've got camouflage so it should be okay,* I thought to myself as I nervously continued the drive through the concrete jungle. This was a far cry from the backcountry adventure I had just experienced in Arizona with Kenny. As I arrived at my sister's house, which she had just moved into a few weeks before, there were no parking spots so I called her and she gave me the code to park in the garage at her old house. After driving through traffic, I arrived at the garage and learned my entire truck wouldn't fit into the garage. The back of it stuck out. With my shotgun and all of my turkey hunting gear in the back I knew this wasn't going to work. Not wanting to risk getting all of these items stolen, I decided to break down my shotgun and place it inside my duffle bag along with my turkey vest and all my other gear. This made for a very nerve wracking walk down the sidewalks of Philly toting a shotgun with a camouflage shirt and hat on all the while hoping that nothing bad was going to happen. Oh well, I didn't have any other options at this point and my sister's place was only a couple of blocks away.

I called my sister who was still out to dinner and feeling two sheets to the wind. She gave me the code to get inside of her new house, but also wanted me to call an Uber and drive down to have dinner and meet her friends. I thought, *Do I really have to do this!?* I finally reached her house and dropped off all of my gear. First, I had to download an Uber app and figure out how to use the damn thing first.

Later on, an Uber driver finally picked me up and took me to the restaurant. As I looked through the window I found my sister sitting at a table in a dress with all of her fancy doctor friends. There I was donning camouflage, looking like an idiot. As I walked in there I felt like an animal at the zoo. These people were mesmerized by my accent and the camouflage I was wearing, along with the fact that I was there to turkey hunt.

As I sat there having a few drinks amongst all the doctors, they asked me a million questions and to my surprise it ended up being quite fun. All of them were very enthralled with the fact that I was there to turkey hunt in New Jersey. Even though my sister stayed there until 11 p.m. and knowing that I would only get three hours of sleep, I was still willing to suck it up and spend time with her. Instead of taking the Uber back, my sister insisted on taking a subway home, which I had never ridden before. The subway pulled up and as it was preparing to leave my sister and her husband hollered, "Run! Try to get on it!" As soon as those words came out I took off at a sprint. Being in turkey hunting shape I left both of them in the dust. Just as the subway doors closed I expected them to be right behind me, but they didn't make it in time. I could see my sister through the glass and both of us started laughing and waving at each other as the subway took off. With no cell phone service I decided to get off at the next stop and waited for my sister to get there. After all of us reconvened, it ended up taking an hour to get to her house. We should've just taken the Uber. It was a funny experience, however it cost me one hour of sleep with my alarm set for 3 a.m. Oh well, as you know, lack of sleep is typical for the spring turkey hunter. This was a fun little precursor to a more comical experience in New Jersey.

In no time I found myself out of bed and walking down the streets of Philadelphia with my broke down shotgun in my duffle bag and turkey hunting gear back to my truck. In no time I arrived at the private property. After looking at the map I soon realized I only had a couple hundred yard walk to hunt. Based on this guy's property I could quickly tell it looked like an area that would hold turkeys.

Daybreak came and I didn't hear anything right off the bat. However, eventually some turkeys started gobbling over on the neighbor's property. I figured maybe three or four of them. Soon the gobblers flew down and joined up with some hens. Because I was limited on where I could hunt, I began calling in hopes of drawing them within shotgun range. However, as it closed in on 10 a.m. the gobblers refused to cross the property line. I was becoming concerned that I hadn't heard the gobblers for what seemed like hours and started formulating my next plan.

After walking through the edge of the woods, I took out my binoculars and glassed the back of the guy's house and saw him washing out his pool. I decided that it would be a great time to introduce myself to the landowner. As I approached him he waved and said, "Man, I can't believe you haven't killed one yet!" I explained to him that they were over on his neighbor's property. "They'll be over here eventually!" He assured me.

I responded, "Well, maybe it will be okay." As we continued to talk I looked up and through the breezeway of his house stood a gobbler strutting only 60 yards away in his driveway. The lone gobbler paraded back and forth like a mouse teasing a cat. I asked the landowner, "I know this might be kind of weird, but if I can maneuver on that turkey and shoot him right there would that be a big deal to you?"

He said, "If you want, you can get in my vehicle and we'll take off down the driveway and you can just shoot him like that." I instantly declined to do so. Shooting a turkey out of a vehicle wasn't even a thought for me. It cracked me up how gung ho he was about it. "Well, suit yourself!" He said. I decided to walk back into his woods and wait them out, figuring they had to leave the guy's yard at some point in the day. As I closed in on the woods, I discovered a little ditch that ran up about five yards into the wood line beside his house. To my surprise, as I looked back over my shoulder I saw the lone gobbler now had been joined by four longbeards and a bunch of hens. I knew that calling to a flock was pointless, plus, I've never had any success calling to them in this particular situation. Just my luck, the ditch was full of water and mosquitoes.

At this point, I didn't even care. *The hell with it, I'm going into the ditch,* I thought to myself. I took my vest off and laid it on the ground before entering the ditch. I waded through the water trying to at least get even with the turkeys. Hopefully, this would allow me to take a shot at them on their way to the woods or out in the field as long as I was careful not to shoot at this guy's house. Soaking wet, I continued wading through the water closing in on about 150 yards. Besides being soaked, the mosquitoes ate me alive. Thoughts of West Nile Virus crossed my mind. Finally, I was even with the turkeys that stood about 75 yards out in the field. I laid there in this water-filled ditch for at least two hours, waiting for them to leave the field. Eventually, around mid-morning the flock started meandering over in my direction. All of them were just outside shotgun range and got a free pass. The big strutter I had seen earlier was bringing up the rear. He was an absolute dandy. For whatever reason, this particular gobbler had decided to take a different route, which was going to be a little bit closer to me. This forced me to climb back down into the ditch and crawl 10 more yards. I knew that when I popped up over the edge of the ditch it was going to be another one of those situations where we would both see each other and I was going to take a shot without hesitation.

However, when I came up my gun wasn't facing the right direction. The gob-
bler saw me and began walking fast. I made a last second adjustment swinging my shotgun over towards his head and dropped him in-stantly. He was a hefty gobbler, probably from eating bird seed at the neighbor's.

After I grabbed the bird the flock dispersed and I began walking

May 5, 2018

through the field and up the guy's driveway. I could see the owner through the glass window of his house. He was so excited for me that he stood there with his hands up in a "Rocky Balboa" stance, which made me start laughing. The landowner said that he had watched part of my stalk as I moved through the ditch and was amazed that I had snuck up on the gobbler. Because he had been so generous allowing me to hunt on his property, I gave him $200.

After the hunt I decided to drive over to my future in-laws that live in New Jersey a couple hours away. My girlfriend, who is currently my wife, was visiting them also. Because the turkey I shot was still whole, I showed it to them and they were amazed that I had shot it that morning. They aren't hunters so once again, I felt like a zoo animal. ↓

LESSONS LEARNED

While hunting in New Jersey there were a couple of key tactics I deployed in order to fill my tag. The first one was to be patient when going after gobblers in a smaller area. Although you would think that it would be easier to seal the deal on these types of birds, don't underestimate them. Oftentimes, a smaller area can mean there are fewer trees, brush, and other natural features to conceal you. However, in my case the ditch was the ticket allowing me to close the distance on the gobbler while remaining hidden. Although this entire ambush took about two hours to complete, it was well worth remaining patient.

Lastly, I've learned through the years that turkeys will oftentimes exit the field from the same general area they entered it. Therefore, set up shop where they entered the field and wait patiently.

Chapter 32

Nebraska

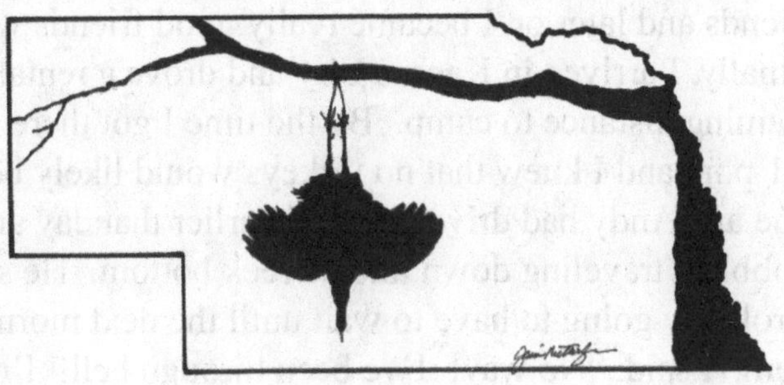

At the time Nebraska and Kansas, weren't even on my radar, however I had been keeping in contact with Joe from my South Dakota and Florida hunts and decided to have a long week-end of turkey hunting. Kenny and I had inspired Joe to complete the Super Slam and to date he is almost finished. This particular spring Joe mentioned he had some private land in these two states that we could hunt. I only allowed two days for this hunt and would fly out Friday night and returning on Sunday. Without taking any extra days off I thought the best case scenario would be to knock at least one of these states off. My plan was to hunt Nebraska on Saturday and Kansas on Sunday before I had to catch my plane.

Joe had talked with the landowner who was okay with me joining him on this property. I purchased a ticket and boarded the plane Friday evening. Unfortunately, my flight didn't go straight to Kansas. Instead I had a layover in Atlanta. At this point I should have known that something bad was going to happen. And sure enough, it did. There was an issue with the connecting flight to Kansas City and they didn't have another flight leaving until Saturday morning at 9 a.m. I was instantly pissed and debated on whether or not I should turn around and drive home, but I had already purchased my hunting licenses. My two day trip was really cut short now because I wouldn't be able to start hunting until Saturday afternoon. Because of the delay, I ended up staying in a hotel in Atlanta. I called the guys who had already set up camp and were waiting on me to arrive. Another gentleman by the name of Andy Orlando had also joined Joe at camp. Both of them were good friends and later on I became really good friends with him also. Finally, I arrived in Kansas City and drove a rental vehicle the remaining distance to camp. By the time I got there it was around 1 p.m. and I knew that no turkeys would likely be gobbling then. Joe and Andy had driven around earlier that day and spotted some gobblers traveling down into a creek bottom. He said they we're probably going to have to wait until the next morning to go after them. I said, "No way! I've been through hell! I'm going in the creek bottom with them." I wanted to kill one of them that evening. Joe agreed and soon he got out a map of the property showing me the boundary lines and we came up with a game plan. It appeared that the creek bottom ran about a mile through the landowner's property.

The plan was for Joe and Andy to drop me off at one end of the creek, which would allow me to slowly work my way along the bottom in hopes of roosting a bird for the morning hunt. Once I got dropped off, I began working my way down the creek bottom. After about two hours of walking I didn't hear a single gobble, but when I looked out into the field I spotted a lone gobbler. I attempted to call him in closer, but unfortunately he remained stubborn and decided to keep to his business. It reached about 4 p.m. when I heard a faint gobble in the distance. It had the typical Rio/Merriam cross gobble and I thought, *I'm in the game now!* My spirits suddenly picked up. When I heard him I couldn't pick out exactly where it came from so I pulled out my glass call and yelped to him. The first time I yelped he instantly gobbled. I soon discovered that they were down the creek bottom along the field edge about 500 yards. I figured I could probably call them in, but first I needed to cut the distance so I continued walking another 200 yards. I reached in my pocket and pulled out my glass call again. When I called I realized the gobblers were only 50 yards in front of me. I was shocked they had closed the distance so fast. When they gobbled, I panicked and hit the dirt in the thick creek bottom right next to the cut corn field. It sounded as if they were right in the thick brush with me. As I prepared to kill one of the gobblers I heard drumming nearby. I kept looking in the thick brush expecting them to appear at any time when I caught a glimpse of one of their heads coming down the edge of the field. Suddenly, I spotted three gobblers together. It was so thick along the edge that only my head was sticking up while the rest of my body remained hidden. I let them get about 25 yards when I picked out a gobbler and raised my gun up out of the thick cover and fired a shot, which instantly rolled him.

May 12, 2018

The beginning of a terrible trip had turned into an awesome first four hours of hunting in Nebraska. I ran out and grabbed him, thinking how things went from zero to hero in a heartbeat.

Finally, I arrived back to where Andy and Joe had set up camp on the landowner's property. Both of them had heard me shoot and were amazed that I had got it done so fast. A successful first day was cause for a celebratory evening in camp.

LESSONS LEARNED

Like turkey hunting, traveling also presents many challenges such as a flat tire and plane delays. You need to keep on keeping on, no matter what. Just like an old gobbler spotting you feels deflating, you need to keep going after him and never give up. Being persistent on this trip paid off big time for me and allowed me to fill my tag.

Another thing that I learned is if you are hunting out west and a Rio Grande or Merriam's answers you from far away it is best to hang out in that spot for awhile and give them time to close the distance. They aren't like Easterns. They will come across a county road, up a cliff, and are willing to cross all types of obstacles in order to reach you if they are in the right mood. In the back of my mind I knew this at the time, but became too impatient and it almost cost me a bird.

Chapter 33

Kansas

It was about 5 p.m. and with plenty of daylight left, we decided to drive down to Kansas and try to put some birds to bed for the following morning. My hope was to shoot two birds in two days, which was ambitious but doable. My flight was scheduled to leave Sunday night so this would allow me most of the day to hunt. Filling my tag on this weekend trip was looking like a possibility. After driving around for awhile and glassing, we finally spotted a gobbler strutting in a farm field from the road. This was the bird that I decided to make a play on. There was a little drainage ditch that ran out to the area the gobbler was hanging out. We stopped and I began traveling along the ditch to see if I could get within shotgun range of him. Unfortunately, though, I moved a little too fast and the gobbler saw me and spooked. I had gotten a little too lackadaisical, which sometimes happens after shooting a bird. However, we did see the area where the bird flew, so we were hoping we could roost him.

We continued to drive around looking for birds. Andy began searching in one place while Joe and I traveled to another area, hoping to roost some turkeys in areas that we could hunt. Unfortunately, though, the only birds we spotted were on property we didn't have permission to hunt.

Once we arrived back at camp, which was located next to the landowner's house, Andy heard a gobbler on a nearby ridge. I instantly knew this would be the bird I would go after. We stayed up late that night, eating some good food and sitting around turkey camp enjoying the moment.

Morning arrived and after breakfast I gathered my gear and made the 15-minute hike to the area where we had roosted the gobbler. I thought I had a pretty good pin on his location and decided to walk through a farm field and into the woods where he was roosting. Once I arrived and set up, just before daybreak he began gobbling and drumming from his roost. I made a few more moves in order to close the distance a little more. I soon realized that I was set up a little too close – about 30 yards from this turkey's limb on the side of a hill.

I could see him as plain as day. He was an old Rio turkey with long spurs that stood out and caught my attention. I knew at that point I wasn't dealing with a typical turkey. This was an old wise gobbler that had survived several seasons. Fortunately, the turkey had absolutely no idea I was even there the entire morning and I knew that he could pitch anywhere in the woods that he so desired. It was just a matter of time. Finally, the gobbler decided to fly down. Instead of flying into the woods and walking to the farm field like I had anticipated he hopped off the limb and pitched straight down out of the tree. Just like that he completely disappeared like some magician's trick, and he side-hilled it around me before I could even lift my gun. I hadn't called to him while he was on the limb because he was too close, however once he hit the ground I threw a couple of yelps at him. He responded, but soon ceased gobbling and already had a destination in mind as a Rio is known for. I began to wonder if he had some hens with him. An hour or two passed, and at that point with just a few sporadic gobbles I knew that I was out of the game and it was time to move on.

After reaching another block of woods, I began hearing a turkey gobble. In order to cut the distance, I crossed over a creek and arrived at the back side of a field in a little piece of woods. As I reached this spot I noticed a longbeard strutting in the field. On the opposite side of the field were four jakes, which ran over to the gobbler, bullying him, and ran him off. I knew this was a different gobbler because I was in an entirely new area. As I laid there on my belly debating on what I needed to do, the jakes walked past me and left the field, having returned from their fight with the gobbler. At this point my wheels started spinning and I thought that with the jakes gone and the gobbler all by his lonesome he might be susceptible to calling. However, I was prepared for him to come in silent so as not to draw attention to himself and risk another fight with the gang of jakes. The last time I had laid eyes on the gobbler, he disappeared behind a hill in the field and traveled over to some woods. With this in mind, I started to ease in his direction after determining that the jakes were out of the picture and began softly calling in hopes of drawing him in closer for a shot. There was no response, but that didn't surprise me.

It wasn't but a couple of minutes when I spotted him coming up over the rise where the jakes had run him off. Because of his bad experience with the jakes earlier, he was on pins and needles. He popped his head up and looked around, making sure things were safe before moving any further. As he stretched his neck out I turned my head to the right and threw a call out, making him think a hen was down in the woods. When he heard that, he instantly started walking down the edge of the field toward me. At this point it was about 10 a.m. As he continued to cut the distance I was still laying on my belly because there were no good trees where I could set up. Finally, he reached about 40 yards and I squeezed the trigger and sent the gobbler tumbling.

I couldn't believe that I had pulled it off at this point in both Nebraska and Kansas. I had only been on this trip for 24 hours and had killed two birds in two different states.

I sat in the woods with him for about an hour or so, soaking in the moment and feeling extremely thankful. At this point I was on a good roll for the season and felt like I was in a groove.

I called up Joe and Andy who met me by the road that bordered the property. We took several pictures and was able to take a group photo of all of us. It was too short of a trip, which seemed to be the norm while completing the Super Slam. I could have stayed in

May 13, 2018

those woods admiring that turkey all day.

After Mexican food for dinner and saying our goodbyes, I left for the airport where I boarded the plane around 7 p.m. Because of a layover before landing in Pittsburgh, I was super late getting back home. I was so late I didn't even have a chance to shower before heading to work. I just threw on some clothes and was off to go teach. I wasn't thrilled about this, considering that I hadn't showered in a couple of days at this point. I was running on about two hours of sleep, which I got on the plane. *It's turkey season! Gotta love it!*, I thought to myself.

It started out a stressful day because I hadn't gotten there an hour early like I usually do to make lesson plans. About half way through the work day I was dog tired. At lunch time I felt something funny around my waist line. I lifted up my shirt and there were about 30 or 40 ticks attached to my belt line. I figured that I probably had gotten them while crawling during my Kansas hunt. That is the most ticks I have ever seen on a human being. I spent my entire lunch break pulling ticks off of me and washed them down the sink in my room. If ever there was a time to catch Lyme disease this would be it, or I figured I would never get it. ↓

LESSONS LEARNED

If you've got some bully jakes running around an area, which does happen from time to time, and they're doing the gobbling and have taken over the hen(s) there is a chance of killing a lone gobbler if one is in the area. However, don't expect him to gobble. More than likely he is probably going to come in silently for fear of the jakes picking a fight with him. If you can call to him you can kill him.

Chapter 34

New Hampshire

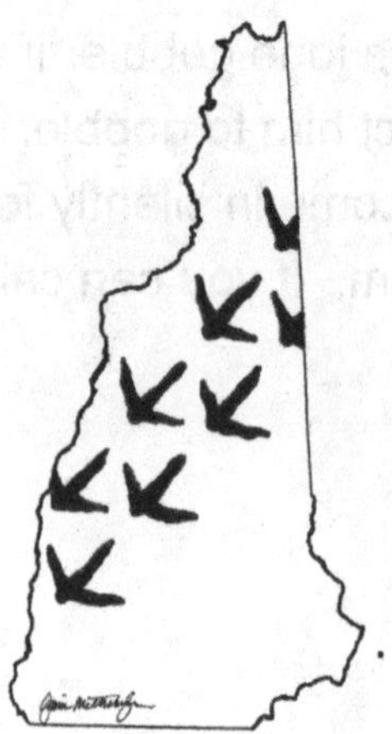

As my momentum moved along during the spring of 2018, I decided to use my extra time off during the Memorial Day Weekend to tackle New Hampshire. This was turning out to be one of the best, if not the best, turkey seasons I will likely ever experience.

During this three-day weekend my hope was to fill my tag in just one state or possibly two at best. The stars had aligned for me once again. Like I had done many times before, I decided to leave right after school got out. My goal was to arrive in New Hampshire by daylight if possible so I would be able to start hunting immediately. Time management was crucial on these short weekend trips, and I needed to make the most of this one, especially since the season was winding down. As an obsessed turkey hunter, I figured I could make it with no sleep and catch a nap during the middle of the day. By the time I got out of school at 3:30 p.m. and drove all through the night, I arrived in New Hampshire around two hours before gobble time. I've noticed that the birds in this state gobble early, around 4:30 or 5 a.m., because it gets daylight in this area sooner than most of the places I've hunted.

I wish I'd arrived right at gobble time because when I got there I decided to take an hour long nap, which made me feel even more tired.

After hiking up to a field which wasn't too far from my truck, I found a pine tree perfect for concealment and leaned against it, settling in for the morning to listen. As the sun started to rise, it appeared it was going to be a nice day, but unfortunately I still felt terrible. I started to regret that I pushed myself this hard. It wasn't long before I heard a turkey gobble across the road and suddenly all of those feelings of being tired disappeared and I was ready to rock.

By 2018 I had started using OnX Hunt, which allowed me to easily navigate areas open to hunting. As I looked at the app, trying to determine where the gobbler was, I quickly figured out he was on public land and a long ways away. I would need to cross the main road in order to reach him near a power line. As I was cutting the distance toward the gobbler, I spotted my first ever porcupine, which ran up a tree after I videotaped him for a few minutes.

It was 6 a.m. and finally I reached the area where I had heard him gobble. Soon I realized he was on the ground and up on a nearby ridge. Because of the terrain I was not able to get above him or parallel with him. However, I was able to position myself below him and thought, *What the hell! I'm going to try and call this turkey downhill.* When I began calling to him he immediately answered me. I discovered he had a hen with him that was answering too. As usual, I was lying on my belly in a prone position behind a dirt mound. Eventually, I saw the gobbler and the hen coming towards me, but they hung up about 70 yards out and refused to come any closer. Because the woods were pretty open, I decided to stop calling. Eventually, the turkeys began to lose interest in the so-called hen, and that's when I decided to scratch the leaves and make some soft hen yelps. That was all it took for the hen to come towards me to investigate. However, the gobbler decided to swing to the right instead of walking straight to me. The problem was, my gun was facing towards the hen where I was expecting the tom to come also. So, I had two problems. One, my gun was facing left and the gobbler was coming from the right and two, the hen was about to step on top of me and the gobbler wasn't even in range.

The hen was closing in fast and was now a mere 10 yards in front of me while the gobbler continued to swing right. By the time the hen had reached 10 yards the gobbler was to the right and

May 26, 2018

within range. I was going to have to swing my gun to the right and hope that I could out gun him. The moment of truth had arrived. Coming up slightly from my belly I swung the gun to the right, scaring the nearby hen into flight. Although the gobbler was on high alert and tried to get out of there, I was too quick, and rolled him.

He had been hunted before because when I skinned him I found a couple of pellets in his wing that weren't TSS. It always makes you feel good knowing you shot a turkey that had been previously messed with by other hunters.

I couldn't believe it. It was close to 6 a.m. and New Hampshire was in the books. I sat there on the ridge with him, smoking a cigar and enjoying the moment, giving thanks for another bird down on my journey. ↓

LESSONS LEARNED

Rarely does it work for a gobbler to come downhill to calling because they have more visibility. The best position to set up is either above or parallel with them.

Chapter 35

Vermont

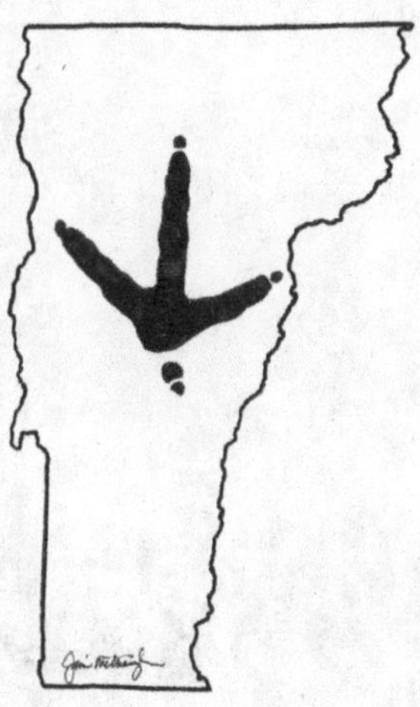

After New Hampshire, I was so tired I decided to rent a motel room and catch up on some much needed-sleep. Around 1 p.m. I woke up and decided to drive over to the location in Vermont where I had planned on hunting. The map showed a lot of fields and once I arrived I noticed a little knob that stood out, which I thought could have been an old farmstead. There were a bunch of buildings in this area. The knob in this area was open to the public so I thought that I would head over there and skin my New Hampshire gobbler for a mount because he was in such good shape and also glass for turkeys. I also needed to check my bird in to a check station, which is a requirement in New Hampshire.

During mid-afternoon I walked to the knob and began skinning the gobbler. I found the perfect tree to hang my turkey from. I was no more than 20 minutes into skinning when I suddenly noticed a black blob as far as I could see. I thought, *Man, that looks like a turkey strutting.* I quickly grabbed my binoculars and I'll be damned, it was a gobbler and three hens out there in the distance.

It's game on, I thought.

Just before fly up came I saw a vehicle driving towards mine. I prayed it wasn't another turkey hunter. Later, I found out it was a guy from Vermont that was basically the caretaker for this piece of public land. He enjoyed driving around the area and keeping an eye on things. He couldn't believe I was from West Virginia and in Vermont turkey hunting.

Tacoma on a roosting mission in Vermont.

He carried a little signature book or what appeared to be a guest book at a wedding and asked me, "Could you sign this book and say why you're up here? I can't wait to tell people about this." I'm thinking, *Man, this is weird!* But I still signed my name and wrote down that I was up there turkey hunting along with the year. He was a really nice guy and told me that he had seen a lot of turkeys in the area. I didn't tell him that as we were talking the bird I had been watching was at that moment still strutting. Fortunately, he had no idea it was even there.

After the gentleman left, the gobbler eventually drifted out of sight. I decided to glass the field and found another knob in the distance that would give me a different angle to the lower field where he had gone. I took a gamble and decided to get up on the other knob. I caught glimpses of him in the lower field at a distance of around 600 yards or so. Finally, I noticed him fly up from the field. However, I wasn't sure if I needed to get on the side of the woods where he was roosted or set up in the woods opposite the roost. These two separate woods were about 100 yards apart. I waited until it was completely dark and walked down to the field, arguing back and forth with myself about which side he would land closest to and where I should set up in the morning.

The following morning in total darkness I walked in and opted to set up on the opposite side of the woods from where he was roosted. After gobbling just two or three times, he read the script and flew down into the field just like I had thought. However, when he landed he was out of range at 70 yards. Had I chosen the side where he was roosted I would have been right in his wheelhouse. So now I had a serious problem on my hands. I had a turkey in the wide open field along with very little terrain that would allow me to sneak up on him without being seen and to top it off, several hens surrounded him. It seemed like the ingredients for failure. Like many times before, I resorted to crawling on my belly, which was the only option in this situation. Although it wasn't an ideal option, considering that the ground was soaking wet from some precipitation the night before.

Just when I would gain ground the turkeys would drift off and I would continue to crawl to their previous location, then I would pop up and they would be out of range. This cat and mouse game went on for three hours. It was reaching 10 a.m. when I came to the conclusion that this gobbler basically lived in this field avoiding any temptation to go into the woods. It was a grueling hunt. Soaking wet and cold, I was about to call it quits. But it wasn't like me to quit so I continued to push on. Eventually I lost sight of him. I wasn't quite sure what had happened to him. I figured there was one of two places he must have gone so I decided to use the woods and began to walk below the edge of the field. Eventually I slowly raised my head up so I could scan the field when suddenly I caught a glimpse of his tail fan heading over towards the equipment and the old barn that I had spotted the previous day. There was also an old rundown building in this location. I soon realized that the turkey was taking a route that would put him behind this particular building. At this point I did some risky business. My plan was to take off on a dead sprint and gain ground on the turkey as he passed the building.

The hens were in the lead and the gobbler trailed about 10 yards behind them as they crossed the field and went out of sight behind the building. This was my cue. I sprinted at least 200 yards across the field, praying to God that I would reach the structure before they cleared the building and I had all of those eyeballs staring at me. Finally, I reached the backside of the building, but needed to work my way around it in order to take a shot. As I slowly walked around the perimeter and reached the final wall I peeked around the corner and there they stood. At 50 or 60 yards they were just out of range and I debated whether or not to take the shot. I decided to pass. However, there was still hope. The path that they were taking would take them up a hill and out-of-sight. Once they disappeared over the hill I took off on a sprint again. This time it was only 80 yards. Just before I was about to break the knoll during the last 10 yards I got down on my belly and started to crawl. As I reached the end of my army crawl I slowly peeked up over the knoll and saw the hens were way too close. The damage was done and they saw me, instantly flushing and flying off. During the commotion I got on my knees and expected the gobbler to be in sight. However, during the time it had taken me to reach the knoll he had drifted to the right and out of sight of the hens that had scattered. This was pure blind luck. The gobbler appeared to be completely oblivious to what just occurred. It was the perfect scenario. I had flushed the hens and now the gobbler was all alone. I continued to shoulder my gun, pointing it in the nine or ten o'clock direction, but soon caught a glimpse of him to my right. I slowly shifted my gun to the three o'clock position. It was apparent the gobbler had heard all of the commotion. His curiosity had gotten the best of him. Finally, the gobbler reached the top of the knoll, instantly spotting me. It was another split-second decision to take the shot. Just like rabbit hunting, I wheeled to my right and the gobbler took off running. However, it was too late. My shot proved deadly, instantly tipping over the turkey. It was a grueling hunt that had lasted around six hours. I had just killed two birds in two days in both New Hampshire and Vermont.

Later that evening after I spent time reflecting on the hunt and showing my appreciation for the gobbler, I was thinking Maine was a possibility and my wheels started turning. ↓

One of the things I love most about turkey hunting is roosting birds the evening before the hunt. May 27, 2018.

LESSONS LEARNED

This hunt was another example of using the terrain to get the job done. But more importantly, I think about the shot that I didn't take. I learned that if the gobbler is teetering on the edge of your shooting range, don't take the shot. A wise man once told me when turkey hunting if there is any doubt then there is no doubt. Basically, if there is even the smallest voice in your head saying the shot might not be a good idea then you need to listen to it. A lot of times it pays off. Sometimes it doesn't, but more times than not being patient with your shot when it comes to being in range is extremely important.

Chapter 36

Maine

With one day remaining in my three-day weekend I debated on whether or not to press on and try to fit Maine in or driving back home to West Virginia since I had already filled two tags in two states. After all, I hadn't done any prior research whatsoever on where to hunt in Maine and was unfamiliar with where to even begin. Regardless, I got on the road and started driving in that direction, wondering what I was even doing. After driving for awhile I discovered a Bass Pro Shop and pulled into the parking lot. I decided to call Kenny and fill him in on the hunts during the previous two days. He was really stoked for me. I explained I was between a rock and a hard place and only had one day to hunt. He said, "You have a day to hunt? Well, that answers your question. You need to go hunt!" I walked into Bass Pro and bought a Maine license. I think if it hadn't been for Kenny I might have turned around and driven back home. Four hours of driving later, I found myself in an area I had read about in an article about some guys that had killed turkeys in a particular county.

When I arrived, I started to focus on this area because I knew that birds had been killed here. However, it was going to be challenging because it was Memorial Day Weekend and there wasn't much public land. This meant I would have to knock on some doors in order to hunt on private land during a holiday weekend, when most people are out of town on vacation. I drove around that evening focused more on finding birds. Evening arrived and I wasn't having any luck spotting turkeys, so I got out a map and found a large farm with fields and timber, which looked very promising. Finally, I found the property. As I drove in there were at least 30 people hanging out on the porch grilling and drinking beer. I thought to myself, *I can only imagine how this is going to go.* I had the landowner's name, which I had gotten from OnX Hunt, so at least I would be able to greet them properly. "Here goes nothing!" I mumbled as I exited my truck and strolled up onto the porch. With my southern accent I asked for the landowner. He responded, "Yeah, I'm him. What can I do for you?"

I responded, "I'd like to do some turkey hunting on your farm if you allow it. I'm responsible and only have a day to hunt." Without hesitation he agreed and gave me permission along with an ice cold beer. That's always a good sign. As we talked over a beer he explained the layout of his property. I asked him if it was okay if I hunted the last two hours of daylight and besides that I was also going to work on roosting a bird.

There was a state policeman at the party and he explained to me that you can't hunt after a certain time. Fortunately, he spoke up or else I would have broken the law that evening. I spent some time listening and went out to look for sign with no luck. The landowner saw turkeys from time to time, but I still was feeling a little discouraged. With no other options, I went back to the hotel that evening and prepared for the day ahead.

Once I arrived the next morning at the farm, I parked behind their house and decided to walk back to a knob that I had discovered. I heard absolutely nothing. It was 5 a.m. and if there were turkeys there I should have heard them, but instead silence filled the air. As I sat there the first 45 minutes the sun displayed the beauty of the surrounding farm. *Man, it looks like there should be turkeys everywhere*, I thought to myself. Before leaving, I pulled out my glass call and began cutting on it. Suddenly, as far as I could hear a distant gobbler broke the silence on the same ridge I was on. "You've got to be kidding me!" I whispered to myself. I knew I needed to cut some distance on him so I got up on the ridge and began walking down a road on top of it. After about 100 yards I called again and by the sound of him, he had cut the distance also and was eager to find the hen. I called a few more times and he was on fire, gobbling every single time I called. I quickly found a big pine tree to set up against and figured he would continue to bebop on down the road right toward me just like he scripted it. I spotted him at around 80 yards walking directly down the road. However, for whatever reason, he veered off of the road and was hanging off towards the left like he was going to walk off of the ridge. "What are you doing!?" I grimaced suddenly. I had a mouth call in and turned my head to the right in hopes of steering

May 28, 2018

him back to the road, but he was too stubborn and failed to change his course. However, he refused to walk back onto the road. As bad luck would have it, there was a huge mound of dirt to my left, which the gobbler decided to walk behind. To make matters worse he was within shotgun range. With a big pile of dirt between me and him, there was obviously no shot. He was gobbling and strutting away. At one point I could momentarily see his bright red head make an appearance, as if to tease me. I knew it was time to make a move if I was going to kill him. I debated whether or not to crawl up to the dirt pile and try taking a shot, but knew that it would be too risky. I opted to raise my body and get as tall as I could while sitting down. When he was out of strut he would on occasion stretch out his head just enough where I could see the top third of his head. I figured the next time he brought his head up I would take a shot. Sure enough, as I squeezed the trigger he folded and I got my third gobbler in three days in three different states.

It was one of those trips for the books. This was probably the best turkey hunting trip I'd ever had. It was absolutely unreal. I sat there with him on that ridge admiring him, knowing this would be the last turkey of the year. ↓

LESSONS LEARNED

If you just have one day to hunt, don't hesitate. You never know what might happen. A full day to hunt meant the difference in getting a new state checked off, not to mention the cost of returning to Maine at a later date in a different season.

If anything you'll learn valuable intel for the return trip.

Chapter 37

Illinois

Going into the 2019 season, I was naïve enough to think that I could wrap up the Super Slam. However, little did I know this was going to be a lot more challenging than I anticipated. In reality I only knocked out six states during this spring season. I guess I was riding high off the banner 2018 season and feeling bulletproof. My Illinois tag was only good for four days, so there was some pressure, but it was something I was growing accustomed to during my journey.

My plan was to hunt in the southern portion of the state during the first season. I was unaware of anyone who had hunted this tract of land, however I knew it was a county with a healthy population. My season started on a Monday so my thought was to arrive early and scout on Saturday and Sunday, which would give me a pretty good idea of where I needed to be on Monday. I should have stuck with this plan. About halfway there, I realized the Oklahoma season started on Saturday, so I could hunt there first before driving to Illinois. This is where the bad luck started.

I drove all night, arriving in northeastern Oklahoma for the opener. Unfortunately, I didn't know anyone who had been in this area, either. However, I had done some research and figured there should be a few turkeys in this location. I arrived and parked by a gate sometime in the middle of the night. At best, I got around two hours of sleep. A couple of hours before daylight, people started rolling in and I noticed headlights coming my way. That's when I realized that Oklahoma turkey hunters don't mess around. I hurried up and got my turkey clothes and gear on so I could start walking. After reaching a river bottom, it started to get daylight when I heard a nearby turkey gobble and another one gobble, causing my heart to beat faster.

I decided to make a play on one of the gobblers but I soon realized he was across the river. The river was too deep to wade so the only way to reach the other side would be to swim. I wasn't quite willing to do this yet. I tried to figure out how I could drive around it. At one point I actually got even with the gobbler and I could see him in a tree towards my left. I kept thinking, *Man I wish I could find a way around this river!* The river had a bend upstream so I went for a walk and found a log jam, which I was able to walk across. *Oklahoma here I come!* I thought with confidence. So I walked across the log jam and reached the side where the turkey was roosted. He pitched almost directly down beneath his roost. I had to move about 150 yards in order to get even with him. The turkey started to gobble on the ground just over the bank. It was almost going to be too easy. I got to within shotgun range of the turkey and decided to take off my vest and leave it before I crawled up there. As I got about halfway through taking my vest off a shotgun blast went off. Another hunter had beat me to the gobbler. I was so close I could hear the bird flopping on the ground. I'm lucky I didn't get shot. It was a scary situation and I'm glad I hadn't crawled up there and been in the line of fire. I decided not to say anything and turned around and walked back the way I had come from. Along the way I heard another bird gobble near the river a few times, but nothing had transpired.

The remaining two days in Oklahoma were spent wandering around trying to find a turkey to go after, but I never heard another one. I did cut some tracks, but that was about it.

This was the beginning of my bad luck – people shooting turkeys out from under me.

Sunday evening rolled around and I decided to drive to Illinois. After arriving I was delighted to see lots of farm fields and was hoping to make quick work of this trip. Boy, was I wrong again. That evening I drove around and saw some turkeys in a field, but didn't get any roosted. However, I did see a lone gobbler and another area with some turkeys, so I figured this would be where I would start. Little did I know there was a farm field along the edge of it by the road and the rest of it was a swamp. It was a nasty one, and those turkeys were living in it. When you think of Illinois you don't generally think of swamps, but this area had one.

The following morning I walked to the edge of the field where I had seen the turkeys, and shortly after setting up I heard turkeys gobbling back in the swamp. From what I could tell there were at least two or three of them. I got in close and as I closed the distance I realized there was a large creek between me and them, which I became very familiar with crossing during the course of my four-day hunt. I also stayed very wet, because the creek was deep. I felt that I was in the perfect spot. The turkeys could either fly across it or walk along its edge. I was close enough to be able to call to them and shoot across it. As soon as I began hitting them with the call they ate it up. Gobble after gobble rang out throughout the creek bottom. It wasn't long before a gobbler came right towards me. I was in a predicament. Not only did I have a creek in front of me, but he was almost going to have to come to the edge of it in order to get within range. Soon the turkey started skirting me to the point where I needed to move in about 10 yards. Eventually, he started bearing to his right where I had an opening between two trees, which I estimated to be around 50 yards. I thought, *When he hits that opening I'm going to kill him right there.* However, when I shot him in the opening he flew away instead of flopping on the ground. The other gobbler he was with flew away as well. I hadn't even hunted Illinois an hour. Now that I'd missed a turkey, they were going to be extra difficult to kill, and they were.

Even though I had scared the gobblers, I decided to head back to this location in the evening and ended up roosting some turkeys in this swamp. I did a fly-up cackle and made a turkey gobble. However, this swamp wasn't easy to get into in the dark. There was all kinds of obstacles you had to navigate. I ended up walking down an old railroad track and cutting in. It was a long ordeal getting in and out of there every day.

The next morning when I entered the swamp I ended up hearing four gobblers while sitting about 20 yards from their tree. I thought, *As soon as you fly down, I'm going to kill you.* However, they ended up flying out of gun range and joining the other group of gobblers and hens. I tried to call them in without any success. I began to crawl in closer, but never did get within range. I felt like I spent the entire time in Illinois on my belly and knees, trying to get close to this flock of turkeys.

During the evening of day 2, I went back to the same area to roost a gobbler again. This time the turkey roosted back near a swamp pond and a creek that led to it. I'm not sure what happened to his three buddies from the previous morning, but there was just a lone gobbler in there.

Day 3 found me once again making the hour-long trek, through the swamp once again. I saw a lot of non-poisonous snakes throughout this area, which made the adventure even more interesting. I ended up getting about 40 yards from this gobbler on the limb. I figured he was going to fly somewhere in the opening offering a shot, but it never happened. Some hens started calling about 100 yards down the river and he flew that direction. Soon, I found out there was another gobbler down there with the hens. They got together and did some good gobbling, but I could never turn them around and catch up with them. It's like once they hit the ground they had a destination in mind and it was end of story.

Later on, at the end of day 3, I went back to the same location, but failed to see any birds roost. At that point I thought they'd had enough. I'm sure I had bumped some turkeys and spent too much time in there. I was feeling pretty defeated. I had one day left to fill my tag and that would be it.

On day 4, I decided to hike in to a completely different area, which can be the ticket sometimes. I got this bright idea that I was going to hike in there deep. On a positive note, I hadn't seen a whole lot of pressure on this particular piece of land. I ended up hiking in so deep I ran into another road where a parking lot was before daylight, which defeated the purpose of me hiking in so far. As I stood there in the parking lot after well over an hour of hiking in the dark, I thought, *This trip can't get any worse.* Lo and behold, as I stood there feeling dejected I heard a turkey gobble about 100 yards from me. There was just a little strip of woods, which had a creek running through it with a farm field. This covered me as I slipped down into the bottom and called to the turkey. He answered me, but failed to advance, which told me he had hens. I started to crawl towards him and reached a point in the terrain where I could see his tail fan and soon realized he wasn't alone. There were three other gobblers with him, all within 60 yards and on the other side of the creek. Seeing how I was feeling crazy and in desperate mode, I took off my vest and entered the creek with my gun raised over my head. When I walked into the creek the water was up to my chest. However, it was the last day and time was running out. As I reached the other side and crawled up the bank, the turkeys had already traveled from the strip of woods out into the field, which was no man's land. Hens, jakes, and gobblers – the entire freaking flock was out there. It was the early season and the turkeys were still grouped up. I decided to just watch them out in the field. A couple of hours passed and the gobblers continued to strut in the field. There was a cluster of trees on the right side of the field, which eventually the birds drifted into. It looked thick and nasty, so I decided now was my chance to get into those trees with them and see if I could kill one of them. After crawling a few hundred yards across the open field I arrived at the edge of the trees. It was really thick and there was no shot, but I could hear the turkeys gobble within shotgun range. As I continued to remain behind cover along the edge of the thicket with my gun shouldered, I looked to my left and a lone gobbler was walking directly towards me at 35 yards. He had absolutely no clue I was there. I slowly pulled my gun to the left waiting for his head to pick up and I pulled off a shot. Just like that on day four I filled my Illinois tag.

As I sat there soaking wet I thought, *Boy, if I didn't earn that one!*

April 11, 2019

I had spent a total of five or six hours crawling and watching across the farm field down the wood line to get to the gobblers.

This was my first trip of the year and I had two weeks off between spring break and a week off for vacation. My plan was to knock out four states during this timeframe, or as many as I could. However, this was the end of day six and things weren't looking good. I wasn't off to a good start. ↓

LESSONS LEARNED

Don't get caught up hunting the same turkeys every day. Even if the turkeys are there find a different place to hunt. Sometimes all you need is a change of scenery.

It was the change of scenery on the last day that was the ticket and made the difference between going home empty-handed or with a gobbler draped over my shoulder.

Louisiana

Prior to arriving in Louisiana I drew a tag on a WMA (Wildlife Management Area). Typically these draw tags are known for pretty good hunts. However, Louisiana is notoriously known as a tough State to hunt for turkey hunters going after the Super Slam because the turkey population is struggling in this particular state. Therefore, going into this trip I knew that it was going to be challenging.

After I killed my bird in Illinois my draw tag didn't start for another three days. I had some back up areas that I wanted to try two days before it started so I planned on hunting a section of Louisiana that I had heard was good and also had read about online. I don't have much to report on these two days while hunting in this area. I only saw a couple of hens, didn't cut any tracks or hear any birds on the roost. It was a rough two days.

When the season started for my draw tag I was feeling pretty optimistic. The evening before my season started I decided to learn the area and try and roost a turkey, as funny as that sounds now looking back. Once I arrived at the WMA I couldn't understand why this was a draw WMA. The best way to describe this place is that it looked like a test area for nuclear bombs. It was nothing, but a barren wasteland. There was no turkey habitat and the woods were thick. I could quickly tell that this WMA was not taken care of at all. Hunters were required to check in by filling out a form with your license information and drop it in at a kiosk. After a day and a half of hunting this place I wrote them a very long letter out of frustration on just how bad it was. I had read a NWTF article about how this place had been clear cut and how the understory had been allowed to grow back up. It was a haven for predators.

At the beginning of day two I ran into some hunters from Louisiana and they were camping near this area. In an effort to pick their brain for information I asked them, "Hey man, have you guys hunted this before?" They replied, "Yeah, we usually draw this tag every year and hunt. At least one of us does." "Do you guys kill a lot of turkeys?" I asked in desperation. "No, we've heard a couple, but never killed one." I'm thinking, *you've got to be kidding me*. I can't imagine hunting a place for six or seven years and not killing a turkey. Fast forward to day five of my trip and I knew that I've got to get out there and make a move.

I just happened to know someone online that was from Louisiana who hunted mostly private, but not a lot of public so he really couldn't help me out. However, he did reply, "I heard my dentist talking the other day about a piece of public land where he heard some turkeys. Why don't you go check it out." "Well, it's better than nothing." I replied.

After gathering the information I pulled up to this WMA on day five walking into the area blind and I was impressed. It actually looked like turkeys should live there. My optimism was starting to go up. The birds were chirping and I could tell that it was one of those spring mornings where if there was a turkey there it was going to gobble. I believe it was during the second or third week of the Louisiana season so it had been running for awhile. Believe it or not, I ended up hearing two turkeys. Now I had to figure out a way to kill them. The two that I heard were towards the front part of the property. On my way there I found a bunch of boot tacks and found someone's mouth call lying in the road so I knew that these turkeys had been messed with. Eventually, I ended up crawling towards one of the gobblers to within 80 yards, but failed to get within shotgun range of him. However, while I was crawling up to this turkey deeper within the property I heard another turkey. After I had lost track of this turkey in the timber that I had been crawling up on I decided to go in after them. And these turkeys were far back around three miles from where I had parked hanging out in an area that had been recently burned. This particular year was a little unique on this property because there is usually an access on that side but the access had gotten flooded. So anyone that wanted to hunt that area had to walk a long ways just like I did. I believe those turkeys were living there because hunters couldn't access it like they normally could. Once I got back in there I started putting two and two together. When I arrived near the burn I called and the toms hammered out a gobble. I continued to work the gobblers and I could quickly tell that they were coming towards me. However, here is the bad thing about calling turkeys that are in a burn out in the open. I don't use decoys so once they got close to me touching off a shot with my 20 gauge the two gobblers failed to see a hen as they stood about 60 yards from me and got nervous meandering out of the opening. The rest of the morning I didn't hear anymore gobbling from them so I guess that I did indeed bump them. Regardless, these two gobblers were going to be my targets for however long it would take for me to kill them even though it was day five.

The morning of day six found me back in the same location where a fire had scorched the entire area. At daylight I heard one of them, but I wasn't sure where the other one had disappeared to. There was a little grassy woods road that ran back to this location and as I was walking along it I noticed a bunch of turkey droppings and tracks. I could tell that they were living in this little area beside the burn. They were moving back and forth between the burn and the green grass. The gobbler would walk out into the opening and answer my call, but he refused to come down the road to me. He had flown down here, but I could never get him to commit the rest the rest of the way. However, I took note of where the gobbler had roosted and decided to go back there towards evening since you could hunt all day in Louisiana and try to bushwhack him in that burn or on the edge of the green grass without doing any calling.

After sitting for a couple of hours my hopes were dwindling. Something bad happens when you sit for this long of a period. It's hard to keep your guard up at all times. Anyways, I'm sitting back in there by the burn messing around on my phone when I look up and the turkeys are walking towards me in the burn a mere 30 yards away. Fortunately, they don't have a clue that I'm there. However, my shotgun is on my lap. Well, by now you've heard a bunch of stories of me having just that one second opportunity and being able to capitalize on it, but this was not one of them. When I went to pull my shotgun up I tried lifting it up as fast as possible, but the turkeys took off running. I may have been able to take a shot at them on the run, but I elected not to. I didn't have a good shot on them. After all, these were my only options and I didn't want to risk screwing it up. I had scared them and they ran out of the area. I was disgusted. Had I not been playing on my phone I would have seen those turkeys coming from a long ways out. If only I had been paying better attention and had my guard up. It was day six and this was a hard lesson learned having them within shotgun range and I blew it. To make matter worse there was a monsoon coming in towards evening and it was suppose to rain for the next two days straight.

I turned in that night at the cheap hotel where I was staying Sitting on the edge of the bed and decided to give my Dad a call. He said, "Just go on to the next State. There isn't any shame in not killing one. People go to states all of the time and don't kill one." I just couldn't let it go. I debated about moving on to Oklahoma, but I didn't want to throw in the towel just yet. I didn't want to quit until I had to go back to work even if it meant staying here for another three or four days and hunting in the nasty weather. I knew that with the heavy rain coming there was a good chance those turkeys were going to come out into that grass field beside the burn.

When I woke up to the alarm on day six it's raining cats and dogs. Despite the rain I proceeded to make the three mile walk back to the burn. I can't remember if I slept in or what, but when I arrived it was well past fly down time. Not that those turkeys were going to gobble anyway because it was raining so hard. As soon as I got back to the burn I spotted the two gobblers out in the grassy field about 150 yards from me. I knew I had to belly crawl and figured the rain will help cover my movement. I removed my turkey vest and all that I had with me was my shotgun and a poncho on and I started crawling. Eventually, I reached the woods that paralleled the grassy road and I saw that they were working away from me. So I used my map and dropped a pin where they were at in the road and walked into the woods 100 yards where they couldn't see me. As I was making the big circle I could walk most of it, but then I had to crawl a hundred yards to get within the edge of the road. The plan appears like it is going to work to perfection. I hadn't been sitting there very long when I see one of the hens that's with them pop out over the hill and then the two gobblers, which are working their way towards me. They quickly close the distance. Then for whatever reason one of the hens turns and decides to go back the other way where I had just came from on the road. "You've got to be kidding me!" I muttered under my breath. So, I decided to do the same thing once again. I wait until they're out of sight and drop back in the woods away from the road and try and make a big circle and then crawl the remainder of the way to get on the edge of the road. Talking about this it seems quick, but in reality I've got at least two or three hours invested in this movement. I've confirmed that there are two hens and two gobblers in this group. Déjà vu happens once again. I get to a point where I think that I'm in front of them, but it was hard telling because I had lost sight of them and couldn't see all of the way down the road. I hadn't been sitting there long and I catch one of the hens walking right towards me and then I hear one of the gobblers drumming. The rain had let up just enough for me to hear him. He was strutting and looked like a wet rat. Well, the hens started to walk by me, but there is a lot of trash along the edge of the field and I had to let them get about 20 before I would be able to shoot one of the gobblers in tote. The first hen walks through the opening with no problem. The second hen smells a rat. There was something about the situation that she didn't like and she started putting. The gobblers don't know what happened, but soon I lost track of them. The hens stepped into the burn, which was across the grassy road from me and they're standing in the woods knowing that something isn't right on my side. The entire time I'm looking to my hard right trying to see where the gobblers went. Well, the hens start working back to the right, so I'm thinking, *I'm going to have to drop back in the woods and get in front of them again.* However, my vision continues to stay focused on my right the entire time because that's where I think that the turkeys are coming and it's the last place that I spotted them. However, to this day I don't know how both gobblers got to my left, but they did. I was just getting ready to crawl away and I looked to my left and there stood the gobblers in the wide open at 25 yards on that grassy road. I'm not sure how they got to the left, but they did. Unfortunately, my gun is facing right so I had to shift positions quickly with my gun. Fortunately, the turkeys didn't see me. They just threw their head up

April 18, 2019

and walked fast away allowing me to take a shot at the second one directly in the back of the head on the grassy road.

Out of the entire Slam I came unglued on this gobbler. I yelled, "I got him! I got him!" It felt so good to shoot that turkey on day seven. What a grind it was to kill this gobbler. I was in disbelief. The toughest hunt of the entire Super Slam was definitely Louisiana.

It was one of those moments where I couldn't even smoke a cigar and enjoy the moment because I was soaking wet right to the bone and tired. I threw the turkey over my shoulder and was heading back to the truck. As I got closer to where I parked I heard another vehicle idling next to mine and discovered that it was a game warden who had been waiting on me. He stepped out of his truck and saw that I had a turkey and said, "Man, I was just making sure that you were okay. I was waiting here for you. I can't believe that you were out hunting in this rain." I responded, "Yeah, I've been after a couple of them back there." He was blown away that I had been hunting in the rain. The weather was borderline dangerous that I had been hunting in. We stood there laughing about how crazy I was to be hunting in these conditions. He checked my license, congratulated me, and was on his way.

With all of the time spent on this Louisiana gobbler it allowed me only two days in Oklahoma to kill a gobbler during this two week trip. ↓

LESSONS LEARNED

If you're waiting a turkey out while calling to it or trying to bushwhack it you need to keep your guard up at all times. There is no room for error when the moment of truth is nearing. This was a tough pill to swallow. On day six I had a gobbler within shotgun range and missed my opportunity.

Chapter 39

Michigan

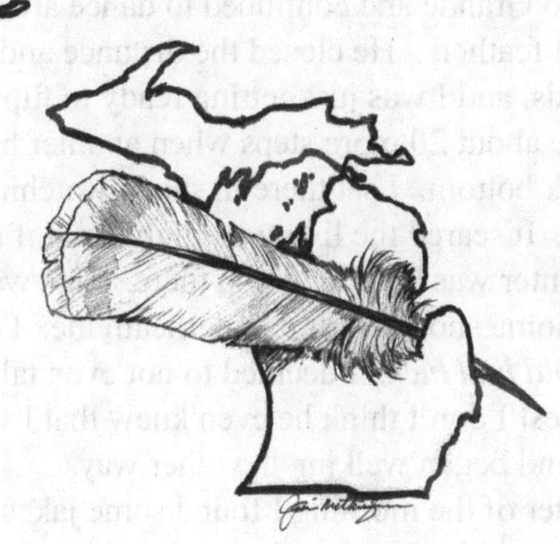

Oklahoma Disaster

After leaving Louisiana I drove to Oklahoma with just two mornings to hunt before heading back home to work. In Chapter 37 I had already gotten my butt kicked in this state, but it was time to head to a new area and redeem myself before heading to the Great Lakes State. Once I arrived, I didn't have any time to roost that evening so I was just going to head straight out in the morning and go for it. I was in the western portion of Oklahoma. When I arrived I climbed up on a knoll overlooking plains with vast areas of treetops down below. It was super windy, which made it extremely difficult to listen for any birds. Unable to hear any turkeys, I decided to climb back down into the bottoms to see if that made a difference. Once I reached the bottom I called on my box call and instantly heard a gobble. I thought, *That's him! I don't care what it takes, I'm killing him.* Because the turkey was relatively close I got down on my belly and knew I needed to close about 50 yards towards him. As I started crawling and trying to get in position, I spotted him out in front of me strutting. I called and he answered again, but this time I could see he was slowly making his way towards me. At this point I was still on my belly and hadn't even set up yet against a tree. I thought, *Well, this is good enough. I'll kill you right here.*

He was a Rio Grande and continued to dance around and show off his beautiful feathers. He closed the distance and approached to about 70 yards, and I was just getting ready to flip the safety and let him take about 20 more steps when another hunter fired a shot in the creek bottom. I sat there in shock watching the gobbler fold up and die. It scared the living daylights out of me. I had no clue another hunter was hunting down there. This was the second turkey in Oklahoma shot out from underneath me. I thought, *This was just plain old bad luck.* I decided to not even talk with the guy. To be honest I don't think he even knew that I was there. I got up, turned and began walking the other way.

The remainder of the morning I found some jakes, but never did find another gobbler. In the evening I ended up traveling to a new section and heard a turkey gobble on the ground. Having one last morning left, I knew I had to get him roosted no matter what because I had to make the 18 hour drive back to West Virginia so I could go to work. I had a coyote howler which he kept answering, allowing me to keep tabs on him. As it was getting close to dark I continued to call on the howler and kept him gobbling. About the time I thought he was in a tree I found myself still clear across the valley from this turkey. I knew I had to get closer to him in order to find out his exact location so I could set up on him in the morning. I was overly aggressive on this one because when I started going to him he wasn't even in the tree yet, but I thought he was. After reaching a point where I figured I was getting too close for comfort I decided to pop up over a little rise.

As I peaked, turkeys flew everywhere. Apparently they had been hanging out on the knoll waiting to fly up. When the flock scattered I noticed a bunch of hens along with the gobbler I was after. I thought to myself, *Man, why didn't I stay over there!?* When you're an aggressive turkey hunter sometimes things like that happen. You roll the dice anytime you're being super-aggressive like the way I hunt. This time it came back to bite me in the butt. However, I was still optimistic. I said, "You know what, he'll gobble in the morning! There's only so many places that he could've gone."

When I went back in there the following morning he never gobbled again. I decided it was time to pull the plug and drove the lonely 18-hour drive back to West Virginia all through the night without stopping for any sleep. On the drive back I made the decision to turkey hunt when I got home since the West Virginia turkey season had already commenced...

I ended up killing a bird shortly after arriving and then made it to school just in time to teach. A nice consultation prize for an ass beating in Oklahoma.

Michigan

A week later I decided it was time to head to Michigan and hunt. Things were finally starting to turn around for me. My buddy Joe Diestal had a friend who lived in Michigan named Wade Childs. My plan was to drive to Michigan with Joe and meet up with Wade, who said he could put us on some birds. As the calendar worked out, I was going to arrive a half-day before Joe, so I would be able to hunt in the morning before he got there. On a Friday, after school got out, I drove to Michigan and didn't get to Wade's house until really late. Realizing this, Wade left the door unlocked and told me to let myself in and to sleep on the couch. I felt this was very odd considering that up to this point I'd never even met the guy. However, once we both woke up at 4 a.m. and met each other with sleepy eyes, we laughed and shook hands. It was almost as if we were old friends. Wade is another great friend I made while working on the Slam.

After the introduction and some breakfast, we were off to some private property Wade bowhunted on. Wade was a big bowhunter and liked to make fun of us turkey hunters, and Joe and I would poke fun back at him even though we both enjoyed deer hunting also. It's what buddies do, make fun of each other. Once we arrived at the location Wade explained, "Turkeys always like to hang out here. I just saw them the other day, so we'll just wait to hear one and then do our thing." There was a small woodlot, so I mentioned getting inside of it a little ways and trying to catch them before they entered the field. We decided not to do any calling unless absolutely necessary for fear of changing their direction or putting them on alert if they walked through the area looking for a hen.

Not far away was a house that had a goat and every couple of seconds it would go, "Baa!" Eventually, as the sun rose and it began getting lighter, the turkeys in the woodlot began answering this goat. Wade and I determined there were at least four gobblers in the group. They weren't all together, but in the general area. As they gobbled the goat would answer or vice versa. Wade and I couldn't contain ourselves and began laughing so hard in the dark. To this day, Wade still sends me Snapchats with videos of the goat heard in the distance while he is bowhunting in the fall. We always have a good laugh about that. This was the "goat turkey" for sure.

It was apparent these turkeys hadn't been pressured by the way they were throwing all of their gobbles towards the field. There wasn't a whole lot of real estate for them to go to other than this location. As Wade and I sat there I readied my gun, waiting for the turkeys to fly down. The hens flew down first, which caused me to worry we would get busted. However, we had great cover and they walked by, making their way to the field. It wasn't long when the gobblers followed suit. As one of the gobblers approached a slight roll in a hill, I could tell by its gobble and head that it was a mature tom even though I couldn't see its entire body. I placed the sights of my shotgun on the bird's red head, clicked off the safety and fired a shot, checking off Michigan from the list.

He had inch-and-a-half spurs but what impressed me the most is that he weighed 28 pounds. To date he is the heaviest turkey I've ever killed.

I was super-grateful for Wade taking me to a spot with unpressured turkeys. Best of all, it was the beginning of a lasting friendship.

We called Joe and both of us could tell he was a little perturbed

April 26, 2019

that he wasn't there celebrating with us. You know how it is when your buddies are hunting and you're still on your way to camp. He was ready to be there.

When Joe arrived in the early afternoon, Wade was unable to join us so we drove around to a couple of different spots Wade had directed us to. We found turkeys at all of them. Eventually, we caught a gobbler out in a field and Joe used a nearby ditch to crawl to within shooting range and was able to secure the bird.

It was only the first day and both of us had filled our Michigan tags. With only a one-bird limit and no plan to travel to another state, we were wondering what else we could do with our extra time. Wade had just the answer. He happened to have some buddies that liked to walleye fish so he invited Joe and me. This was my first experience fishing for walleye. We traveled to the Detroit River for the day and ended up catching a few. Afterwards, we filleted the walleyes and cooked them with some of the turkey we had harvested. This combination was very pleasing to the palate and a great way to end the trip.

This Michigan bird sits in the show room of my taxidermy shop and is one of my top five turkeys as far as spurs go, but number one for weight. ↓

LESSONS LEARNED

A few of the things I learned from this trip is not to get impatient when you're between a turkey and where he wants to go. Calling could have changed the direction or demeanor of the gobbler that I eventually killed. Sometimes it's best to just sit tight in cover without doing any calling at all.

Lastly, private land turkeys are not the same as public land turkeys. I doubt we would have gotten by with those hens coming by us on public land or in a heavily-pressured area.

Chapter 40

Indiana

The next state on the docket for my 2019 season was Indiana, which was convenient since it was so close. This particular hunt is another good story of a friendship made along the trail of my Super Slam journey. About three weeks before I planned on hunting Indiana, I received a call from a gentleman in West Virginia who inquired about getting his buddy's turkey mounted. His friend, who lived in Cincinnati, had recently killed a six-bearded gobbler in the Hoosier State. I told them to come down to my shop. His friend was a mountain of a man. He stood about 6' 5" and looked like he could be a professional wrestler. His name was TJ Johnson. We started talking and I could quickly tell it was a magnificent bird with its six beards. TJ was the type of person that didn't like to brag about himself, however he didn't have to because his buddy informed me TJ made some of the best box calls in the entire country. I hear a lot of different information in the shop from people so I was a little skeptical. Then the customer tells me TJ use to play for the Cincinnati Bengals. It was surreal to have an NFL football player and also one of the best box call makers in the country standing in my taxidermy shop. I began to tell him a little about my Super Slam and how far along I was on the journey when he asked me if I had ever hunted in Indiana. I responded, "Well, I'm actually getting ready to go to Indiana within the next week or two."

He instantly replied, "Dude, I live in Cincinnati and I've got a spot just across the river there with a lot of turkeys. I'd love it if you came up and hunted with me."

I found it hard to believe that I just met this guy and he was already willing to let me hunt on his property and stay at his house. However, he was truly serious about it and I could tell he was the real deal. Not wanting to turn down an opportunity to hunt on some private land I told him I would think about it and get back with him. He handed me his six-bearded gobbler along with a down payment and left for Ohio. I decided to look up this TJ Johnson guy on the Internet just to confirm he was a former NFL football player and a box call maker. Both were true. In fact, there was a year-long waiting list if you wanted him to make you a box call. As for the NFL, he was a starter and had quite an impressive resume. Also, he was a very religious man and became a minister after retiring. To top it off, he has a great family. After reading all of this, I decided to take TJ up on his offer. He actually texted after he and his buddy had left and said, "Hey man, I enjoyed meeting you. I can tell you're a real passionate turkey hunter and so am I." I always thought that it was real nice of him to send that message and it meant a lot to me.

A couple of weeks rolled by and then one day after teaching I drove to Indiana. For once, it wasn't a long drive at all. I made it well before dark, around six o'clock. I met TJ's family and early the next morning as we were both getting ready he said, "I'm going to take you over to the farm where I killed that big six-bearded turkey."

Once we arrived at the property, we discovered the landowner was already up, which surprised both of us. However, he was an old farmer and probably used to waking early every day. After meeting him, I could quickly tell he was a gentleman and I felt blessed that he allowed me to tag along with TJ. Afterwards we walked over to an area where he typically heard turkeys. As it got close to gobble time, we noticed the turkeys hadn't gotten the memo and were behind this morning. We didn't hear anything. TJ had a nice owl hooter that carried a great tune, and as we reached another spot he let out the prettiest owl hoot I've ever heard, which caused a nearby turkey to gobble. I said, "Well, there he is!" Before hunting with TJ I rarely used one, but once I heard him use it I had to buy one for myself.

After the same turkey gobbled twice more, we decided to set up semi-close to where the bird was roosted. TJ found a spot behind me and then used his box call, creating some beautiful sounds in the turkey woods. I figured how cool it would be to shoot a turkey TJ had called in using a box call he had made. However, it would have to wait because the gobbler flew in the opposite direction and joined up with some hens. Eventually, we lost tabs of him. In the meantime, another turkey started gobbling across the property a ridge over. When we walked towards the turkey we realized the turkey was beneath us in the bottom while we stood above him on the ridge. As TJ called to him from the ridge, he was eating it up and gobbled every single time. I figured the gobbler would eventually break, but he stayed put and we both figured he must be with hens. I even broke out one of my glass calls. However, all of our calling efforts still wasn't enough to make the gobbler budge. Eventually, after numerous attempts to call him in, he went silent and we finally decided to head back to the truck and break for lunch. So far, the hunt felt productive after hearing a couple of gobblers, and there was no need to panic considering it was only noon and I still had three days remaining to fill my tag. As we were walking back to the truck, we passed a little section of woods. TJ decided to hit his box call and boom! Two gobbles rang out. These gobblers were slightly more cooperative than the others. However, they hung up once they reached about 70 yards. TJ continued to work these birds with his box call from 15 yards behind me, but it was a standoff and we failed to gain any ground with them. After an honest effort I finally said, "Hey man, they aren't coming to us, we're going to have to go to them. I'm going to start crawling and I want you to hit that box call about every minute or two so they answer and I can keep tabs on them." TJ looked over at me like I was crazy and said, "You think that's going to work?" Desperately I responded, "It's the only option we've got!" TJ agreed and soon I found myself snaking over a couple of logs and easing my way towards the gobblers as he periodically hit his box call. The two gobblers continued to gobble and were holding tight, which allowed me to pinpoint their whereabouts. There was a large tree I had in my sights that acted as a beacon for my desired destination. Keeping my eye on the tree, I continued to inch forward a little at a time. Finally, I made it to the tree and looked to the right. Sure enough, there they stood, well within shotgun range. As I slowly raised my shotgun from the awkward prone position I was in, I somehow hooked my gun on my facemask, pulling it over my eyes. With my vision blocked, I took my left hand and in a last-ditch effort attempted to lower it in order to see. All the while the turkeys were staring right at me. At this point, I was flustered and so were the turkeys. It was another situation where I was going to pull my gun up quickly with just seconds to take a shot. Finally, I got my red dot scope on one of the gobbler's heads and squeezed the trigger. Both turkeys flew off. The turkey I shot flew about 20 feet and fell. I figured I must have caught him with some shot in the lungs or something. Regardless, I wasn't going to take any chances. I took off on a sprint towards him. When I reached him he

TJ and I soaking in the moment after a successful hunt in Indiana. May 10, 2019.

had his head up and looked like he was well on his way to dying right there. However, because he was still pretty mobile I decided to shoot him again. Afterwards, I went back to see where TJ was and I found him with a million-dollar smile. He said, "Man, you're the most crawling son of a gun I've ever seen. I can't believe that worked out!" We looked at each other and started laughing. The combination of TJ on his box call and me getting aggressive and crawling in got the job done in the Hoosier State.

It was around lunch time and I decided to smoke a celebratory cigar and thanked TJ for bringing me to such a nice piece of property. Since it was still really early in the day TJ insisted that I stay one more night even though I didn't want to inconvenience him or his family more than I already had. On the drive back to his house we stopped by a store and picked up some steaks and some sweet potatoes and the two of us along with his family enjoyed a really nice dinner together.

TJ is a stand up-guy and since I've known him he's won many awards for call making. One of them was "Call Maker of the Year." ↓

LESSONS LEARNED

If you have a situation where you're hunting with another person and you have a turkey that continues to gobble at the call but hangs up, that's a prime opportunity to get aggressive and crawl towards him like I did in order to gain some ground. It's important in this scenario to have the other person continue to call in order for you to keep tabs on the gobbler. This is a deadly tactic to use on those stubborn gobblers that refuse to come closer.

Chapter 41

Wisconsin

On Memorial Day Weekend of 2019, my buddy Eric, drove up from North Carolina and met me in West Virginia. We left on Friday when I finished teaching and drove to hunt Wisconsin and Minnesota during the three-day weekend.

We drove all through the night and it was a very grueling trip. I'll never forget, we were about an hour away from Wisconsin when Eric, who spoke with a real slow southern accent said, "The same thing driving this truck right now is the same thing killing those turkeys, determination." He couldn't have been more accurate. One thing is for sure, we were both determined to reach Wisconsin before daylight. In my opinion, determination is the main thing that kills turkeys.

Both of us were exhausted by the time we arrived in Wisconsin. We decided to hunt on a piece of private land, which I discovered from a friend of a friend. He was an old farmer who said we could come up and hunt. He had a little loft in his barn that would be our home for the weekend hunt. It was a cool deal. However, we got there so late that we didn't even go to sleep. We just threw on our camouflage and left to go hunting. I felt like we were in the movie, "*Dazed and Confused,*" just wandering through the woods. Despite a lack of sleep and feeling like a couple of zombies we pushed on opting to hunt together on the first morning. A storm had rolled through during the evening, which I believe had slowed down any activity off the roost. We started to work the edge of a large field which sat up high. Below was a valley with a bunch of ravines. As we navigated along the edge, we periodically called with hopes of striking up a nearby gobbler. After about an hour of working the edge and casting our calls into all the nooks and crannies, boom, two gobblers hit it together in unison. *Now we're in business!* I thought to myself. We had to crawl about 40 yards before we could set up. They were just out of sight and we had flipped our guns off safety. However, they decided to circle us and when we finally caught sight of them they were 70 yards, out of range.

We were on a knoll and there was nothing we could do except watch them strut along the edge of the field, taunting us as they walked by. Once they disappeared, Eric and I tried to re-position and negotiate the rugged terrain, but they had hens with them and didn't budge. At this point it seemed to be a losing battle.

Around mid-morning we decided to split up. I walked across the road while Eric elected to hang in there and see if he couldn't spot the two gobblers that had eluded us earlier in the morning. No sooner had I reached the other side of this place than I spotted four gobblers with some hens in a cut corn field. About the time I started to get into position on these birds I heard Eric's gun crack. I thought, *Well, he got one of those birds!* Now I really had to work things out and get a bird. I started to get close to these gobblers, but they seemed to always stay just out of shotgun range. Eventually, they worked their way to a corner of the field where I thought they would exit. At that point, I knew I needed to get to where these turkeys would leave the field and try and get a shot at them. I didn't even bother calling, but I probably should have. When they finally left the field they were once again out of range. I assumed they decided to do some mid-day loafing in another area.

Overcome by defeat once again, I headed back to our camp house and was greeted by Eric who, sure enough, had drilled one of those two gobblers we had seen earlier in the morning. He had set up along the field edge and they eventually walked in. He was in the right place at the right time.

Between an evening with no sleep and hunting in the morning, both of us were completely drained so we took a nap. Afterwards, I returned to the same spot and they were back in the field. I continued to watch them all evening in hopes of figuring out their roost location. However, when they left the field to roost I never heard them fly up or gobble. At that point it was a guessing game on where they were roosting and how far they traveled, but I was confident they would return to the same field in the morning since I had already seen them twice. I was feeling optimistic and when I arrived back at camp I filled Eric in on my plan for the morning hunt. I would go back to the spot and listen for them to gobble and set up between them and the field.

Once it started cracking daylight around 4 a.m. it was time to implement my plan. I decided to go solo because my plan required a stealthy approach and with two people there were too many risks in making noise and ruining the hunt. Eric got into a position several hundred yards away to keep an eye on the field and keep track of the situation. Although the birds from earlier in the day failed to gobble, two new turkeys in the distance started hammering away, burning the woods down with every breath. I patiently waited for these distant gobblers to come closer, but it never happened. A bunch of scenarios started going through my mind. *Man, did those turkeys really go that far?* I pondered. Because I never did hear them fly up or gobble. For a turkey to cover that distance is nothing, so maybe they preferred roosting in that area. So I sat there, debating all of this in my head, and continued to wait for a bird to gobble closer. I figured these distant turkeys were the ones I saw in the field the previous night or they would have gobbled next to it. I was 100% convinced they were the same turkeys. Once I realized this, I went tearing off through the woods towards these gobblers. After covering a distance of 200 to 300 yards I looked up and there in the trees was the entire flock of gobblers and hens that had left the field last night. And of course they flew every which direction there was.

I kicked myself for being so impatient. I knew those turkeys couldn't have gone that far right before dark and I should have been more patient. However, I knew I had two other gobblers near the area. I muttered a few cuss words under my breath and kept moving, cutting ridges for about 45 minutes. These gobblers were the kind that you dream about. When they flew down they were still gobbling on the ground. I finally reached a point where I was about 100 yards from them. I knew the way they were acting and gobbling they probably didn't have hens. I found a large tree that I got behind and then peeked out from around it and gave them a few yelps from my mouth call. Boom! They cut it off. One more yelp and they instantly gobbled again. I slid around to the front of the tree and no sooner had I sat down than I heard leaves crunch-

Although Eric and I were sleep deprived, determination killed birds for us. May 26, 2019.

ing and it was getting gradually louder. I thought, *Alright, this is about to work out. Here comes my Wisconsin turkey.* There was a downed tree in front of me and I had my gun facing in that general direction. Sure enough, I saw a big red head stick up from behind the downed tree and then I saw his beard. The second gobbler never appeared, but it didn't matter. After identifying this turkey as a gobbler, my shot reached its mark rolling the Wisconsin bird over. The other out-of-sight gobbler flew off to the next ridge. I was happy as a lark. Once he quit flopping I walked out to retrieve my bird. As I was sitting there smoking a cigar and reflecting on the hunt, I looked around and noticed I was sitting amongst one of the largest morel mushroom patches I had ever seen. I'm talking softball-sized morels everywhere. I filled my turkey vest with them and we gave some to the landowner and ate the rest later on.

If I had the option of ambushing one of those gobblers on its way to the field or calling in the gobbler like I did, I would choose the latter. Either one of these is obviously fun to me, but I would prefer calling one in. ↓

LESSONS LEARNED

Towards the beginning of the hunt, my gut told me that it was a different group of turkeys, but I had listened to them for too long and convinced myself otherwise. Therefore it's important to always go with your gut feeling.

Sometimes if you have a turkey that is far off gobbling, you have to go to him even if you think there might be another gobbler nearby. Choosing the receptive turkey is the best option even if he is further away.

Chapter 42

Minnesota

Because we left for Minnesota directly from Wisconsin, we only had a two-hour drive. This state would complete my 2019 turkey season. We found a nice cabin and we rented it for two nights, close to where we would be hunting. Once again a friend of a friend had connected us with a landowner who allowed us to hunt on his property. After arriving, we started looking at OnX Hunt and realized his property butted up against public land, so we would be spending our time hunting on a mixture of both public and private. As we drove through the valley where we would be hunting I was blown away by the beauty of the area. It was one of the most stunning places I have ever hunted. There was a trout stream running through the bottom with rolling hills on the sides. I could tell this area was made for turkeys.

The anticipation was high for Eric and me and we figured we stood a decent chance of killing one that evening. Sure enough, as we went back to our cabin and started unpacking we looked out behind the cabin and there were some strutters along with some jakes in a cut cornfield. I was going to be up to bat. I quickly planned my route and figured I would drop down in the creek and began working my way over to the area in the middle of the cornfield and pop up over the bank within shotgun range. However, while in route the terrain was higher than I anticipated and the turkeys somehow saw me. As I climbed up out of the creek to see where they were they had already run off of the cornfield and it was game over. Eric watched the entire thing from behind the cabin. Later on we noticed some other turkey hunters that were in the area so we knew there would be a little bit of competition to deal with. After I messed up the hunt I told Eric I was going to head back out towards evening and see if I could get one roosted. I figured I hadn't scared the gobblers too bad and hopefully they would be around somewhere. Eric opted to travel in another direction and try to roost some birds.

Later, it was getting close to dark and I hadn't seen or heard any of the turkeys. At that moment I had to make a decision. I told Eric we could probably get in the car and ride the valley, covering more ground instead of me trying to roost just the one turkey. It seemed like a smarter decision than putting all our eggs in one basket. We knew there had to be more birds in the area. Prior to hitting the roads we heard a bird gobble across the main road directly across from the cabin on public land. We both knew he was going to be right there. This is where Eric would be hunting in the morning. With just 15 minutes of daylight left, all of the turkeys in the area were probably already on the roost so we started driving down the road, stopping occasionally to howl in a few locations and listen for any gobbles like we did out west. Doubt was slowly creeping in when at our last spot I let out one last howl and a turkey gobbled directly above the road. He couldn't have been 30 yards from me when I howled. I looked at Eric and we both grinned, our eyes as wide as frying pans. We got that oh shit look on our face. I got back in the vehicle and dropped a pin on the location, which was on public. It was a no brainer. This is where I would be hunting in the morning. Unfortunately, when I looked in the direction where I heard him roost it was thicker than hell.

I'm not sure why he was up in there. However, below him was obviously the road we drove in on and there was a big field, but we didn't have permission to hunt there.

The next morning Eric went across the road while I was going to hunt the turkey we had roosted right above the road. But I had a sneaking suspicion he was going to fly into the field across the road. I knew it was a long shot, but Eric took me over there since we only had one vehicle and dropped me off down the road, a short walk from where the bird had roosted. Once I arrived I walked into the woods towards the turkey and Eric went back to his spot. We didn't have any cell phone service so there was no way we could communicate, which of course wasn't ideal. Therefore, Eric told me he would swing by and pick me up at lunch time.

I hadn't been sitting for more than a half-hour when I heard drumming directly above me. I elected not to get above him because of how thick it was and I felt he was going to travel to the field after he flew down. This gobbler was probably 30 yards from me on the limb and he was a battleship. This turkey was heavy and had big old long spurs, which I could see in the twilight from my position. He continued to gobble and drum. I soon realized he was alone. However, as the morning wore on, just as I expected he sailed right over my head and landed in the field. My nightmare had become a reality. At this point, I figured I might as well try calling him back up into this thick stuff. It was a shot in the dark, but despite the circumstances I started calling to him. He answered, but wasn't leaving the field. I had a decision to make. He was the only gobbler I was hearing in the area, so my mind started drifting back to the turkeys I had seen the evening before behind the cabin. Because I had two hours before Eric planned to pick me up I decided to walk back to the cabin. Eric and I had a gobbler on both sides of the cabin, so we were still in the game. I felt optimistic even though things hadn't worked out with the gobbler earlier that morning.

Unfortunately, with no cell service, I wasn't sure if Eric had tagged a gobbler. Once I arrived at the cabin I decided to go in for a quick cup of coffee and a bite to eat. I just about reached the door when I heard the turkey Eric was hunting across the road gobble. By this time it was about three hours after daylight. I thought, *What the hell is he doing? Why isn't that turkey dead yet?!* I had enough cell phone service now and decided to text him. "Are you on that turkey across the road? I just heard him gobble."

He replied, "No, I'm on a different one deeper in. Go kill him!" I grabbed my stuff and I was off. I hadn't been in the game all morning and was down in the dumps, so it was like a match was lit under me. I started wondering what had happened. *Why had Eric not gotten on this bird, but went to a different one?* However, I trusted him and started walking across the road. The cover in this area was also thick, but it was late spring so that was to be expected.

I quickly found an area in the woods with a field down in the bottom. I was really hoping the gobbler wouldn't come out into the field even though I thought he had the evening before. I hadn't sat there long when he gobbled behind me a few hundred yards. It was apparent he was up in the thick stuff. I decided to gain 50 on him, but there really wasn't any good spot to try and call to him. Finally, I found a spot with a 20-yard opening. It was going to be hand to hand combat. I yelped to him and boom, he cut it off. I yelped to him twice and once again he gobbled. As I sat there in the thickest cover imaginable I heard him drumming and knew he was on his way. As he continued to drum I threw all of my calls down the hill to the right, hoping he would take the high ground, which would put him directly in front of me. Well, he was apparently an old and wise turkey, because instead of coming directly at me or below me he worked his way to higher ground. This was bad news because I could only see about 20 yards above me. I continued to hear him drumming and he swung left and at that point I knew it wasn't going to work out. Finally, I begin to catch glimpses of him through some autumn olive along with other thick vegetation and thought, *If I see his head I need to go for the shot.* I might mow down some briars, but I was willing to take the chance.

Suddenly, I saw this big, bright red-head pop up behind a patch of briars and decided to take the shot. At first I wasn't sure what had happened. All I saw was a bunch of vegetation and other debris come down from the aftermath of the shot. I thought, *Please*

God tell me I got this turkey! I got up and ran towards him and there he was, flopping around behind the green briars.

My mind quickly drifted to Eric. *Man, I hope he got one!* I pulled out my phone and saw that about 10 minutes before I shot I had received a text from Eric that read, "I got his ass!" So we ended up killing two gobblers within a few minutes of each other, which made the entire hunt that much better. At that point I went from cloud nine to a notch higher because we both had got it done. I continued to sit there and pay my respects to the turkey while reflecting on the hunt. I couldn't wait to talk with Eric to hear his story. Eventually, I got up and walked back to the cabin and hung the gobbler up. It wasn't long before Eric showed up. I asked him, "This was your turkey! What ended up happening?"

May 27, 2019

Eric replied, "That sucker didn't gobble on the limb! I never heard that turkey. When it started cracking daylight a turkey started gobbling way up in there so I just assumed that it had been that turkey across the road that I heard yesterday." He went after this particular gobbler, which took him several hours to kill. Eric said it caught him by surprise when I texted him there was a gobbler directly across the road gobbling because he thought he was on that turkey the entire time. He figured the gobbler had gone deeper into roost. For whatever reason that bird didn't gobble on the limb, so Eric inadvertently went after another gobbler. Talk about a good problem to have. It was one of those hunts where the stars had aligned for both of us.

That evening we hung out at the cabin, knowing this hunt was our last trigger pull of the season for 2019. I grilled steak number 42 and was staring down the barrel of finishing my Super Slam journey the following spring. Along with the steak, Eric and I fried up a turkey breast along with some morels and washed it down with a few cold ones.

There is nothing like being a traveling turkey hunter and sharing the moment with your buddies when you both kill a gobbler. Those are some of the best days. ↓

LESSONS LEARNED

I use TSS shot. Most hunters use this type of shot to shoot at longer ranges. However, I use it because of situations like my Minnesota hunt when the gobbler is in thicker cover. If you take a shot on a turkey from 20 to 40 yards, he doesn't have to be in the complete wide open. I'm not condoning sketchy or unsafe shots, but opportunities happen sometimes where you can identify it is a longbeard, but just its head is exposed fully. I shoot TSS because I want the maximum pay load I can throw at a gobbler's head. Would I have shot this turkey with other types of shot? Possibly, but I'm not willing to take a chance. By shooting TSS, I feel confident and with the high pellet count in one of those shells I'm able to fully maximize my opportunity to kill a gobbler.

You don't shoot TSS shot to shoot further, but rather for situations where you're in thicker cover and need more penetration. This may have saved me on this particular turkey hunt in Minnesota.

Chapter 43

Oklahoma

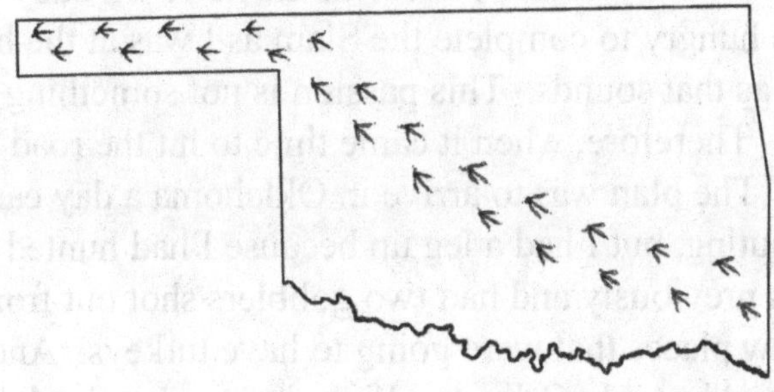

To say things had changed going into 2020 is an understatement. My wife and I had our son in November of 2019, so by the time turkey season arrived he was only four months old. This was our first child, so it was something new for both of us. Another major event was the Covid pandemic, which changed the world. Going into 2020 I had seven states left in my journey for the Super Slam. I had to make a decision before the season began on whether or not to go to Hawaii and try to hunt all seven in one year or hunt six and save Hawaii for last. I opted to not hunt Hawaii that spring. Within the six states I wasn't worried about any except Arkansas. If I failed to connect with a turkey there I would just have Arkansas and Hawaii left for the 2021 season. Another reason I elected not to hunt Hawaii that year is that the group going weren't my real close buddies and I hadn't traveled with them much. I wanted to go there with Kenny, Eric, and Dave, the main guys that had been with me on my journey for the Super Slam. Plus, while hunting in Hawaii you're going to have to burn at least a week, and with my four- month old, that would be tough on my wife.

My first state on the list was Oklahoma. When Covid hit in

March, it shut the school down where I was teaching and I began working virtually. This meant I could go anywhere I wanted. The pandemic by no means was a good thing, but it definitely gave me some traveling flexibility going into this spring.

After my son was born, my traveling was not the same as before. I was carefree for the most part when I was on the road, but now I had the guilt of leaving my wife and kid at home. However, I'd be lying if I told you that even with the newborn baby at home I was just as hungry to complete the Slam as I was at the beginning of it, as bad as that sounds. This passion is not something you can just turn off. Therefore, when it came time to hit the road I was ready to go. The plan was to arrive in Oklahoma a day early to do some scouting, but I had a leg up because I had hunted there for two days previously and had two gobblers shot out from under me, so I knew places that were going to have turkeys. Another leg up was my buddy Andy Orlando. If you remember, back in the Kansas and Nebraska chapters my buddy Joe had introduced me to Andy, who was also going to be in Oklahoma. Andy was going to get there three days early to scout and planned on hunting the same area, which would help me tremendously if he heard some birds. So I was feeling pretty good heading into Oklahoma.

I finally hit the road and tried driving the entire distance, but ended up stopping and sleeping because I had gotten such a late start in the evening. Once I arrived, I talked with Andy and we were all going to get a motel there. My buddy Ryan, whom I had hunted with before, was planning on showing up a couple of days later after the start of the season. Once I got my bird I would try to help him get one, too. Because it was so late when I arrived I wasn't able to put my ears on anything at daylight. During this week I had off, my goal was to hunt Oklahoma and Arkansas. I was banking on getting Oklahoma done in a day or two and then have at least two days to scout Arkansas and about five days to hunt there if necessary.

After arriving around mid-day Andy told me about two turkeys he heard while scouting on a piece of public ground the prior evening so I decided to dive right into the hunt and start there.

After about a mile walk from the parking area I got into an area with some trees and draws and started to glass the surrounding area. Unfortunately, I couldn't see or hear the turkeys that he had been talking about during the 40 minutes I sat there. I had a box call with me and for whatever reason I decided to give it a try and see if that would get them to talk. It's a good thing I did, because they instantly gobbled less than 100 yards away. If I would have taken 10 more steps over the knoll I would have gotten busted. After they gobbled I didn't dare call to them for fear that they would continue to come closer and see me so I decided to lay on my belly. I knew that I would see them come out of the draw. It wasn't long before I saw two big strutters and a bunch of hens. At that point my plan was to stay with them until dark so I could see where they roosted and figure out my set up for the morning hunt. When daylight faded and they finally decided to roost they flew up over a ridge and I lost sight of them. Afterwards, I quickly made a big circle to get a higher vantage point. Once again, I laid in a prone position with my binoculars and was able to spot them right as they were flying up just before dark in a little group of trees. Because these gobblers had hens, I knew I needed to get in front of them right in their landing zone the next morning. The problem was where they flew up from and where they were going to fly down to was completely wide open. I waited until it got completely dark and snuck down in there from the area they had flown up. They were about 50 yards from me and I was trying to figure out how in the world to kill these turkeys. There was some sage grass in this area along with a couple of little bushes, which I decided I would use to hide in. I thought maybe I could lay down and make it work. I used my pruners to carve out the bushes and basically made a little blind in the wide open. There was also a little depression there, which would help conceal me. It was a crap shoot, but this was going to be my setup in the morning.

This was also the first time I used the 12 gauge my Dad had bought me the previous Christmas. Prior to that, I had been carrying a 20 gauge for the duration of the Slam. This new gun was special to me so I decided to give it a try on this trip. However, I was hunting with a gun I had never shot a turkey with, and that sat in the back of my mind. I had been used to the 20 and was super confident with it. Now I had a new gun that I had to get used to.

When I got back to the hotel, everybody had roosted a turkey and had gobblers to hunt the next morning. After I talked to the guys about my set up I still didn't feel real good about it. I felt those turkeys I had roosted were going to see me from the tree when it got close to fly down time and could possibly change their direction.

Morning arrived. Because I arrived so early I had to wait awhile for the turkeys to wake up. Soon, they started to gobble and I noticed both the gobblers and the hens were in one tree. The non-strutter of the two gobblers was off to the left while the dominant gobbler stayed with the hens. I could see the subordinate bird get antsy on the limb. He had been facing me the entire morning. I knew he was getting ready to fly down any second and land in range. My plan was to pull my gun up when he was in the air because there was no way I was going to have my gun in the ready position for two hours. When they're in the air they've got a lot going on and can't detect movement as much. Plus, it's a little too late if they do.

As the non-dominant bird took to the air and was flying from my left to right, I raised my gun. Everything was going perfect except that he decided to land almost directly behind me so I had to swing my gun hand to my right to get on him, but he was plenty close enough. As soon as his feet hit the deck at 35 yards I shot him. The shot caused all of the other turkeys to scatter and fly everywhere.

There was a lot of preparation that went into this hunt and I was glad everything came together, allowing me to fill my Oklahoma tag on the first day. Because my Arkansas season didn't open for another week and there was only a one bird limit in the area I was hunting in Oklahoma, I spent the next couple of days helping my buddies Andy and Ryan get their birds. Andy actually killed the strutter that was with the turkey I had shot. It took awhile, because after I killed his buddy he was a wily son of a gun and didn't want to cooperate right away. It took Andy three days to kill him.

This trip reminded me of my Nevada hunt where I crawled into my setup several hours before daylight with no light and tried to

April 6, 2020

get in front of the turkeys' landing zone.

A lot of hunters look down on shooting turkeys when they fly down, but you can obviously see by what I've told you how much effort has gone into this crawling around in the dark. Anyone that puts down hunting them like that doesn't know how to put in the work and can't crawl in the dark and can't do the things that it takes to kill them with this approach. Because by no means is this a full proof system or an easy way to shoot a turkey. ↓

LESSONS LEARNED

Because I hunted this area the previous year, I already had knowledge on where I could find turkeys. Plus, I knew the type of terrain I would be dealing with, which allowed me to plan my approach on the roosted turkeys I found the evening before my hunt. This was a huge time saver, allowing me to get on a gobbler quickly and fill my Oklahoma tag.

Chapter 44

Arkansas

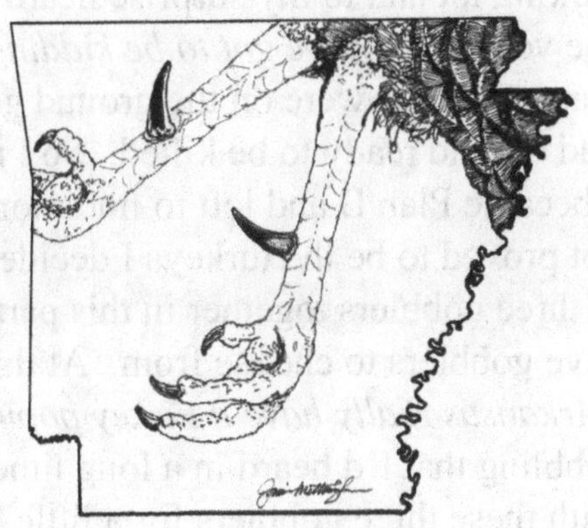

Since I had been successful in Oklahoma early on, I was able to dedicate two full days to scout Arkansas, which I figured I was going to need. Unfortunately, I didn't know anything about the area I was going to hunt. I knew of a few people that had been there, but that was it. My buddy Ryan Bennett came with me this time and both of us were excited at having two days to scout in such a tough state. Arkansas has beautiful turkey country, however the population has plummeted in the last 10 years and their season is only two weeks long. I couldn't stay there the entire time because of my child, but I was prepared to spend at least one week if necessary.

Once Ryan and I arrived on Arkansas soil and began scouting we heard some gobbles, which erased any doubts we previously had.

The following morning we headed out on a scouting mission, parting ways and scouting two separate areas. Right at daylight I heard two gobblers together, which made it easy to pick out a spot. I began slowly walking towards them on the roost so I could pinpoint their exact location in case I was heading back to this location. I ended up marking this spot and listening to them for awhile and waiting to see what they did when they flew down when a light bulb went off in my head. *Man, you need to find more! Plan A, B, C, and D, and E with all of these days to go.* So, this was the number one spot on my map. After arriving at a new area I parked my truck in a parking lot and to my surprise heard a turkey gobble when I exited the vehicle. *You've got to be kidding me!* I thought. Obviously, at that point they were on the ground gobbling. He was gobbling his head off and ready to be killed. So I marked this location too, which became Plan B and left to find more birds.

The third spot proved to be the turkeys I decided to hunt on the opener. I found three gobblers together in this particular location. Already, I had five gobblers to choose from. At this point I was thinking, *Does Arkansas really have a turkey population issue?* It was the most gobbling that I'd heard in a long time.

I hung out with these three gobblers for a little bit and liked the fact that they were difficult to access. It was quite a hike to access this area and there were many obstacles to negotiate along the way. Of all the spots so far, this was looking to be the most promising. After all, 3 gobblers is better than 2 or 1, which was how many I had located in the other spots.

About mid-morning I traveled to a different location and heard another turkey gobble. With all of these different options I felt confident in filling my tag. Obviously, It was two days before the season so there wasn't any hunting pressure in these areas yet so that made a difference in the turkey activity I was seeing.

Ryan and I regrouped later and we compared notes. Unfortunately, he didn't find nearly as much action as I had.

On day two, my mission was to hike into the spot where I had heard the three turkeys and find exactly where they were roosting so I could set up near them the next morning and try to kill them off of the limb.

I arrived at the area where they had been gobbling on the ground. Sure enough, all three of them were only a few hundred yards from me and I knew the exact spot they roosted in. Unfortunately, they were roosted on a private and public boundary line.

However, this setup was still doable. I needed these birds to stay on the public, which is where they were when I arrived, but they ended up traveling to private. It was youth season and I watched some people on private land hunting these turkeys and knew that this was going to create an obstacle for my setup on these birds. As ashamed as I am to admit this, I was hoping the kid who was hunting didn't kill one of them. I was being selfish, but I wanted an Arkansas turkey very bad.

I ended up hanging out there almost the entire morning, keeping an eye on the trio of toms along with keeping my ears open for gun shots. Fortunately, I never heard any shots and the hunters I had seen earlier that morning didn't see me, which was perfect. I didn't want to give them any reason to hunt harder than they were.

Evening arrived and I went back to this spot to try and roost them.

There was a fairly large creek I had to cross to reach this particular section, which is one of the reasons I chose it. The creek was deep enough that rubber boots wouldn't cut it, so I had to switch to my pair of Crocs, which I had in my turkey vest. I even had to take off my pants in order to successfully cross it without soaking my hunting clothes. However, just before I stepped foot in the water I noticed there was a little field on the other side, so I decided to glass it for turkeys so I didn't bump any out of it. I'm not sure why I had gotten the feeling to do so, but when I raised up my binos I instantly saw a red head and it was obviously one of the birds I was after. He stood in the field about 100 yards out. If I had taken just one more step I most certainly would have bumped him and who knows what would have happened. This is the reason going into an area to roost birds in the evening can be so dangerous, you run the risk of bumping them.

As I stood there glassing the gobblers it wasn't long until I heard one of them gobble on the ground. When they did this I cringed because I didn't want them to attract anyone else in the surrounding area. Soon, all three of them gobbled. I thought, *So much for keeping them a secret.*

Eventually, they moved out of the field and I was able to finally cross the creek. When I reached the other side, I began belly-crawling a few hundred yards along the edge of the field. I wasn't about to take any chances on spooking these turkeys. When I finally reached the area I thought they were, it wasn't long until I spotted them. They continued to gobble letting me know their whereabouts the entire time. I had a good feeling they would fly down in this creek bottom in the morning. There were a few trees, but it was fairly open.

Finally, the turkeys decided to fly up. One gobbler roosted directly above the boundary line fence separating private from public, so I knew he could fly down on either side of it. His two buddies were 50 yards on public, which was encouraging for the morning. I figured I had a good chance of catching them in the morning before they drifted onto private. Plus, I didn't see the youth hunters from the day before. I felt like my scouting had paid off.

I hung out there until it got completely dark and followed my usual tactic of finding a place to set up under the cover of darkness and brush in a natural blind. I decided I would set up right along the fence line with my back against one of the posts facing public land. However, as I was waiting for it to get dark a severe thunderstorm moved in. I thought, *well at least there is less of a chance of the turkeys seeing me.* Of course, every time it thundered they were gobbling their heads off, which made me nervous knowing another hunter might hear them. Then I quickly realized, nobody is going to be listening for turkeys in the pouring rain. As I was constructing my little ground blind along the fence line the thunder continued to cause them to gobble just 50 yards away.

I was hoping one of the gobblers would either land in front of me or I could bushwhack one while it was traveling. The gobblers had a bunch of hens with them so I didn't plan on doing any calling unless I had to. I knew these birds had been spooked the day before, so the last thing I wanted to do was to let them know I was there.

It was almost ten o'clock by the time I made it out of the area because I was back and forth on where to set up along the fence line. But after walking out of the area, I felt confident about my set up.

After crossing the creek I decided that I would leave my Crocs along the bank so that I didn't have to carry them in my vest all morning. Well, that was a mistake. When I returned at the creek the next morning all of the rain that we got that evening brought the water level up and washed my Crocs away. So, if you're ever in Arkansas and happen to find a pair of Mossy Oak Bottomland Crocs, those belong to me. Because of this mishap I was forced to walk across the creek in bare feet. It was dangerously high. I put my rubber boots in my vest and carefully waded out in the creek that now was up to my waist. Luckily, it didn't get my vest wet. I figured no one else would be willing to cross at this point because of how treacherous it was, unless the other hunters that I had seen came in from the private side. I was really hoping I had the place to myself.

Finally, I reached my little blind along the fence line well before daylight and soon the turkeys began gobbling. At that point I still didn't see anyone coming in from the private and figured that I would have seen them by now if they were going to hunt. My heart sank. Shortly afterwards, about 30 minutes before fly-down, some hunters walked down a hill on the private, directly towards me. I figured, these turkeys are definitely going to see them and spoil the whole hunt for everyone.

Eventually, the two hunters walked down the boundary line and set up 50 yards behind me on the wood line. They had no idea I was nearby. Somehow they remained hidden from the view of the roosted turkeys. Unfortunately, I couldn't move to let them know I was there because the gobbler was 40 yards from me. The other hunters were 40 yards from the gobbler also, but on the private side. Then I watched in disbelief as they walked out into the open and set up a bunch of decoys. I don't know to this day how the turkeys didn't see them. I guess they had enough grey light or the turkey's vision must have been obstructed. To make matters worse, they set up the decoys directly at my back. If they shot at the decoys there was a chance that I could get shot. So, I had some decisions to make. I would love nothing more than to let this gobbler land in front of me on public and kill that joker before the other hunters had a chance. However, they were too close and it wasn't worth the risk. I knew I had to move and more than likely it would scare off the gobbler. I sat there contemplating what to do and reluctantly decided I couldn't have those decoys at my back in case one landed over there. As badly as I wanted to fill my Arkansas tag, no turkey is worth the risk of getting shot. I began crawling to the next available tree that would be best to set up at, which was about 30 yards in front of me. Fly down time was approaching fast and I knew that by crawling over to the tree I was probably going to spook the turkeys. But as I slowly began crawling I remained undetected. He continued to sit up there and gobble, so I knew that he wasn't on to me. Once I reached the tree, out of the line of fire from where those guys had set up the decoys, the turkey was still gobbling and starting to get antsy on the limb. At that point I'm thinking, *Please God let him land on my side.* Well, he didn't land on my side. When that joker's feet hit the ground he was right in the middle of the decoy spread. He wasn't going to the decoys, nor did he know that they were there. That's just where he happen to land. Upon landing just onto private, he got toasted by one of the hunters. I thought, *Well, he landed over on private and I wouldn't have been able to shoot him anyways.* However, I was still pretty mad because when one of them shot the other two gobblers that were down the fence line flew away. On a positive note, they flew further down onto public. I figured that eventually they would settle down after all the commotion.

After fuming some more I got up and walked over to the fence line to retrieve my turkey vest where I had left it before crawling.

Despite this setback I had the other two gobblers in the back of my mind. I walked away from the boundary line and hunkered down for a bit, letting the turkey woods settle. I hadn't been there for more than 30 minutes when I heard one of the other two turkeys gobble. It was time to go after him. I didn't find this out until later, but little did I know the other two hunters came over onto public land and also went after the longbeard, trying to fill their second tag. I thought, *Come on man!* The woods are open enough where I can kind of see what they're doing. Obviously, they had heard the bird gobble too because they started to gather up their gear. That's when I knew that I had to get there before they did so I got up and basically took off on a dead sprint to the area that I needed to. I was able to get even with the gobbler on this hill. He was on the side of a pretty steep ridge where a bench stuck out and he continued to gobble from that position. Because he continued to gobble I began to call to him in hopes of drawing him in closer for a shot. He would answer it, but not budge an inch. Probably in light of everything that had just happened earlier on. It didn't take me long to realize I needed to sneak up on this turkey if I wanted to kill him. I decided to drop down off the bench and get to the low ground beneath him, belly crawl up the hill and get even with him, but below him, and then crawl up to the bench, pop my head up and pray to God that he'd be within shotgun range.

Meantime, in the middle of doing this I heard the other guys who were still about 200 yards back. They weren't nearly as tight, but they were calling to him also. The gobbler answered every time, but still didn't budge. In truth these guys actually were helping me out because every time they called the tom gobbled, allowing me to keep tabs on his whereabouts.

I continued to crawl beneath the vertical bench inch by inch while the other hunters continued to call, but the gobbler didn't gain any ground. I knew when I popped up I needed to take a safe shot, knowing the other two hunters were nearby, but then I realized they were still to my left over 100 yards away, so if I shot to my right there was no risk. I continued to climb the bench and finally reached the edge. I anticipated seeing the gobbler when I popped my head up. I began to inch my head up just about as slow as humanly possible. Once my eyes cleared the edge, I slowly scanned and didn't see the gobbler. I knew that when I spotted him he should be within shotgun range. As I patiently stayed in position waiting for him to gobble again I heard the sound every turkey hunter dreads, putt-putt-putt about 45 yards up the hill. I thought, *How in the heck did that joker see me!?* Somehow he saw me inch my head up the hill, but when he started putting he gave me a line of sight to him. Although he was putting, he didn't hightail it out of there.

As he stepped out from behind a tree I shot and rolled him at 45 yards. I thought, *Oh my gosh! Did that really just work out in light of everything that had just happened!?*

I was so pumped up. I ran out after him, picking him up, and was so excited that all of my prior frustrations and disappointments were quickly forgotten.

April 13, 2020

The two hunters ended up coming over to me and we had a good laugh together. They were completely cool. They wondered how I had gotten back in there. I explained how I had been on the fence line and had to crawl out of there for fear of getting shot. They had no clue I was even there or had crawled away until I came back for the turkey vest.

From a safety stand point, I felt everything I did was smart. The only thing I could have done differently was to let those fellows know I was there, but it was at risk of spooking the turkey. And I knew once I got to the other set-up there was no chance of them shooting me. I also knew that when I shot up on that bench I wasn't shooting in the direction they were calling from. ↓

LESSONS LEARNED

A major lesson I learned on my trip to Arkansas is that if you're ever in doubt that another hunter is nearby and you might be set up in an unsafe location, get out of there. You need to be aware of what is in front and in back of you and plan your set up accordingly. Be aware of your surroundings at all times. There is no turkey worth losing your life or compromising your safety.

As for strategy, because the turkey I was after had been pressured, he wasn't going to commit to any calling, so I had to be aggressive and go to him. Like many other turkeys I've hunted, it paid off by using the terrain to my advantage and going after the gobbler.

Lastly, having all of those turkeys in my back pocket from scouting gave me options. I could have easily found those two turkeys on the first morning while scouting and called it good. But I wanted to have plan A, B, C, and D in order to have several different areas to choose from in case one of them failed. One thing I've learned is that when you're on the road it is essential to have a back up to the back up.

The particular turkeys that I was after were in the best locations as far as public access, even though I faced the challenges of hunting close to private property and ran into the other two hunters.

Chapter 45

Massachusetts

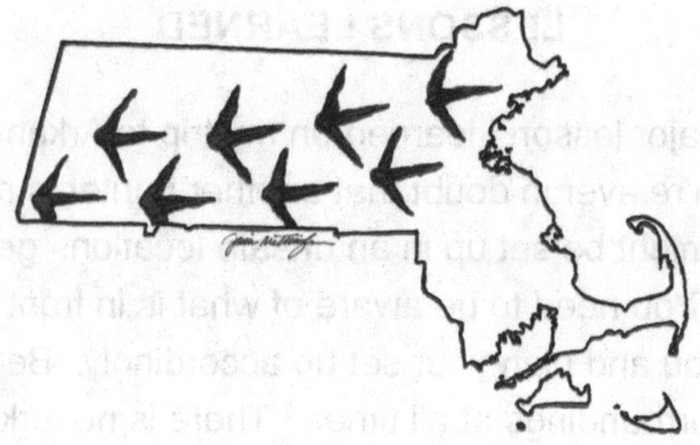

After I left Arkansas I traveled back home and waited for the West Virginia season. My plan was to set aside a week to hunt Massachusetts, Rhode Island, and Connecticut. Kenny came up and hunted with me for a few days and we had a great time. He killed a couple of turkeys during his hunt. I was also able to get a West Virginia bird during the first week of the season.

Because it was quite a drive to Massachusetts, I had planned on leaving mid-morning, a day before the opener, in order to get there in time to look around. Unfortunately, that didn't happen because Kenny and I hunted until quitting time in West Virginia.

By this time my taxidermy business had exploded and I was mounting close to 100 turkeys per spring. I had five turkeys thawing in the shop and I needed to skin them before I got on the road. We had been hunting hard all week and I was dog tired. After finishing the skinning, I started driving, hoping to make it the entire way so I could arrive in time for the opener, but after putting in about four hours on the road I was too tired to keep going. I knew I had the whole week to hunt these three states, so I didn't want to push it and run myself down. I pulled over about halfway there and slept for longer than I should have. When I woke up it was around 6 a.m. and I still had four more hours to go.

As soon as I crossed the state line, I saw a strutter with two hens behind someone's house. This wasn't the area I planned on hunting, but going back to that "Plan B" thing, I decided to drop a pin on the location. I already had a public land destination in mind, still about 45 minutes away.

When I arrived at the public land, the parking lot was almost full. I thought, *That's not a good sign!* On the other hand, I figured maybe it was a good sign, meaning there must be turkeys in the area. I can't remember when quitting time was in Massachusetts, but I only had a few hours left until dusk so I decided to go for a walk to see if there was any turkey sign. I climbed up on the side of a mountain and didn't like what I saw. There wasn't a lot of sign, however I knew of some people who had hunted here and killed turkeys, but it didn't look promising to me. I figured I might hear one come daylight, but my mind started drifting back to that strutter I had seen behind those people's house. I was instantly drawn to this area and thought about how nice it would be to get permission to hunt there and go after him. After pondering some more on the idea, I finally decided to drive back to that property and see if I could gain permission to hunt.

The first house I came to had a little bit of property and was actually right near the spot I had seen the strutter. I knocked on the door and a young kid answered, "My Dad's not home. You'll have to come back in a couple of hours." As I walked back to my truck I noticed there were some deer targets in the yard and figured he was a hunter and questioned whether or not he would allow me to hunt. Then I looked on the map, and nearby was a big farm, which had over 100 acres and was next door to them. It looked like it had better turkey habitat than the other property. I figured while I was waiting for the other property owner to get home I would see if I could get permission on this farm.

As I was driving down the road, the owners pulled into their driveway and I followed behind. These folks were the nicest old couple you'd ever meet. Without hesitation they gave me permission and showed me where to park when it was time to go hunting.

To my surprise, another guy who I had known also hunted on this property. When the couple mentioned his name I instantly recognized it. I didn't know him personally, but found out about him through social media that he was a turkey hunter. I couldn't believe we got permission to hunt the same farm without knowing each other. We joked what a small world it was. He had hunted towards the end of May the previous year and only heard one gobbler, which he ended up shooting. He also said since I would be hunting on the opener things could be different.

As I stood on the hill overlooking a big field, we continued to message back and forth. It hadn't been very long when I heard a turkey gobble. At this point it was in the evening. I sat there and listened to him, noticing his gobbling was sporadic and he wasn't staying in the same spot. However, he was gobbling enough for me. I had a feeling he was going to continue to gobble until he reached the limb. However, my hopes dwindled about an hour later when three dogs came running through the field barking like crazy. *Perfect, this is all I need,* I thought. If the dogs would have stayed in the field, it wouldn't ruin my hunting. However, they ran right towards where the turkey had gobbled not a minute before. At that point I knew all of the commotion would most definitely cause the turkey to stop gobbling. I was faced with a choice. I looked at a map and found a couple of other spots of public land within 30 minutes of this farm, and I could either hunt there or hope this gobbler got fired back up. I remember sitting up there contemplating what option to go with. Finally I elected to leave, because there was a field and I thought maybe I would spot a gobbler from the road. Well, leaving was a dumb decision because when I got on the road and drove by a couple of those public areas, I didn't see any turkeys out in any fields.

Afterwards, I had just enough time to drive back to the farm. I raced back there, driving way over the speed limit, kicking myself for leaving in the first place. I should have known the gobbler would settle down after those dogs stirred him up. Thank God I did.

After pulling into the driveway of the farm, I ran back up the hill as fast as I could. After only standing there for a minute, Boom! He gobbled from his roost. I confirmed this because he gobbled a couple more times from the same location and I could tell he was in a tree. He was probably 150 yards into the woods. I didn't want to risk moving until it got completely dark, so I sat there and waited. I wanted to get even with him while he was still gobbling so that I was between him and the field in his line of travel when it came fly-down time.

I crawled down to the field edge and placed a stick in the ground when I was even with him that was easy to see. I used an owl hooter a couple of times in order to hear him in the dark. This way, when I returned in the morning I would know where to stop and where to start down into the woods.

Afterwards, I went back to a motel I had seen. I looked at the time for sunrise and it was five-something so that meant I needed to return to the farm around 4 a.m.

The following morning the temperature had dropped and I felt as though I was going to freeze to death. My goal was to set up within 50 yards of the gobbler, in hopes of killing him when he hit the ground. I was probably more like 70 yards out, but I still felt confident in my setup based on hearing all of his gobbling, which was burning the woods down.

When the turkey flew down he flew to my hard left. If he took the route from where he landed to the field he was going to walk by me. He was all by his lonesome and the way he was gobbling I could tell he was looking for a hen. Once his feet hit the ground I gave him about 20 seconds and then I turned my head to the right to steer him a little bit and let out a couple of yelps with my mouth call. He instantly cut me off. At this point he was about 60 yards from me just over a slight roll. I spun to my left a little and then flipped my gun off safety. In no time at all I begin to hear him drum. Suddenly, he appeared at 25 yards, strutting. I took a shot using the 12 gauge my Dad had bought me. When the gobbler had come in from my hard left I wasn't able to shoulder my gun tightly and the gun cracked me right in the nose. The bird instantly tipped over and I ran out and retrieved my Massachusetts bird.

I knew you could kill two birds in this state legally in the same day, so I went back to the same field where I had sat the day before, smoking a cigar and enjoying the beautiful day with my turkey beside me. About 15 minutes had passed and I heard a turkey drum behind me. I turned my head, but didn't see anything. By this point all of the turkeys had quit gobbling. Another minute or two passed and the sound was unmistakable this time. I heard the drum once again. I look behind me and there is a longbeard and three hens. Without really thinking about it, I grabbed my shotgun and wheeled around, killing my second gobbler.

April 29, 2020

At the time I didn't regret it, but looking back I already had a good hunt and felt that I should have left this gobbler for somebody else or for seed. I didn't need to kill that second turkey. This is the only time that I killed two gobblers in the same day and I don't think I will ever do it again. Not because I wouldn't be offered the opportunity, but because it seemed greedy. When I'm on a trip nowadays I'm after a single turkey. If I can kill another a day or two later, great, but it's not the norm for me anymore. I'm not sure if this feeling comes with age or experience.

I walked back down to my truck and the old couple had heard me shoot and were out in their yard amazed that I had killed two gobblers. "My goodness, we didn't realize there were that many turkeys back there!" they said with surprise. We had a nice conversation and I thanked them once again. I was very grateful they had given me permission to hunt.

I credit dropping a pin from the road and having this gobbler as Plan "B" for getting me in there and filling my two tags.   ↓

LESSONS LEARNED

Don't ever be scared to ask for permission. The worst thing someone can say is no. When approaching a landowner, collect yourself and be as polite as possible.

If you get the opportunity to kill two birds in one day, just kill one. This was my biggest regret of this trip. You can always go back another day or year and fill your tag.

Chapter 46

Connecticut

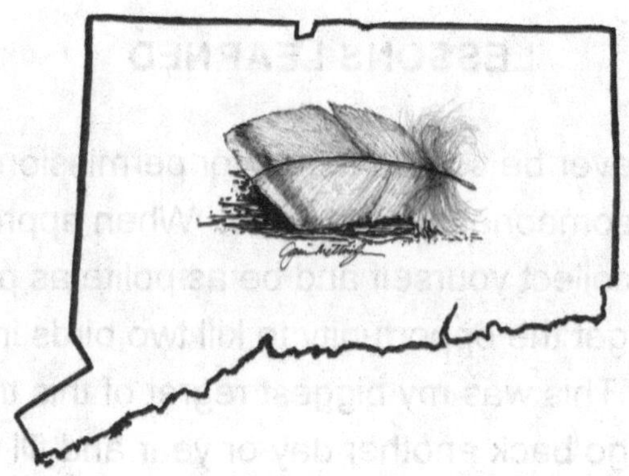

Before arriving in Connecticut I already had a spot picked out, along with the names of a couple of landowners. I had spoken with them on the phone, but still needed to meet in person and get the lowdown on their property and confirm I had permission to hunt. Tagging out early in Massachusetts, coupled with the short two-hour drive, afforded me more time to buy my license and get in the woods to hunt.

I pulled up to the first farm and met the landowner who was out working in his barn. He explained he had some other turkey hunters coming in and where they would be hunting so we wouldn't pressure each other, and also where he had been seeing turkeys that morning. I also had another landowner in my back pocket in case this property didn't work out. By this time it was about midday and all of the other turkey hunters had left.

I put my turkey clothes on, gathered my gear, and dove right in. I hadn't been out of the truck 45 minutes and I already found myself climbing this little knoll where I could scan a field below and view a stand of mature hardwoods to my right. I pulled a glass call from my vest and struck a gobbler right away. However, the turkeys I eventually saw didn't gain any ground on me, so I backed away from the rock wall I was positioned behind to get into some better timber and gave the gobblers the silent treatment. Then unexpectedly, while in the process of backing up, I heard some turkeys in the leaves. *The turkeys had broken!* I thought. One by one they stuck their head up over the rock wall and hopped over, closing the distance. It was five jakes. One of them had a deep gobble, which fooled me into thinking they were toms. In the Northeast turkeys don't have as hearty of a gobble as in the South, so it had thrown me off.

The fifth gobbler that was the caboose of the group never showed his entire body so I decided to crawl up there and lay eyes on the last bird, just to make sure. At that point the turkeys had traveled to my right over a knoll about 20 yards away. After a few minutes of crawling I soon confirmed that he was a jake.

In the meantime, a lone gobbler had come in silent, the same way the jakes had come. I was still facing the knoll and my back was to the rock wall. I heard some heavy walking from behind and when I turned my head a gobbler hopped up on the rock wall. If I would've stayed put he would have given me a 30-yard shot. The gobbler was within range, but it would require me to do a complete 180 degree turn, which is pretty tough to do. I figured, what do I have to lose, so I swung around and as I did he flew straight up, but came back down and landed nearby. Unfortunately, he never presented me with a clear shot. Maybe I could have shot him, but I wasn't willing to take the risk. There was no window of opportunity.

It was going on one o'clock and I almost had killed a third gobbler – two in Massachusetts and now this close encounter in Connecticut.

I decided to let the gobbler calm down for an hour or two. I sat there in the same area, not wanting to leave, killing time on my phone. After two hours, I walked over to the knob and called. I'll be damned if he didn't gobble. I knew he was by himself and very lonely. However, he stopped gobbling, but I could hear him drumming on higher ground on the same knoll I was on probably

75 yards away. After 45 minutes of listening to him drum I got aggressive with my calling, but nothing got him to budge. I elected to inch my way towards him. I hadn't crawled 20 yards when I heard him putt. Now, I had scared this same gobbler for the second time this day.

I decided it was time for a break. I walked out to my truck and drove to get a bite to eat and recharge my batteries for a bit. Brainstorming my next plan of attack, I figured I would go over to the other landowner. He told me he would love to let me hunt, but he already had guys hunting on his land for the next two days. Trying not to be too pushy, I asked him if I could walk around and hunt for a couple of hours that evening. Without hesitation he said that would be fine because there was no one hunting until the next morning.

He mentioned a section where the turkeys had been hanging out, so I drove to that area and started walking the edge of a cornfield. After discovering gobbler tracks throughout the area I quickly decided to set up along the edge and see if any appeared in the field. After sitting for only 20 minutes the wind picked up and the temperature dropped fast. I got up and walked back to my truck to grab a jacket. When I got back, some gobblers beat me to the field and quickly spotted me. They ran to the far end of the field, which had a small roll in it blocking my view. I began cussing myself out and beating myself up for getting my jacket. If I hadn't moved, they might have given me a shot.

Because it was so late in the day, I decided to try and roost some birds in this section and go back to the landowner to see if he would allow me to come back and hunt here in the morning if some gobblers flew up. At this point I was flustered to say the least. I decided to sit tight and give them some more time. *After all, I've bumped turkeys before and killed them later. I had almost done this same thing earlier that day,* I told myself.

It wasn't 20 minutes and I heard one gobble at the end of the far end of the field, where I had seen them run earlier. *Is there a chance I could kill the turkey from right here where I spooked them?* I thought.

I sat between two fields on the rock wall in an elevated position, which would allow me to shoot to the left or right side of the field.

I decided to call to him and he instantly answered, but as I got aggressive and ramped up my calling he failed to respond. Soon he went silent so I put the call away. I thought, either he's coming or something else happened. I anticipated him coming from the right so I got my gun ready. I wasn't in the best position because I was up too high and my shooting lanes weren't that great. Soon, I heard drumming. I looked to my left and here he came, sneaking down the left edge of the field. My gun was still pointed to the right and swinging to the left was going to be difficult. I knew I was in a pickle and feared scaring the third turkey for the day.

The gobbler made it to 40 yards when he smelled a rat and saw me sitting there. At that point I still hadn't gotten my gun moved

April 29, 2020

yet because things transpired so quickly and I didn't think I could get away with it. But when he started putting I decided to go for it. When I swung my gun he started high stepping it, but it was too late. I was able to get the bead of my shotgun on his head and shoot him at 45 yards in the field. *There's no way that I just killed three gobblers in two states in one day,* I thought. Honestly, it felt kind of surreal, but I was happy to have Connecticut under my belt. I didn't know if I would ever again kill gobblers in two states in the same day.

At the time, I needed to get my Slam done and had a wife and kid waiting for me at home, so I was trying to get a gobbler as quickly as I could. However, I was feeling conflicted with myself over the entire hunt. I think it's important to soak in the hunt in each state and not rush on and try and kill a bird in another within the same day. ↓

LESSONS LEARNED

One of the major lessons I learned while hunting Connecticut and other states during my Slam is despite bumping a gobbler, never give up on hunting him. However, if he flies away from one ridge to another or a great distance, then you probably will have to relocate. But if you just bump him a little, stick with him and don't get discouraged. There is always a chance you can kill him.

Chapter 47

Rhode Island

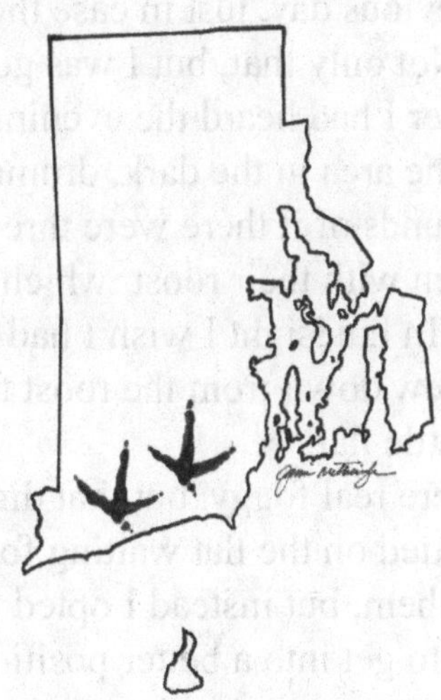

The area I planned on hunting in Rhode Island was only an hour from where I had killed my bird in Connecticut, so I decided to make the short drive and try to roost some turkeys that evening.

Once I arrived, my excitement dwindled a little when I noticed there was a vehicle in the spot where I had planned on parking. I figured someone else was in there hunting, which derailed my plans.

After circling around the property in my truck through the different fields, I returned to the parking lot and the vehicle was gone. You can only hunt until midday so I was certain he must have been roosting birds also.

It was a piece of public land bordering private land, and the turkeys traveled through both areas. With that said, you had to try and ambush them on the public side, which was where they preferred roosting. Typical of turkeys in the Northeast, they spend a lot of time in people's yards and housing areas, so it can be challenging to pull them over onto public land for a shot opportunity.

That evening I heard a distant turkey gobble, and even though it was further away I was able to keep tabs on him. This got my blood pumping and I was hopeful of possibly tagging out in Rhode Island early like I did in the last state.

With a fresh license in my pocket, I ventured out the following morning extra early in order to beat the other person whose vehicle I had seen the previous day, just in case they were planning on hunting there also. Not only that, but I was going to try and get 40 yards from the gobbler I had heard the evening before.

As I approached the area in the dark, drumming cut the air like a knife and by the sounds of it there were three or four gobblers close by. I set up even with their roost, which was in some trees on the side of a hill. In hindsight I wish I had set up behind them, because when they flew down from the roost they landed up above me and got up on a little flat.

The conditions were real foggy, but that didn't stop them from gobbling as they strutted on the flat waiting for the hens. I should have tried calling to them, but instead I opted to crawl closer to the lip of the flat and try to get into a better position for a shot. However, that moment never came. As I began to make my move, one of the gobblers saw me and all of them quickly high-tailed it out of the area. It was game over. They appeared to have been hunted before and pressured.

I spent the rest of the day trying to get on these turkeys and eventually found them in the field on private property, so the chase ended there. It was quitting time, but I had those turkeys' number. Later that day, I walked back into the place and roosted the same gobblers. I was banking on them staying with the same routine as the morning before.

The morning of day two was a redemption hunt, which seems to be the norm in turkey hunting. This time I set up above them in total darkness and once again their gobbles rang out across the valley. However, they failed to cooperate, and instead of flying down onto the flat they sailed completely into the private field. Once again it was game over. *You dirty rats!* I thought to myself. I spent the remainder of the morning calling to them and trying to get one of the gobblers to break off and come into the woods with me onto public land.

Finally, one of the gobblers began gobbling pretty good around mid-morning. I called and he started to cut the distance towards the woods where I could legally shoot him on public. However, he came within shooting range and hung up in the field on private, never fully committing. It's always a challenge trying to get a gobbler to come out of a field and into the woods. It just wasn't happening and I ran out of time. I was really getting tired of messing with these birds, but it's hard to leave turkeys to find other turkeys.

Day three arrived and again they roosted in the same spot. I wasn't feeling very optimistic they were going to fly down onto public with me, like they did the first day. Of course, my prediction was right and they landed on the private field again for the second day in a row. They spent most of their time in the lower portion of the field. However, I was hoping they would travel to the upper portion because it seemed like it had more open woods where they could travel and see better. The lower part was very thick with brush and vegetation. It would be a lot to ask a turkey to come out of an open field into thick cover.

The rest of the morning I spent crawling around the edge of the field in hopes of getting one of the gobblers to break off and come into shooting range, but they continued to hold their ground and didn't take the bait. It was about an hour before hunting hours ended when I decided to call it quits. I began circling back into the woods when suddenly I heard a turkey gobble in the upper field. At this point I'm thinking, *it's day three, my wife is ready for me to get back and I need to step it up fast.* As I peeked into the upper field I was shocked to find a gobbler all by himself. I figured I stood a decent chance of calling this joker in, so I crawled on all fours to get closer. The leaves were so dry that as I was crawling along and approaching the 100 yard mark, the gobbler thought there was a hen in the woods and started gobbling his head off. I never had to call, however I needed him to leave the field so I could shoot him on public. I had another 20 yards before making it to a tree I had picked out where I would set up. In the process, I looked up and saw the gobbler already in the woods coming my way. I was still on all fours and not at the tree, so it was going to be another one of those scenarios where I pull my gun up quick in order to make a shot.

He continued to close the distance fast – 60, 50, 40. As he reached the 30 – yard mark and went behind a tree I slid back and prepared for the shot. Once I could see him again I could tell he sensed danger because he just stopped and stared in my direction. But he wasn't fast enough. My shot had proved fatal and sealed the deal.

After three days of getting whipped, it felt good to walk up and get my hands on him. It was a hell of a trip. As I draped him over my shoulder and walked through the woods my mind was in a whirlwind. Three states in six days. ↓

May 1, 2020

LESSONS LEARNED

Even though this wasn't the first hunt I've been on where I scratched or crunched leaves to get a gobblers attention, this method is just as good as doing some soft calling most times. A turkey and a human sound a lot alike while moving through the leaves and this worked to my advantage during this hunt in Rhode Island, causing the gobbler to come in to investigate. This tactic is another tool you can add to your turkey hunting arsenal.

Chapter 48

Oregon

It was the beginning of May 2020 so there was still plenty of time left to turkey hunt with most seasons in full swing. My plan was to hunt Oregon, however the Covid pandemic caused Oregon to shutdown to non-resident turkey hunters interested in purchasing a license. This was unfortunate because Oregon was the next state on my list to hunt. This meant I would have to wait until 2021 to hunt both Oregon and Hawaii. I was reaching the end of the Super Slam and I was eager to check this state off my list towards the end of May.

As I was driving back from the Northeast I received a text from my buddy Ryan, who saw a post on Facebook that Oregon had opened up to non-residents. Soon afterwards, I made a call to one of their DNR offices and found out that it was legit.

At this point my wife was over me turkey hunting, since I had been gone a lot during the Covid year and just having our new baby. I called her while still on the road telling her about Oregon re-opening and she said, "It's not happening Tanner! You've hunted too much."

I fired back, "I don't care what it's going to take or what I have to do – I'll stay up all night with the baby, but I'm going to Oregon for three days in the end of May so go ahead and put it on your calendar."

Fortunately, my wife got over it just like the wives of many men that hunt a lot. For the next two weeks I did some extra baby chores to help smooth the waters.

I gave my buddy Kenny a call. I hadn't hunted a new state with him in a while and he agreed to head to Oregon towards the end of May. Kenny had planned on hunting in Washington and was going to drive over and meet me in Oregon during my three-day hunt there.

Toward the end of May, I boarded a plane and flew into Portland, where I rented a vehicle. I met Kenny in the area we planned on hunting, which neither one of us had hunted before. It was a beautiful landscape with elk everywhere. Prior to the hunt, Kenny and I did a lot of online research on this area and also gathered information from local biologists. Based on this information, we were both optimistic and concluded this area should have a decent turkey population.

Around midday we checked into the place we were staying, which gave us plenty of time to look for turkeys and try and put a move on one if we could, or at least get one roosted for the following morning.

After spending a couple of hours driving around this beautiful region we failed to spot any turkeys. Our hopes were high of at least seeing some birds from the road or on private property, but to our disappointment we saw absolutely nothing. We began to worry and second guessed the turkey numbers and what everyone had said about the area, however there was a lot more territory to cover.

After continuing to drive around for hours, checking different spots, we finally spotted some jakes so we knew turkeys did exist there. This was encouraging, but we needed to find some longbeards. As we drove along on a national forest road we approached a turn leading to a large clearing and saw a gobbler in full strut with some hens. We decided to drive on by so as not to alarm him, and the tom barely came out of strut. Once we drove about

300 yards past the gobbler, Kenny pulled over and looked at me and said, "What would you like to do?"

I responded, "Are you going to let me out? I'm going to go try and kill him! And if I don't get him killed I'm going to get him roosted."

Kenny replied, "I love your attitude! I'm going to drive around and I'll come and pick you up at dark so you can go put a play on him."

I marked a waypoint at the spot where the gobbler was and where Kenny was going to pick me up at and began walking back down the road towards him. As I got closer to where the birds were at I started crawling. At this point I wasn't sure what these turkeys were doing, yet I was kind of expecting them to still be in the road. The final 100 yards I crawled through some thick stuff providing me with some cover as I approached them. I didn't call because I figured that he wouldn't leave any hens with him. I knew I would have to continue to crawl in order to close the distance for a shot. Once I arrived near the area of road where Kenny and I had seen the turkeys they were nowhere to be found. I kept scanning the area hoping to spot them. Finally, I stood up and continue to look for them. Just as luck would have it the sun gleamed off a hen's back, allowing me to locate the turkeys. They were walking down into the woods. *Ah ha! Gotcha! You guys went that way!* I thought. I began to take it real slow to the last spot where I had seen them. Once again as I approached, I saw them and started crawling, but they had disappeared. I thought, *Man, these Merriam's never stay in the same spot!* However, it was day one and I really wasn't expecting much. I didn't want to mess things up because if I got them roosted then I figured I could probably get one killed. Merriam's turkeys like to gobble, so hopefully it wouldn't be difficult to roost them.

I decided to sit there for a bit and play it safe, waiting for them to fly up. However, desperate times call for desperate measures, so after 10 or 15 minutes passed I rolled the dice and threw a call out to the gobbler with my mouth call. It was risky because a lot of times when hens hear you call out West they start dragging the gobbler the opposite direction. They don't want any competition from another hen. I don't know that I've ever heard of anybody calling a Merriam's gobbler away from hens, but I was willing to try.

After a couple of yelps from my mouth call the longbeard let out a gobble. He was probably 250 yards away. I dropped and began crawling towards him, trying to keep up with him. I didn't want to call any more than I had to. Fortunately, it was pretty open country, which made crawling a little easier. Eventually, I saw him strutting with the same hens angling towards me. By this point I had gotten near some thick cover, which allowed me to gain some ground undetected. I continued to crawl on my belly cutting the distance to 100 yards. I couldn't believe the amount of hens scattered throughout the area. There were too many eyeballs and soon some nearby hens saw me and started putting. This caused the gobbler to come out of strut and be on high alert. As I remained on all fours like a statue, hoping to not scare off the turkeys, my fist somehow managed to end up right smack in the middle of an ant hill. As I looked down I began to cringe at the thought of them biting me. Fortunately, I had gloves, a face mask, and a long sleeve shirt on so I figured they would have a hard time reaching my skin. I still had a hen at 20 yards so I wasn't about to smack these ants off me and ruin my chances at the gobbler. Moving only my eyes, I looked down at the ants and up at the hen, praying that she moved along soon. Eventually, I was able to move my hand out of the ant hill. However, the standoff went on long enough that a few of these ants made their way to the corner of my eye lid and started biting me. I remember thinking, *This is ridiculous! I need to smack these ants off me.* But I never did. I wanted an Oregon turkey so bad that I let those ants sit there and chew on me. Looking back now, I'm pretty sure I was a psychopath. I should have just smacked them.

Eventually both the hens and the gobbler walked off and by now they were alarmed, leaving me frustrated, yet relieved that I could finally brush the ants off and move away from the ant hill. As I sat there kicking myself for screwing up the hunt I heard him gobble and immediately felt as though I was back in the game once again. At this point he was so far away that I didn't need to crawl so I began walking in their general direction and again I lost them with 45 minutes left of shooting light. He continued to gobble every now and then, but he moved so much I couldn't gain any ground on him. I knew if I was persistent and kept up with them they would eventually hang out in one spot.

As I moved through the open terrain I finally reached a point where I hadn't heard from a turkey in awhile so I broke out my call and gave it one last try for the day. He instantly gobbled a buck twenty five from me.

The turkeys were over a little rise, so I was able to use the terrain to my advantage like I had done so many times before. I began crawling uphill, figuring they should be within shotgun range once I peeked over the rise. After I reached this high point I began to slowly raise my head. As I peeked over the rise, I could see the hens to my right, but there were so many of them in the way I couldn't see the gobbler. Finally, as I cut my eyes to the left I spotted him behind a large deadfall at 30 yards. He was within shotgun range, but I had to wait for him to clear it before taking a shot. At this point I was on my knees watching the gobbler as he moved from left to right behind the deadfall waiting patiently for a clear shot. Suddenly one of his hens flew up into a nearby tree to roost. I thought, *I've got to get him out from behind this deadfall before he flies up and I can't kill him!* Then a minute or so later another hen flew up. However, there was still hope. In my experience, most of the time a gobbler will be either the last one to fly up and roost or the first. With the gobbler still holding tight behind the deadfall I made the executive decision to raise up from my knees to a half standing position. This caused him to raise his head above the deadfall just long enough for a shot. Instantly, he tipped over. The shot caused the entire flock to scatter everywhere. In the blink of an eye my Oregon tag was filled the same day I flew in, right before fly up time.

With three days left, I was able to shoot a second gobbler, and Kenny ended up filling his tag as well.

As I walked up to the pick-up spot with the Merriam's and its snow white tail fan draped over my shoulder, I remember thinking, Kenny isn't going to believe this. Kenny pulled up at dark as I

May 24, 2020

stood there holding the turkey and said, "I knew his ass was done and you would kill him tonight!" Like a proud dad he gave me a great big bear hug.

It was great to be on the road with my old mentor once again. By this time I was an extremely different turkey hunter than when we had started hunting together. My knowledge of turkey hunting had grown as my journey continued throughout the U.S.

By this stage of the Super Slam I had a lot of people following along on Instagram and most people in my home town and West Virginia knew what I was doing as I approached the end of the Super Slam.

I could tell when I walked up to Kenny that evening he was

really proud of me for filling my Oregon tag and the turkey hunter that I had become. ↓

> **LESSONS LEARNED**
>
> The huge lesson I learned on this trip is to never take the first evening of a trip for granted. We could have easily unpacked our things and settled in for the next day, but instead we were aggressive. If given the opportunity, don't just stop at spotting and roosting a turkey. Try getting aggressive like we did and make a play on one if you have the chance.

Chapter 49

Hawaii

A wave of excitement and anticipation overwhelmed me as I entered the spring of 2021. I was sitting on 48 states with just, Hawaii left. After the previous year's hunt in Oregon I had all the time in the world to think about this hunt. During the entire off season my taxidermy business was exploding and I was mounting over 100 turkeys per year. This gave me a lot of time to think about my final hunt to complete the Slam. It's almost as though I conjured up a turkey because I can remember working in my shop and thinking, *There's a turkey right now in Hawaii that has a date with destiny.*

I knew I wasn't going to come home until I shot a gobbler in this state. Somewhere on that island out in the Pacific was a turkey that had my name on him. As weird as it sounds, I would think about this gobbler periodically throughout each day in my shop. Here I am 4,600 miles away, thinking about a bird with my name on it. I thought this was weird to think about the entire year, but visualizing the hunt helped me to mentally prepare for it.

Later that summer, Dave Owens had gotten in contact with me, wanting to join me and film this hunt for an episode of the *Pinhoti Project*. This hunt can be viewed on the *Pinhoti Project's YouTube Channel*.

The crew heading to Hawaii with me consisted of Dave and my friend Eric. Kenny decided at the last minute he wasn't going to join us. He thought four people would be too many and a five-day hunt wasn't worth going. This caused us to have a little bit of a disagreement because I really wanted him to be in Hawaii for the end of the Slam. I wish Kenny would have been alongside me on this final hunt. To this day I'm still a little sour he chose not to go.

Leading up to the hunt, we scouted and talked to people to gather information, however, Eric and I had never hunted in Hawaii. Fortunately, because Dave turkey hunts for a living, he had already hunted there so he had information on this state. The way Dave's schedule worked out, he was able to arrive in Hawaii three days early and scout. He figured he would have some gobblers nailed down come opening day, but unfortunately the turkeys he located moved around constantly and were difficult to pattern. However, he did hear some turkeys, which was encouraging.

Leading up to our hunt Dave and I were in constant contact as he kept us up to speed on his scouting adventures and his findings. On one particular outing at the end of day two, Dave texted, "You're never going to believe what I saw?! I saw a white gobbler and it had two other gobblers with it."

Unfortunately, as Dave was filming the gobblers on the roost while standing in the middle of the road, he heard a vehicle coming. Because he was afraid it was another turkey hunter, he stopped videoing and hid in the brush alongside the road in order to avoid the risk of getting spotted. All this commotion blew the white gobbler off the roost, causing it to fly for miles. This was no exaggeration, considering the area where we hunted was 9,000 feet above sea level.

It was at least a two-hour drive to this particular area. On any given day you could expect rain, snow, fog, and high winds. It was a different world up there and I still find it hard to believe turkeys could even live in such a rugged environment, but they did.

After Dave told us about the white gobbler, I would be lying to you if the thought didn't cross my mind for a second, *Man, what would it be like to finish with a white one?*

I remember getting excited and texting two of my buddies back home about this unusual bird Dave had seen on the island. I thought, *How big of a deal would it be if I shot a white turkey for the 49th?!* Obviously I wasn't holding out for this turkey. Any turkey that came by me with a long beard was getting killed.

In order to arrive in Hawaii from the continental United States, you had to go to a Covid-certified establishment to get tested and upload a negative Covid test to a Hawaii medical website within 48 hours of your flight. This test had to be from a certified place. Unfortunately, you couldn't just go to any doctor's office and get a Covid test. Because of this I had to drive three hours to a Walgreens in Marietta, Ohio, which was the closest certified place to where I lived. You had to get tested not only before the flight, but also when you landed in Hawaii.

It was quite the rodeo we had to go through. Because Covid was hot and heavy, I figured maybe all of these hoops would help mitigate some of the pressure and the amount of turkey hunters heading to Hawaii that year. However, people were still out on the island turkey hunting. You can't slow turkey hunters down. We're crazy!

After Dave picked me up at the airport, we met up with two other turkey hunters Dave knew who were on the island and hung out with them for a while waiting on Eric's flight. Because of arriving on the island a day ahead of schedule I had plenty of time to meet with the game warden and buy all the tags I needed and get squared away.

Dave showed me the video footage he had gotten of the white gobbler along with other gobblers he had seen prior to our arrival, which got me really excited for the hunt to begin.

The following morning the three of us elected to all split up in order to find as many turkeys as we could. After regrouping, we discovered that all of us had heard some turkeys, which was encouraging for the upcoming hunt. It was a long drive up there and none of us had ever driven two hours one way to hunt before.

We ended up renting a Jeep, which is almost essential in order to hunt this type of rugged terrain. The evening before, we weren't able to make it out to roost any birds, however, despite this we felt confident in the scouting we had done.

Opening morning arrived and we headed out really early, making the two-hour drive up the mountain. It was finally turkey season and anticipation was running high among all of us.

After reaching our hunting destination we exited the vehicle and were instantly greeted by windy conditions. The air up there was super thin. It was like you were breathing through a straw. I hadn't gotten adjusted to it yet. Every time I climbed a hill on our scouting day I thought, *Man, am I really this out of shape?!*

On the YouTube video you can hear how rough our breathing is. It was apparent that all of us weren't accustomed to this type of elevation. However, in our defense, it was our first hunt of the year so we probably weren't in the greatest shape. For a couple of days it was rough until we finally got adjusted to it.

After parking the Jeep we walked toward where we heard a couple of turkeys the day before. It was sprinkling, but overall the weather conditions were decent.

Because the air was so thin, it made the gobbles sound much closer. You might hear a turkey and think, *Oh, okay he's a couple of ridges over,* when in actuality you could walk all day long towards that turkey and never reach him. Unfortunately, at the time we didn't realize this, but as the week pressed on we soon found out that you could hear a turkey from a longer distance than normal from this elevation.

Fortunately, we ended up hearing a turkey that was fairly close. By this I mean about 400 or 500 yards away. After fly-down time we began to make our way towards him, closing the distance while he continued to gobble. After taking a few more steps up the ridge, I heard a turkey start putting. I looked to my right and there stood a turkey and it looks like it has a big head, which made me think that it was a gobbler. However, I wasn't about to take a chance and shoot. The turkey was well within shotgun range. I turned to ask Dave if it was a gobbler, but unfortunately he was far enough behind me that he couldn't hear me. After the turkey putted about 20

The gobbler that had a date with destiny.

times it meandered on down the ridge. The turkey that was above us quit gobbling so I soon realized we had gotten too close to them. I felt bad and apologized to the guys that I had been too aggressive.

At this point it was a couple of hours into the morning, so we decided to take a break in the area we had bumped the turkeys. As we sat there a turkey started gobbling below us pretty consistently so we began to call. He instantly answered us, however he failed to get any closer. Eventually we laid eyes on him with our binoculars and we could see him walking down there all alone. He continued to gobble, but he wanted nothing to do with us from where we were at.

In the middle of calling to that turkey one of the birds I had bumped up above me 40 minutes prior began to gobble, and it sounded as though he was 100 yards away. Without hesitation I begin walking towards the gobbler alone while Dave stayed behind and did his best to keep the turkey gobbling while I tried to get within shotgun range.

I began crawling in the pouring rain without any rain gear. Because I was in sneak mode the rain was welcome, helping to cover any noise. As I continued to cut the distance, I slowly raised my head up and saw white. While still on my belly I brought my binoculars up and there before me stood the all white gobbler. I could see his beard, which was around nine inches along, with two other gobblers standing close by.

A lot of people have asked me since then, *How did I keep it together?* My response was simple, *I had tunnel vision and at this point I was all business.* I had one mission and that was to get within shotgun range of one of these turkeys. Even when I saw the white one I wasn't holding out for him. Whichever one of these birds I could get a shot at I would be happy with. At this point I remember thinking, *I wonder what the guys will think if I shoot one of the normal ones and not the white one and understand exactly what is going through my head right now?* I was also starting to think, *Should I hold out for the white one?*

All of this was going through my head as I crawled up there. To this day I firmly believe whatever turkey would have presented itself first I would've shot.

When I spotted the three gobblers, I was up above them as they hung out down in an old lava wash. I had the high ground on them, which is not good because when you're trying to crawl up on a turkey you want to be below them most of the time so you can use the terrain. I was probably about 80 yards from the turkeys and out of any terrain which could hide me. As they continued to mill around in the wash, they stopped gobbling. Dave and Eric had no clue where I was at they just knew that I was going towards the turkey. However, the video shows them spotting the white gobbler while I was lying there on my belly watching it.

Soon, the turkeys began walking off towards a distant hill. I looked at the hill and the gobblers through my binoculars and made one of the best moves I've ever made while turkey hunting, which was fitting for the end. I thought, *as soon as they go up on that little knob I'm going to give them just a couple of seconds for their eyes to clear the backside and then I'm going to make a running break for the hill. Hopefully when I reach the hill and crawl up over it they'll be within shotgun range.*

As I kept an eye on the turkeys, one of them flew up in a tree, eating for a little bit, but soon rejoined the rest of the turkeys. Finally, they ended up going to the top of the hill and disappeared off the backside. I remember thinking, *It's now or never!*

By this time they're around 300 yards from me, which meant I had to sprint this distance in order to pull off a shot. As I started to make a run for it I got about halfway there and my lungs felt like they were on fire. I physically had to drop down on a knee to recover and catch my breath. It occurred to me that I might die trying to go after these turkeys. I thought, *What a story that would be if I died on my 49th!* It was rough, but I gave myself a pep talk and pushed on. I continued to sprint to the break of the hill. Once I arrived I had to collect myself again and catch my breath. At this point I wasn't sure how much time had passed, but it couldn't have been as long as I imagined.

When they went over the hill I thought they would keep going on their line so when I reached the top of it I wasn't even crawling. I had my shotgun shouldered and just waited to see a head. However, when I broke the hill I failed to see anything. Then I cut my eyes down to the left and about 40 yards away were all three gobblers standing in another wash. Somehow, even though I was standing there like an idiot, they failed to spot me as I came over the top of the hill. Fortunately, there were some bushes and vegetation between us, which helped hide me as I crawled to the back side of them for a clean shot.

When I initially saw them I melted into the ground, dropping onto my belly. Fortunately, they still didn't see me so I knew I had a chance. I looked through my red dot scope I had been using for years and it was drenched with water, completely blocking my vision.

I was still not focusing on the white gobbler because when I sank down I lost sight of the turkeys, so I had a couple of seconds to think. First off, I looked at my sight to make sure it was good, but it wasn't good and there was no time left to dry it off. However, luckily I had my red dot setting high enough where I could still see the bead of my shotgun barrel under the red dot. I'm not sure I would have killed this turkey had I not set up my fast fire so that I could still see the bead in case of an emergency like this.

The next thing that went through my mind was I needed to crawl three feet to those bushes and when I popped up behind them there was a good chance they would see me because I'd be more exposed. The reason they hadn't seen me before is because I had those bushes between me and them. With this in mind I knew that when I popped up on my knees it was going to be a quick shot. Therefore, I planned on shooting the first gobbler that presented itself.

I remember thinking, *Well, here we go!* I get amped up just thinking about it right now. I crawled about four feet and then came up on one knee. When I did this sure enough, they all saw me, but guess who's in the wide open at about 35 or 40 yards in the absolute primo position – the white gobbler. He was just standing there, but when he saw me he threw his head up and turned a little

Flanked by Dave (left) and Eric (right) after completing my Super Slam with an all white gobbler. March 1, 2021.

so that his back was facing me. I figured they were going to walk out of their fast. However, the white gobbler didn't have a chance. I pulled my gun up and put my bead right on the back of his head and pulled the trigger, dropping him, while the other two gobblers flew off. I just stood there for a second thinking, *What just happened?* I ran down the hill in the pouring rain and grabbed him by the head as he continued to flop. The bird only lost one feather and was in pristine shape besides the blood on the back of his feathers from when his head laid on his back after I had shot him. The rain caused all of the blood to disperse throughout his body within a matter of a few minutes so he was a rough looking bird. However, at this point it really didn't matter what he looked like.

I was still in disbelief when I grabbed him and stood there for a couple of seconds. I didn't stay there long though because I wanted to go find the guys. As I came running out of the wash I saw this huge boulder laying there so I climbed up on top of it to see if I could spot them. It must have been about 10 feet tall. When I reached the top of it here came all of the guys running towards me. At this point I was physically exhausted. Outside the birth of my child this is one of those special moments I had been waiting for. When Dave ran up I said, "I've been waiting for that shot my whole life!"

I looked over at Eric and I'll never forget the big tears running down his face. He looked at me and had a look of pure joy with a big smile on his face as tears continued to run down his cheeks. Dave was also excited for me. All three of us exchanged hugs and celebrated. We were all fired up. This was one of the best days afield in my life.

Because we had gotten split up I didn't realize it at the time, but they had videotaped the shot, which you can hear in the video. Eric and Dave had been laying down with the camera rolling, watching the white gobbler, and they saw me as I came across the wash. They also saw the other two birds fly off after the shot. While in the background you can hear Eric say in his North Carolina accent, "The white one's dead, boss!" I didn't realize he said this until the video came out because obviously I wasn't with them.

I wish Dave could have filmed the shot over my shoulder, but it would have been too much of a risk. I had enough odds against me and Dave knew it.

After the adrenaline wore off, which I don't think completely went away, we realized just how cold and wet all of us were. Because it had been raining hard, we were completely drenched. We couldn't stand around and celebrate any longer, so we made the half-mile walk back to the jeep. Once we got inside, we lit up some cigars, cranked up some music, and continued to celebrate. We still couldn't believe what had just happened.

As we headed back down we realized we needed to take some pictures of me with the turkey. Afterwards, I sent a picture to my Dad. He was really confused at first about the bird being an all-white turkey. Based on his initial response, I knew I would probably get some flak from everyone, saying I had shot a tame turkey because most tame turkeys are white. Also, anytime a customer drops off an all-white bird at my shop, they too have received some flak from critics. However, one thing I've noticed while being a taxidermist and mounting some tame turkeys for people and around a thousand wild turkeys, is the bone structure for each is very different. Tame turkeys have big, fat heads and legs, which immediately stand out and I can always quickly tell them apart.

Obviously, I knew right away my turkey was wild, however I was prepared for people not to understand the difference and that only a select few would. For someone that had hunted them as hard as me to even say I had killed a tame one for my 49th really lit a fire under me, but I knew that some would think that nonetheless. I still let people have it when they say I killed a tame one.

After reaching the hotel and letting Kenny and everybody that needed to know I had killed number 49, we thought, *"How are we going to get this turkey in better shape for photos?"* The turkey was still wet and covered with blood. I knew Dave was really good at taking photos so I felt confident these would turn out great. Besides that, I wanted to mount the white gobbler. I decided to take it in the shower, add some Tide laundry detergent, rinse it off, and then blow-dry him, which took a couple of hours. However, it was worth it. I got him back to looking pristine. As mentioned before, because I do this for a living, I knew this process was going to take awhile.

Later in the evening, we decided to drive back up the mountain and take some pictures with the gobbler. We didn't go to the spot where I had killed him because it was a two-hour drive, but we went close to the area. By this time the nasty weather had moved out and the sun was shining. Afterwards, Dave videoed us for the *Pinhoti Project* up on the mountain while we smoked cigars and reflected on the hunt earlier that morning.

It felt good to be up there without a worry in the world, thinking about the hunt along with my wife and kids at home. In that moment I wasn't worried about anything else. I also thought about the camaraderie, the journey, and how cool it was to end the Super Slam in Hawaii and especially to kill an all-white gobbler for the last state.

To this day the entire hunt was surreal. I periodically watch this hunt on YouTube where Dave shared the hunt, reliving the moment and reflecting on the turkey that had a date with destiny. I still find it hard to believe the all-white gobbler was number 49 and it completed my Super Slam.

When I skinned the turkey, I found three pellets in his breast where someone else had previously shot him. It was only a two-year-old gobbler, so it had to have been shot as a jake. This caused me to think about the other hunter who had an encounter with this bird. I'm sure glad he missed his mark.

We ended up hunting the remaining five days which we had left in Hawaii, allowing me to kill another gobbler later in the week. Both Dave and Eric ended up killing one so this made the hunt even more special.

When I flew home after the hunt, I placed the white gobbler in my suitcase, which always gave me a chuckle when I boarded a plane. Since I was mounting the bird I wanted to make sure it was well protected, especially since I was going to enter it in a contest at the NWTF Convention.

Fortunately, the gobbler survived the plane flight home and the following year I won the Masters Division at the February 2022 NWTF Convention in Nashville with the white bird, my 49th gobbler. It was a standing mount on top of a pedestal. I mounted him in this pose because this is how he was when I hunted him.

I'm really not sure what the chances are or the genetic anomaly is for shooting an all-white turkey. One in a thousand, one in a million, but I do know that they're not very common. I will say a white turkey that is born in the continental United States has a low likelihood of surviving because obviously they're all white and extremely noticeable to predators. When a white turkey is born in Hawaii, the only way they're getting killed is by hunters or run over by vehicles. Therefore, an all-white turkey has a better chance of survival in Hawaii.

The chances of ending with an all-white gobbler for your 49th are highly unlikely. Only a handful of people have completed the Super Slam, let alone killed an all-white gobbler. Combining these two things caused me to stand there over the bird in complete disbelief. There had to have been some Divine intervention that occurred allowing me to kill this bird. Something bigger than me had a part in it. Things like this just don't happen. Man, is it wild just to think about it now. I've always thought it would be cool to shoot a color phase turkey. I've mounted them before at my taxidermy shop for customers and always was amazed by their uniqueness and beauty.

LESSONS LEARNED

There was a culmination of things involved in finishing my Super Slam in Hawaii. These included; using a piece of terrain to get closer to a gobbler, having someone behind you calling to keep the turkey gobbling and help keep track of his whereabouts, arriving at your hunting destination early so you can scout and establish a game plan, and having the proper equipment.

Lessons learned as far as the U.S. Super Slam itself, if you can dream it you can do it. I'm nobody. If I can do it you can do it. I'm not rich and never have been rich. A lot of people think you need to be rich in order to complete the Slam and that simply isn't true. You just need to put money aside where you can. You can make it happen if you want it bad enough. "You've got to want it to win it." This is what Kenny always would say to me.

Epilogue

To this day a lot of people that I come into contact with ask me, "What are you going to do now?" upon completing the Super Slam. My answer is always the same. I'm going to turkey hunt just like I did before, maybe not quite as fast, but I'm still going to be a crazy turkey hunting guy, traveling all over the country, which I still do to this day. However, I don't hunt 10 or 11 states like I did before having two kids now and taking on taxidermy full-time. I'll do maybe six states per spring now and two or three days in some of my favorite places, which I'll hunt as hard as I did then.

Because the Super Slam is gaining popularity among turkey hunters people also ask, "What advice do you have for someone else doing the Slam?" Most people that completed the Slam said that I should have slowed down and that I went too fast. Once it's over it's over so enjoy it. It's not a race. Would I have done it slower if I had to do it over? Probably not. I loved the adrenaline of only having maybe a couple of days or even a day in a new state with your back up against the wall and trying to get it done. I loved the feeling of being challenged and faced with pressure. Of course, it's easy to say that now, looking back on the hunt.

I thank God every day for making me a turkey hunter, for having a Dad that introduced me to hunting and who fueled my love for it when I was younger, and for a wife that supported me on my journey and let me chase my dream.

As this book is written, the majority of my income is my taxidermist business and mounting wild turkeys for people. I quit teaching so I could focus entirely on taxidermy.

At least once a week in some form or fashion, I eat wild turkey. My life is all turkeys. The blessings I've received because of the wild turkey are incalculable. I don't know where I'm going next and what the next chapter in my life is, but I'm going to continue to work harder. With any success that I've ever had, including whatever success this book brings, my taxidermy business, turkey hunting or in sports, I never let anything go to my head. Anytime someone says anything good about these things I just described I put my head down lower and not higher. I let it drive me. I don't have time to think about the good stuff. I'm always trying to be better whether it's a better turkey hunter, taxidermist, husband, or father I'm always trying to put my head down lower and always striving to do better. And by putting my head down lower I mean remaining humble. This mentality has been a huge part of my success in life. It's the same with taxidermy, with turkey hunting, and anything that has to do with my family. I'm just always trying to do better and work as hard as I can. When I first started the Slam, I was still in the phase of my life where I wanted to be known as a bad-ass hunter, but I grew out of this as the years passed by. Now, I just want to be known as a bad-ass Dad and husband. As for turkey hunting, I would rather be known as a conservationist. Someone who helped save the wild turkey and helped preserve turkey hunting for future generations so that my kids and their kids get a chance to enjoy these birds.

What's next for me? Being a bad-ass Dad and husband, hunting turkeys when I can, and doing everything that I can through the platform that I've been given and the notoriety of the Super Slam to help turkeys.

– Tanner Burns

Acknowledgements

One evening at the end of Michigan's 2021 spring turkey season, I stumbled across a YouTube video of a gentleman from Buckhannon, West Virginia named Tanner Burns. He was featured on the YouTube series *Whitetail Cribs* created by *Exodus Outdoor Gear.*

At the time, Tanner had just a handful of states left to complete the U.S. Super Slam. As I watched the video, which was just over an hour long, I was intrigued by Tanner's passion for turkey hunting and his pursuit to kill a gobbler in all 49 states. To be honest, this was the first time I had heard about the Super Slam. However, I was familiar with the Grand Slam, where a turkey hunter kills all four subspecies of turkeys in the U.S.: Eastern, Osceola, Rio, and Merriam's. But when I heard about the U.S. Super Slam and how Tanner was on track to be the youngest to ever complete it, a light bulb went off. This was an epic journey and I knew at that moment I had to write a book about it. I had always wanted to write a book, but didn't have a subject pinned down. This changed all of that in a heartbeat.

After watching the video I quickly wrote down his name on a sticky note. It wasn't until a few weeks later when I finally got the courage to call up Tanner after he had given me his number on Facebook Messenger.

Tanner answered and I immediately congratulated him on his accomplishment of completing the U.S. Super Slam. As I began asking him questions geared towards a potential article I was thinking of writing, I knew in the back of my mind what the real reason was for making the call. After asking him some questions I could feel butterflies in my stomach much like hearing the first gobble of turkey season. *Here goes nothing,* I thought. Although anxious, I somehow managed to get the words out, "What would you think about me writing a book on your Super Slam quest?" Without delay I continued, "Each chapter would be a different state you shot a turkey in and checked off your list." Without hesitation Tanner agreed and liked the idea of the chapter and state combination.

Shortly after our conversation Tanner began sending me audio recordings beginning with West Virginia and we were off and running. My dream of writing a book was officially underway.

As I listened to Tanner's audio recordings while writing this book, I felt as though I was accompanying him each step of the way, state to state from the hills of West Virginia to the volcanoes in Hawaii.

Tanner's completion of the U.S. Super Slam in essence helped fulfill my dream of writing a book.

Therefore, first and foremost I would like to thank Tanner for allowing me to tag along via audio recording while *Climbing to 49*. Without his drive, determination, and passion for the wild turkey this book would not be in your hands.

Jim Spencer, whose name is widely known throughout the turkey hunting sub-culture, was responsible for proofreading and putting up with my endless messages and phone calls throughout the entire book-writing process. His knowledge and support is greatly appreciated.

My talented friend Jamie Metheringham, with whom I've shared countless mornings together getting shook up by gobblers on the roost, deserves a thank you for all of his amazing illustrations throughout the book. These made each chapter come alive.

Without Kevin Rhoades and the folks at IngramSpark Publishing this book would have never existed. These amazing people gave me the opportunity to share Tanner's Super Slam journey.

Once you spend time in the turkey woods with others, you're forever bonded. Each season I've been blessed to share the turkey woods with many wonderful people; my dad, brother, nephew, and uncle; Alan Potter, Dean Potter, Brock Potter, and Jack Potter respectively. Along with my friends; Tyler Henry, and Matt Winiecki.

While on a camping trip as a youngster in Michigan's Upper Peninsula, my Mom and Dad bought me a notepad, which I used as a journal throughout the entire trip. I recorded mostly fishing out-ings on this trip, however during the following years I wrote down all of my hunting adventures too.

I'd like to thank my Mom and Dad for introducing me to the outdoors and buying the $2 journal, which spun me into outdoor writing. Who knew that a cheap notepad would have such an impact on me.

Lastly, I would like to thank the National Wild Turkey Federation along with all of the organizations, state wildlife agencies, landowners, and hunters who work relentlessly to help turkey populations thrive in each of the 49 states. Without these dedicated individuals turkey hunting wouldn't be possible.

– Darin Potter

Tanner has won numerous taxidermy awards including; Best Turkey WV state show in 2022 and 2023, the People's Choice for best turkey in 2023, and shown here the NWTF Masters for best standing turkey in 2021, which was the Hawaii gobbler that completed his Super Slam.

www.ingramcontent.com/pod-product-compliance
Lightning Source LLC
Chambersburg PA
CBHW012035140726
47990CB00010B/3237